THE CAMBRIDGE HISTORY OF CLASSICAL LITERATURE

GENERAL EDITORS

Mrs P. E. Easterling *Fellow of Newnham College, Cambridge*

E. J. Kenney *Fellow of Peterhouse, Cambridge*

ADVISORY EDITORS

B. M. W. Knox *The Center for Hellenic Studies, Washington*

W. V. Clausen *Department of the Classics, Harvard University*

VOLUME II PART 2
THE LATE REPUBLIC

THE CAMBRIDGE HISTORY OF CLASSICAL LITERATURE

VOLUME II: LATIN LITERATURE

Part 1   The Early Republic
Part 2   The Late Republic
Part 3   The Age of Augustus
Part 4   The Early Principate
Part 5   The Later Principate

THE CAMBRIDGE HISTORY OF CLASSICAL LITERATURE

VOLUME II

PART 2

The Late Republic

EDITED BY

E. J. KENNEY

Fellow of Peterhouse, Cambridge

ADVISORY EDITOR

W. V. CLAUSEN

Professor of Greek and Latin
Harvard University

CAMBRIDGE UNIVERSITY PRESS

CAMBRIDGE

LONDON   NEW YORK   NEW ROCHELLE

MELBOURNE   SYDNEY

Published by the Press Syndicate of the University of Cambridge
The Pitt Building, Trumpington Street, Cambridge CB2 1RP
32 East 57th Street, New York, NY 10022, USA
296 Beaconsfield Parade, Middle Park, Melbourne 3206, Australia

First published 1982 as chapters 8–14 of *The Cambridge History of Classical Literature*, Volume II
First paperback edition 1983

Printed in Great Britain by the University Press, Cambridge

Library of Congress catalogue card number: 82–19781

British Library Cataloguing in Publication Data

The Cambridge history of classical literature.
Vol. 2: Latin literature
The Late republic
1. Classical literature – History and criticism
I. Kenney, E. J. II. Clausen, W. V.
880'.09   PA3001
ISBN 0 521 27374 9

CONTENTS

1   Predecessors   1
     by E. J. KENNEY, *Kennedy Professor of Latin, University of Cambridge*

2   The new direction in poetry   4
     by W. V. CLAUSEN, *Professor of Greek and Latin, Harvard University*
     1   The New Poets and their antecedents   4
     2   The Marriage of Peleus and Thetis   13
     3   *Catulli Veronensis liber*   19
     4   Lesbia, Sirmio, Calvus   24

3   Lucretius   33
     by ALEXANDER DALZELL, *Professor of Classics, Trinity College, University of Toronto*
     1   Background   33
     2   Poet and philosopher   39
     3   The poem   43

4   Cicero and the relationship of oratory to literature   56
     by L. P. WILKINSON, *Emeritus Brereton Reader in Classics, University of Cambridge*
     1   Cicero's attitude to culture   56
     2   Oratorical theory and practice as Cicero found it   59
     3   Oratorical theory and practice in Cicero and his contemporaries   62
     4   Verse   71
     5   Letters   73
     6   Speeches   76
     7   Dialogues and treatises   82
     8   Literary influence in antiquity   92

5   Sallust   94
     by F. R. D. GOODYEAR, *Hildred Carlile Professor of Latin, Bedford College, University of London*

CONTENTS

6   Caesar   107
    by R. M. OGILVIE, *Sometime Professor of Humanity, St Salvator's
    College, University of St Andrews*

7   Prose and mime   112
    by NICHOLAS HORSFALL, *Lecturer in Greek and Latin, University
    College London*
    1   Varro   112
    2   Cornelius Nepos   116
    3   The literary mime   119

    Appendix of authors and works   121
    compiled by MARTIN DRURY

    Metrical appendix   138
    by MARTIN DRURY

    Abbreviations   142

    Works cited in the text   146

    Index   150

1

PREDECESSORS

The short poems of Catullus, which he himself calls *nugae* 'trifles' (1.4), confront the critic with a paradox: poetry of obviously major significance and power which belongs formally to a minor genre. Only poems 11 and 51, written in the metre associated with Sappho herself, were entitled to lay claim to real lyric status; Catullus' preferred metres – the elegiac couplet, the hendecasyllable, the scazon (limping) iambus – belonged outside the grand tradition. Narrative elegy had of course been written by Callimachus, Philetas and Hermesianax; and Propertius in particular (3.1.1) acknowledged Callimachus and Philetas as his masters.[1] It was, however, the short elegiac epigram that first served Roman poets as a model for a new kind of personal poetry, as it eventually became. Aulus Gellius and Cicero have preserved five short epigrams by a trio of accomplished amateurs, Valerius Aedituus, Porcius Licinus and Quintus Lutatius Catulus. These are freely adapted from Hellenistic Greek originals, most of which can be identified in the Greek Anthology. This trio may have been writing as early as 150 B.C.; the fact that they are cited as a group by Gellius does not prove that they formed a literary coterie,[2] but at least it shows that there existed in the latter part of the second century B.C. a class of Roman *literati* who were actively interested in exploiting the short personal poem in Latin. That this was not a flash in the pan and that this sort of piece continued to be written during the first century is shown by the fragments of nine similar, though less polished compositions unearthed among the Pompeian graffiti.[3] There must have been also continuing stimulation from Greece. More than one anthology of Greek epigram was circulating in Italy during the century or so before Catullus; one of the most influential must have been the Garland (Στέφανος) of Meleager, whose own poems flaunted many of the ideas and images singled out for attack by Lucretius in his famous polemic against false manifestations of love.[4]

More original than such adaptive exercises was the highly experimental Muse

---

[1] The extent of his debt to Philetas is obscure: Ross (1975) 120 n. 2.
[2] Ross (1969a) 140–2 and n. 61.　　　　[3] Ross (1969b), (1969a) 147–9.
[4] Kenney (1970) 381–5.

of Laevius, who appears to have written in the early part of the first century B.C.
At first sight the nearly thirty fragments which survive seem to have a good
deal in common with Catullus in subject matter, metre and diction, and
Laevius has been conventionally counted among the predecessors or harbingers
of the 'new' poetry. Closer analysis reveals important points of difference;
and though it must remain probable *a priori* that Catullus and his contemporaries knew Laevius, direct indebtedness is difficult to demonstrate.[1]
'That Laevius provides a link with the neoterics cannot be denied, but that
Catullus owed more to him than a vague suggestion of certain possibilities is
unlikely.'[2]

Cicero, it is generally agreed, was no poet. He is, however, a more important
figure in the history of Latin poetry than is commonly acknowledged. No
Roman writer was more keenly alive to the rhythmical and sonorous properties
of the Latin language; and it is only to be expected that Cicero should have had
something to contribute to poetry also in the sphere of technique – even if, as
must be admitted, he had nothing to say in his own poetry that posterity much
wanted to hear. For it is the surviving fragments of his translations from the
Greek that are of most interest to the historian of Latin literature, especially his
version of Aratus' *Phaenomena*. This was a work of his youth (*Nat. D.* 2.104),[3]
the first Latin version of this much-translated and (to modern ways of thinking)
unexpectedly popular work; and it seems probable that it enjoyed a considerable
circulation. Certainly it was known to and indeed imitated by Lucretius. What
is perhaps less to be expected is that it shows Cicero to have been, in spite of his
apparent reservations about the 'new' poetry – or about certain of its characteristics and practitioners at all events[4] – what might be called a pre- or proto-
neoteric poet himself, much more so than Laevius. For one of the hallmarks of
the 'new' school of poets was their (Callimachean) insistence on careful and
exact craftsmanship; and Cicero's hexameters, flat and lifeless as they read, are
technically much more like those of Catullus than those of Ennius or even
Lucretius. In part the resemblance is due to stricter metrical observances,
especially in the matter of caesuras and the treatment of the end of the verse.
This process of self-discipline, however, goes hand in hand with and contributes to an increased awareness and realization of the artistic possibilities of
word-order in the verse-sentence structure, such as are normally associated with
Catullus and the Augustans.[5] The precise part played by Cicero in the development of Latin poetry is bound to remain obscure, given the fragmentary nature
of the evidence; but the 'modern' character of his hexameters is unmistakable

---

[1] Ross (1969a) 155–60.   [2] Ibid. 160.
[3] On the dating see Ross (1969a) 134 n. 48.
[4] Below, pp. 4–5.
[5] Ross (1969a) 133–4; for analyses of the Ciceronian hexameter see Ewbank (1933) 40–71,
Duckworth (1969) 37–45.

even to a twentieth-century reader and must have leapt (so to say) to the ear of his contemporaries. No account of the genesis of the 'new' poetry of Catullus and his school should omit mention of Rome's greatest orator. If Catullus himself was conscious of any debt, he does not own it. A reader of poem 49 ignorant of the *Aratea* would not readily guess that the poet might have had any reason to be grateful to Cicero other than the one so carefully not explained in that enigmatic poem.

2

THE NEW DIRECTION
IN POETRY

1. THE NEW POETS AND THEIR ANTECEDENTS

The New Poets, as they are conventionally and conveniently called, were so called by an older poet who disliked them, at least some of them. Cicero, *Orat.* 161 (46–45 B.C.), observes that the suppression of final *s* was, at one time, a characteristic of refined speech but that now it seems somewhat countrified, *subrusticum*; and the new poets now shun it, *nunc fugiunt poetae noui.* 'We used to talk like this', he adds, quoting from Ennius' *Annals* and Lucilius. A year or so later, *Tusc. disp.* 3.45 (45–44 B.C.), he again refers to these poets while extolling the virtues of Ennius. *O poetam egregium! quamquam ab his cantoribus Euphorionis nunc contemnitur* 'What an outstanding poet! although he is despised by these choristers of Euphorion.' Who were these poets, *cantores Euphorionis?* Not Catullus certainly, who had been dead for nearly a decade. Probably his friend Cinna, a sedulous imitator of Euphorion,[1] and contemporary poetasters who imitated Cinna; possibly Cornelius Gallus, now in his mid twenties, who 'translated' Euphorion.[2]

It is a mistake, often made, to speak of 'Cicero's poetry' as if it were a body of work in which a consistent development might be traced from beginning to end. Cicero was serious about poetry, whenever the mood seized him. To an exceptional degree, and at a very early age, he mastered poetic form, and produced, in his youthful version of Aratus' *Phaenomena*, the first elegant hexameters written in Latin. That one unfortunate verse, written years later, should be forgiven him and forgotten:

O fortunatam natam me consule Romam!

O happy Roman state born in my consulate!

Neither as a poet nor as a critic of poetry is Cicero to be ridiculed: he was a shrewd and knowledgeable critic, and as good a poet as a highly intelligent man who has never experienced the sacred rage can be.

---

[1] See below, pp. 12–13.
[2] Servius on *Ecl.* 10.50–1; Ross (1975) 40–3.

In 50 B.C. Cicero begins a letter to Atticus with a playful reference to a mannerism of the New Poets, the spondaic hexameter. *Brundisium uenimus VII Kal. Dec. usi tua felicitate nauigandi; ita belle nobis 'flauit ab Epiro lenissimus Onchesmites'. hunc* σπονδειάζοντα *si cui uoles* τῶν νεωτέρων *pro tuo uendito* 'We arrived at Brundisium on 24 November, as favoured in the crossing as yourself. "Softly, softly, from Epirus blew the Onchesmitic breeze." There! vend that spondaic as your own to any of the Neoterics you like.'[1] Cicero's witty fabrication (the verse must be his own) is perfect of its kind, closing with a 'learned' geographical allusion to an insignificant port on the coast of Epirus. The spondaic hexameter is as old as Homer, but in Homer infrequent and casual; in the Hellenistic poets – Aratus, Callimachus, Apollonius, Euphorion, and others – and in their Latin imitators it becomes frequent and designed.[2] Cicero was well aware of this device, for he had taken pains to avoid it, with a single exception that could hardly be avoided, in his version of Aratus.[3]

The New Poets were a group of young and impressionable poets in the generation after Cicero's who shared a literary attitude relating even to stylistic minutiae, of which Cicero chose to notice two. They wished to change Latin poetry, and to a considerable extent they succeeded in their purpose. The only one of their small number who survives, all but entire, is Catullus; of the others there are meagre remains.[4] It is easy and safe to assume that Catullus survives because he was their best: ancient readers, who were in a position to judge, evidently thought so. At the time, however, Calvus may have seemed the more imposing figure: a poet like Catullus, an accomplished orator, whose attacks on Caesar's henchman Vatinius were still read and studied in Tacitus' day (*Dial.* 21.4), and a Roman noble. Catullus was a provincial, but of a family that must have been prominent in Verona and well connected; otherwise Caesar would not have been a guest in his father's house. Caesar complained of the 'permanent scars' inflicted on his reputation by Catullus' pungent lampoons (poems 29 and 57?). The son apologized: that same day Caesar invited him to dinner and continued to enjoy the father's hospitality.[5] In one of his latest poems Catullus made amends, on a grand scale:

> siue trans altas gradietur Alpes,
> Caesaris uisens monimenta magni,
> Gallicum Rhenum, horribile aequor ulti-
> mosque Britannos...   (11.9–12)

or whether he [*Catullus*] *shall traverse the lofty Alps to view great Caesar's monuments, the Gallic Rhine, the rough strait, and the utmost Britons...*

---

[1] *Att.* 7.2.1; adapted from Shackleton Bailey (1965–70) III.
[2] A survey in Norden (1916) 441–6.
[3] *Oriona* in line 3. In the corresponding lines of Aratus there are 66 spondaic hexameters.
[4] Collected in *FPL* 80–91.   [5] Suet. *Div. Iul.* 73; Gelzer (1968) 134.

That Calvus and Catullus were intimate friends appears from several poems (14, 50, 53, 96); and their names are coupled by later writers. Cinna was another friend, a fellow-Transpadane; Catullus' praise of his *Zmyrna* could scarcely be warmer (95). It is odd that Catullus nowhere alludes to Calvus' *Io*. Perhaps it was written after Catullus' death; if so, then Cinna was the first of the trio to write an epyllion, a miniature epic in the new style; and hence Catullus' enthusiasm. Catullus and Cinna were members of the cohort or entourage that accompanied the propraetor Memmius to Bithynia in 57 B.C. Cinna brought home some sedan-bearers and Aratus' *Phaenomena* copied on mallow bast;[1] Catullus only an abiding sense of outrage (10 and 28).

And there were others, shadowy figures, about whom very little is known. There was Cornificius, like Calvus a poet and an orator; to him Catullus addresses an amusingly rueful little poem (38). Furius Bibaculus was older and lived a long while; he was to be remembered for his lampoons on Caesar, with Catullus, and Octavian (Tac. *Ann.* 4.34.8). Two slight, affectionate poems of his are preserved on the bankrupt old age of the renowned teacher (*grammaticus*) and poet Valerius Cato, 'the Latin siren, who alone reads and makes poets' (Suet. *Gramm.* 11) – and who was not, perhaps, too dignified to be the recipient of Catullus 56. (Ovid, *Trist.* 2.436, cites Cato for his indecent verse in company with Catullus, Calvus, Ticidas, Memmius, Cinna, Cornificius.) A *Dictynna* is praised by Cinna, a *Lydia* by Ticidas. Ticidas composed an epithalamium in the metre of Catullus 61, as did Calvus. Caecilius is known only from Catullus 35: a native of nearby Novum Comum whom Catullus invites to visit Verona, if ever he can disentangle himself from the embrace of that girl who so passionately loves his poetry. The wit of Catullus' poem lies in the repetition *incohatam* (14)...*incohata* (18), the last line:

> est enim uenuste
> Magna Caecilio incohata Mater.   (17–18)

The beginning of Caecilius' Magna Mater *is indeed lovely.*

In circumstances so time-beguiling Caecilius may never have finished his *Magna Mater*. It is not unlikely that Catullus followed Caecilius' progress, or lack of it, with special interest because of his own poem on the subject (63).

The New Poetry cannot be understood simply as issuing from the Latin literary tradition – almost no new form of Latin poetry can: the impulse comes from Greek, in this case later Greek, poetry. Of Hellenistic poets the one who meant most to the New Poets was Callimachus – Callimachus 'the chief classic of an unclassical art';[2] although to Catullus writing his epyllion (64) Apollonius was

---

[1] *FPL* 89; Tränkle (1967) 87–9.   [2] Wilamowitz (1924) I 170.

as important, and to Virgil, a second-generation New Poet, writing his *Eclogues* Theocritus necessarily more important. Still, Callimachus remained the type and ideal of Alexandrian elegance; but for his poetry and the aesthetic attitudes professed or implied in it much of what they wrote – as indeed much of Latin poetry after them – could not have been written.

In Alexandria Callimachus had been a dominant personality; an incredibly learned and industrious scholar of the library, and court poet. A dominant personality, but no literary dictator: Callimachus' position is at once polemical and defensive. Towards the end of his life he made an apologia for his poetic career; he had been attacked – and vehemently attacked, to judge from the vehemence of his retort – by Posidippus and Asclepiades and some others. Callimachus' famous refusal to write an epic suggests a widely held opinion that poets ought to write epics, and some expectation, possibly, on the part of those in high places. Callimachus had no decisive effect on Greek poetry either during his life or, though he was read for centuries, after his death. Epics continued to be written: epics about monarchs or war-lords, epics on mythological themes, epics concerning the history of a people or a region.

Callimachus' idea of poetry is expressed most fully in his apologia, a fastidious and beautiful denunciation of his enemies – the Telchines, as he dubs them, ill-natured literary dwarfs. (The text is defective here and there.)

The Telchines, who are ignorant and no friends of the Muse, murmur at my poetry because I have not made a single song, unbroken, of many thousands of verses about kings and heroes. But I roll my poem forward just a little, like a child, yet the decades of my years are not a few... (The short poems of Philitas and Mimnermus are better than their long.) Let the crane delighting in Pygmies' blood fly far, from Egypt to the Thracians; and let the Massagetes shoot their arrows far, at the Mede: shorter poems – 'nightingales' – are sweeter. Away, deathly brood of Envy! Henceforth judge poetry by its art, not by the Persian surveyor's chain. Don't expect me to produce a great rattling song: thunder is not my job, but Jove's.

καὶ γὰρ ὅτε πρώτιστον ἐμοῖς ἐπὶ δέλτον ἔθηκα
  γούνασιν, Ἀ[πό]λλων εἶπεν ὅ μοι Λύκιος·
'.......]...ἀοιδέ, τὸ μὲν θύος ὅττι πάχιστον
  θρέψαι, τὴ]ν Μοῦσαν δ' ὠγαθὲ λεπταλέην·
πρὸς δέ σε] καὶ τόδ' ἄνωγα, τὰ μὴ πατέουσιν ἅμαξαι
  τὰ στείβειν, ἑτέρων ἴχνια μὴ καθ' ὁμά
δίφρον ἐλ]ᾶν μηδ' οἷμον ἀνὰ πλατύν, ἀλλὰ κελεύθους
  ἀτρίπτο]ψς, εἰ καὶ στεινοτέρην ἐλάσεις.'
                                                        (21–8)

For when first I set a writing-tablet on my knees, Lycian Apollo spoke to me: 'poet, feed your victim as fat as you can, but your Muse, my good fellow, keep her thin. And I tell you this besides: where no wagons pass, walk there; don't drive your cart in the tracks of others or along a wide road, but on ways unworn, even a narrower one.'

Then follow the poignant, wistful lines on the poet's old age. This 'testament' Callimachus placed before the original proem to his *Aetia* ('Causes'), which he had written as a young man: the Hesiodic dream of initiation by the Muses on Helicon. Even in this personal retrospect, literary allusions abound, to Homer, to Herodotus, to Mimnermus, so fearful of growing old, and to Euripides' *Mad Heracles*, written when the tragedian was an old man, as Callimachus the scholar would have known.

It is impossible to read much of Callimachus – his epigrams apart – without being impressed, or depressed, by his multifarious learning; but it would be perverse to wish that his poetry might be dissociated from his pedantry. Callimachus was not a poet and a scholar; he was a poet, or rather could be a poet, because he was a scholar, a γραμματικός, a man whose business was with literature. The earlier literature of Greece being now collected in the great library at Alexandria, men discovered the exquisite pleasure of writing books from books. Now a scholar-poet could scan and compare texts, delicately modify an admired metaphor or simile; follow an obscure variant of a myth or legend while deftly signalling an awareness of the usual version; join an old word with a new in a telling arrangement; choose a unique or rare word or form out of Homer or some other poet and locate it, perhaps with polemical intent, in a context of his own making. As, for instance, Callimachus does at the beginning of the story of Acontius and Cydippe:

Αὐτὸς Ἔρως ἐδίδαξεν Ἀκόντιον, ὁππότε καλῇ
ἤθετο Κυδίππῃ παῖς ἐπὶ παρθενικῇ,
τέχνην – οὐ γὰρ ὅγ᾽ ἔσκε πολύκροτος –   (*Aetia* 67.1–3)

Eros himself taught Acontius, when the youth was burning for the fair maid Cydippe, the craft – for he was not clever – . . .

In line 3 there is an allusion to the opening of the *Odyssey:* Ἄνδρα μοι ἔννεπε Μοῦσα, πολύτροπον . . . 'Speak to me, Muse, of the man . . .'; πολύκροτον is a rare variant. Earlier Greek poets supposed a sizeable group of auditors; Callimachus and his like only a few readers, learned or almost as learned as themselves.

That these umbratile poets were drawn to the composition of didactic poetry is not surprising; for in such poetry they could everywhere display their erudition and artfulness, and please themselves with a performance that owed little or nothing to the subject. Hence their choice of inert or seemingly intractable subjects. They wished to shine, not to persuade: in Nicander's *Theriaca* there breathes no Lucretian fire. The exemplar of such poetry appears to have been Aratus' *Phaenomena*. In one of his epigrams (27) Callimachus hails the subtle, Hesiodic quality of Aratus' verse; so might he have hailed his own *Aetia*.

The attitude of Callimachus to Hesiod and Homer has occasionally been misunderstood: for Callimachus Hesiod was imitable, Homer beyond imitation. Callimachus did not condemn Homer, he condemned Homer's imitators, those who copied whole phrases and tried to reproduce the epic form, not realizing it was by now empty and outworn. Hesiod's poems were relatively short, as, in Callimachus' judgement, poems should be, and told no long tales of kings and heroes. The *Theogony* interested Callimachus especially. It dealt with the true causes or wherefores of things (αἴτια); it was learned, if naively so – but its very naivety would appeal to Callimachus' sophistication; above all, Hesiod's was a personal voice. Hesiod provided Callimachus with the means of describing his own source of inspiration, a matter of deep concern to a late and self-conscious poet. While keeping his flock under Helicon, Hesiod met the Muses, who gave him a laurel branch (the living symbol of poetic inspiration) and breathed into him the divine power of song. While still a young man, Callimachus dreamed that he had been wafted to Helicon and there met the Muses. (Details are uncertain, for only a fragment of the text survives, and the scene cannot be reconstructed with any confidence from Latin imitations – notably that of Propertius 3.3.) The old bard of Ascra[1] seems to describe an actual encounter – strange things happen to shepherds by day in lonely places; but there is some intimation of night and darkness, and the passage was later interpreted allegorically, as a dream. And Callimachus, in Alexandria, could only dream of the Muses of Helicon.

Ennius, who knew so much, knew something of the poetry of Callimachus; he alluded to the famous dream – for reasons now not easy to grasp – at the beginning of his *Annals*, a long epic about kings and heroes. But Callimachus had little or no influence on Latin poetry until the generation of the New Poets. Some time, perhaps a long time, before he was forced to commit suicide in 87 B.C., Lutatius Catulus rendered one of Callimachus' epigrams (41: *FPL* 43); but this, the diversion of an idle hour, should not be taken as evidence of any serious interest in Callimachus' poetry or his aesthetic views. Catulus was a Roman noble with a taste for Greek poetry, an elegant amateur. He would have read many Greek epigrams: one, by Callimachus, caught his fancy and he made a version of it. Meleager's *Garland* had been published a few years before Catulus' death; he could have read the epigram there, or elsewhere; or it might have been shown him by his Greek friend Antipater of Sidon, a fluent epigrammatist who died about 125 B.C. In all probability, Catulus had never read any of the *Aetia*; had he attempted to do so, he would have found the literary polemic and philology either incomprehensible or distasteful. There is, moreover, no

---

[1] Virgil identifies his *Georgics* as belonging to this tradition, 2.176 *Ascraeumque cano Romana per oppida carmen* 'I sing the song of Ascra through Roman towns'.

reason to suppose that Catulus felt any aversion to old-fashioned epic: his circle included a certain Furius, a writer of such poetry, *Annals*.

Callimachus' poetry was brought to Rome by Parthenius of Nicaea, a zealous Callimachean; and arrived there with all the charm and force of novelty. Not that Callimachus had been altogether unknown in Rome; rather that Parthenius introduced him to some young and aspiring poets there, and made him an active part of their education. According to the biographical notice in the Suda, Parthenius was taken prisoner when the Romans defeated Mithridates, becoming the property or prize of Cinna (not further identified); and was later freed because of his learning, διὰ παίδευσιν. Therefore Parthenius arrived in Rome sometime after 73 B.C., the year the Romans captured Nicaea; possibly not until about 65 B.C., when Mithridates was finally defeated. It may be that literary young men in Rome were minded to read Callimachus without prompting; but then the suddenness and intensity of their interest would be difficult to explain; and it is doubtful whether a Cinna or a Calvus or a Catullus could have begun to appreciate Callimachus without a Parthenius at his elbow.

Cinna laboured for nine years to be as obscure as Euphorion, and succeeded brilliantly: his *Zmyrna* required an exegetical commentary.[1] Catullus greeted the publication of Cinna's epyllion with an enthusiasm truly Callimachean (95):

Zmyrna mei Cinnae nonam post denique messem
quam coepta est nonamque edita post hiemem,
milia cum interea quingenta Hortensius uno
. . .
Zmyrna cauas Satrachi penitus mittetur ad undas,
Zmyrnam cana diu saecula peruoluent.
At Volusi Annales Paduam morientur ad ipsam
et laxas scombris saepe dabunt tunicas.

My Cinna's Zmyrna *is finally out, nine summers and nine winters after it was conceived, while in the meantime Hortensius...five hundred thousand...in one...* Zmyrna *will be sent all the way to the Satrachus' curled waves, grey centuries will long peruse* Zmyrna. *But Volusius'* Annals *will perish at Padua itself, and often supply loose wraps for mackerel.*

The technique of the poem is minute. There are, or were, eight lines, divided into two sections of four, each section beginning with the name of Cinna's poem. In the second section two rivers are mentioned, the Satrachus and the Po (Padua was a mouth of the Po, Latin *Padus*): *Satrachi* stands immediately before the caesura, or pause, of the first hexameter, *Paduam* immediately after that of the second, and both hexameters close with similar phrases: *mittetur ad undas*,

[1] By the grammarian Crassicius: Suet. *Gramm.* 18, with an ingenious parody of Catullus 70.

10

morientur ad ipsam. Nor is it fanciful to hear an echo of the first pentameter in the second:

> Zmyrnam cana diu *sae*cula peruoluent.
> et laxas scombris *sae*pe dabunt tunicas.

A polemical poem in the Callimachean style was not merely a confutation; it was, simultaneously, a demonstration of how poetry ought to be written. Catullus wrote another such poem vilifying the wretched Volusius and his *Annals*, 36 *Annales Volusi*, which has not quite been recognized for what it is.[1] Volusius must have been a neighbouring poet; otherwise there would be no point to the emphatic reference, *Paduam . . . ad ipsam*; and the name is attested on inscriptions from that part of Italy. Catullus pays Cinna an artful compliment: his poem will be read even by that far distant river which it celebrates. But there is a piquancy, also, in the oblique comparison of the two rivers: the broad, familiar Po with its mud and flotsam, the exotic Satrachus, swift and clear – this seems to be the implication of *cauus*; Lucan 2.421-2 applies the adjective to the Tiber and the Rutuba where they rush down from the Apennines. Callimachus had used a similar metaphor for long and short, or bad and good, poetry at the end of his second *Hymn*: Envy (Φθόνος) sidles up to Apollo and whispers an anti-Callimachean opinion into his ear; Apollo gives Envy a kick and replies:

> ''Ασσυρίου ποταμοῖο μέγας ῥόος, ἀλλὰ τὰ πολλὰ
> λύματα γῆς καὶ πολλὸν ἐφ᾽ ὕδατι συρφετὸν ἕλκει.
> Δηοῖ δ᾽ οὐκ ἀπὸ παντὸς ὕδωρ φορέουσι μέλισσαι,
> ἀλλ᾽ ἥτις καθαρή τε καὶ ἀχράαντος ἀνέρπει
> πίδακος ἐξ ἱερῆς ὀλίγη λιβὰς ἄκρον ἄωτον.'   (108–12)

'Great is the flood of the Assyrian river, but it drags much filth of earth and much refuse on its water. No common water do the bees bring to Demeter, but that which seeps up pure and undefiled from a sacred spring, a tiny rill, the crest and flower of water.'

What was the subject of Cinna's poem? The incestuous passion of Zmyrna (or Smyrna or Myrrha) for her father Cinyras, her metamorphosis into a tree, and the subsequent birth of Adonis from her trunk. Precisely the kind of tale Parthenius approved of – erotic, morbid, grotesque – as may be conjectured from the fragments of his poetry and from the poetical handbook Περὶ ἐρωτικῶν παθημάτων 'Tales of passion', which he compiled for the use of Cornelius Gallus. One of these (11) tells of the incestuous passion of Byblis for her brother Caunus, on which Parthenius himself had written a poem. And so he quotes, for example, some of his own lines:

> ἡ δ᾽ ὅτε δή ⟨ῥ᾽⟩ ὀλοοῖο κασιγνήτου νόον ἔγνω,
> κλαῖεν ἀηδονίδων θαμινώτερον, αἵ τ᾽ ἐνὶ βήσσῃς
> Σιθονίῳ κούρῳ πέρι μυρίον αἰάζουσιν.

[1] See below, pp. 26–7.

11

καί ῥα κατὰ στυφελοῖο σαρωνίδος αὐτίκα μίτρην
ἀψαμένη δειρὴν ἐνεθήκατο · ταὶ δ' ἐπ' ἐκείνη
βεύδεα παρθενικαὶ Μιλησίδες ἐρρήξαντο.

*And when she knew her brother's cruel mind, she wailed more loudly than the nightin-
gales that in the groves make myriad-lament for the Sithonian boy. And from a sturdy
oak she straightway tied her head-scarf, and therein laid her neck: for her the virgins
of Miletus rent their garments.*

Six hexameters, divided into two sections of three, the third and sixth hexameter
being a spondaic: the phrase ἡ δ' ὅτε δή ῥ' ὀλοοῖο (1) is echoed by καί ῥα κατὰ
στυφελοῖο (4); θαμινώτερον (2) is metrically equivalent to ἐνεθήκατο (5), and
both words are followed by similar phrases: αἵ τ' ἐνὶ βήσσης, ταὶ δ' ἐπ' ἐκείνη.
There are two proper names, carefully disposed: Σιθονίῳ at the beginning of
the third hexameter, and Μιλησίδες immediately after the caesura of the sixth.[1]
The relative dates of Parthenius' poem and Catullus 95 cannot now be determined; or Catullus may not have been thinking of these lines in particular as
he composed 95: yet the technique of 95 evidently owes a good deal to the
example of Parthenius.

The Satrachus (or Σέτραχος) 'surfaces' at only three places in Greek poetry:
Lycophron 448, Nonnus 13.459 with an allusion to Myrrha, and Parthenius frs.
23 and 24 – a recondite river for a young Latin poet to find without an experienced
guide. It is entirely probable that Parthenius suggested this subject to Cinna for
an epyllion, as he later suggested subjects to Gallus for epyllia and elegies.

It remains to characterize Euphorion, *Callimachus dimidiatus*. Euphorion had
Callimachus' interest in philology, mythology, geography, aetiology, and more
than his interest in the epyllion, a form that Callimachus invented but did not
exploit. Callimachus' *Hecale* has almost every feature of the later epyllion, including an αἴτιον (the establishment of the Hecalesian festival) at the end. But one
feature is conspicuously absent: a histrionic woman at centre-stage. It is doubtful whether Callimachus was capable of representing a woman's feelings, or cared
to: his Cydippe is a sort of wax figurine,[2] an artifact manipulated by the poet,
whose concern is for the male attractiveness of Acontius (*Aetia* frs. 68 and 69).
Berenice suffers a similar disregard. Callimachus' *Lock of Berenice* is an elegant
and frigid poem that allows no emotion whatever to the bereft queen and bride;
only in Catullus' hands does she come alive, all the tender feminine touches
having been added, apparently, in his translation (66).[3] Medea, by contrast,
seems to acquire a vitality and will of her own: the confused girl smitten with

[1] Rohde (1914) 102n. failed to appreciate the symmetry of Parthenius' lines or the delicacy and
restraint of his narrative and supposed that some words had been lost after ἐνεθήκατο. Eurydice's
death is presented in the same elliptical style, *Georg.* 4.457–61. Parthenius was Virgil's tutor in Greek,
and Virgil imitated – in effect, transcribed – one of his lines; Clausen (1976a).

[2] Wilamowitz (1924) I 188; contrast the Cydippe of 'Ovid', *Heroides* 21.

[3] Putnam (1960).

love becoming the impassioned, masterful woman – her sentimental education is the achievement of Apollonius in his *Argonautica*. And Euphorion, as did Catullus and Virgil after him, learned from Apollonius. An instructive fragment is preserved.[1] Apriate, while being hotly pursued along a precipice by the hero Trambelus, unburdens herself of an erudite and disdainful speech, and then – in a single hexameter – throws herself into the sea: the occasion of an αἴτιον. Euphorion is not interested in narrative, he is interested rather in obscure mythological allusion and the emotional state of his heroine: his procedure consequently, like that of Catullus in his epyllion (64), is elliptical and abrupt.

2. 'THE MARRIAGE OF PELEUS AND THETIS'

An epyllion was more or less expected of the complete New Poet;[2] and Catullus would have been eager to emulate Cinna, whose *Zmyrna* he so extravagantly admired. *The Marriage of Peleus and Thetis*, as 64 is usually called, is Catullus' longest and most ambitious poem, undoubtedly his intended masterpiece; a beautiful poem only partially successful but necessary to an understanding of Catullus. Catullus did not spend nine years working on it (is there a note of banter in his compliment to Cinna?); but he did not write it in a single mood of excitement, nor easily. 64 is learned and laborious, a specimen of strictly premeditated art.

Formality is established at the outset, and a sense of remoteness from experience:

> Peliaco quondam prognatae uertice pinus
> dicuntur liquidas Neptuni nasse per undas
> Phasidos ad fluctus et fines Aeeteos...   (1–3)

On Pelion's crest once long ago pine-trees were born, and swam (men say) through Neptune's liquid waves to Phasis' waters and the borders of Aeetes...

In these lines there is nothing of the apparent easiness with which, for instance, 50 begins: *Hesterno, Licini, die otiosi...* 'Yesterday, Licinius, at our leisure...'; so might Cicero have begun a letter to an intimate friend, the rhythm of the hendecasyllable being so close to that of ordinary cultivated speech.

It is of the essence of this poetry that there should be no dissimulation of the means by which its effect is attained. Certain features would have been recognized immediately by an ancient reader:

Peliaco quondam: an ornamental adjective with an adverb to summon up the dateless past; a formula invented by Callimachus for the beginning of his *Hecale* and then imitated by Theocritus and Moschus.[3]

---

[1] Easily accessible in Page (1940) 495–7. The tale is essentially the same as that of Britomartis (Dictyna) and Minos, told by Callimachus, *Hymn* 2.189–200, which Valerius Cato probably used for his *Dictynna*.

[2] Furius Bibaculus and Ticidas appear to have been exceptions; Cornificius wrote a *Glaucus*.

[3] Bühler (1960) 47.

prognatae: a word antique even in Plautus' day, here alliterating with *Peliaco* and *pinus* in the high archaic style of Ennius; this entire period (1–7) is in fact reminiscent of the opening of Ennius' famous tragedy, the *Medea exul*.

dicuntur: echoed in lines 19 *fertur*, 76 *perhibent*, 124 *perhibent*, 212 *ferunt*. Callimachus never tires of reminding his reader that whatever he tells him is true, that it can be found (he means) somewhere in a book: ἀμάρτυρον οὐδὲν ἀείδω 'nothing unattested sing I'.[1] Callimachus was that rarity – an original imagination almost wholly nourished on books. Catullus was not an immensely learned man; his scholarly gestures are affected therefore, and are to be taken rather as indications of the kind of poem he aspired to write.

Line 3 has been carefully fabricated from pieces of adjacent lines in Apollonius, *Arg.* 2.1277–8 ῥέεθρα | Φάσιδος 'the waters of the Phasis' and 1279 Αἰήταο 'of Aeetes'. A truly exquisite hexameter results: chiastic, alliterative, spondaic, and enclosed with two Greek names of which the first has a Greek ending.

All this – and these three lines are typical of the poem throughout – might seem but an absurd confusion of Hellenistic artifice, with Ennius doubling for Homer; yet the voice of Catullus does emerge, powerfully if obliquely.

64 is, in many ways, a bewildering poem, a maze difficult to penetrate without a plan of some sort. (It may be that Catullus constructed one for his own guidance while writing.)

1–30: the Argonauts set sail, the Nereids rise from the sea, and Peleus immediately falls in love with Thetis.

31–49: their marriage at Pharsalus; the mortal guests arrive.

50–264: the story of Theseus and Ariadne, the suicide of Aegeus, Adriadne's rescue by Bacchus on the isle of Dia – figures on a tapestry draped over the marriage bed.

265–302: the marriage again; the mortal guests depart, the immortal arrive.

303–81: the Parcae – tremulous crones with bits of wool adhering to their withered lips – weave a strange and fateful wedding song in praise of Achilles, the destined son.

382–408: then and now; Catullus reflects bitterly on the godlessness and degeneracy of his own times.

There is an undeniable awkwardness about the structure of the poem, a ponderosity vaguely sensed. The movement of the hexameter itself is noticeably heavy, with the same rhythmic pattern recurring again and again after the main caesura: *prognatae uertice pinus*. No doubt Catullus managed as best he could; but his skill seems to have been as yet unequal to a composition so relatively large and intricate. (His one other attempt of the kind (68), though shorter, is even more perplexed.) The beauty of 64 is intermittent, showing here and there – in 86–93: the sudden onrush of a first love; in 132–201: 'Ariadne passioning for Theseus' perjury and unjust flight' (Shakespeare), a speech Virgil apparently

[1] Fr. 612 Pf.; Norden (1916) 123–4.

knew by heart;[1] in 268–75: the simile of the west wind rippling the sea at dawn; in 278–84: Chiron, down from Pelion's crest, bringing huge bunches of wild-flowers to the bridal pair (Catullus' own invention?).

The story of Peleus and Thetis was immemorially old; it is depicted on the François vase[2] and was already familiar to Homer's audience (*Il.* 24.534–40): Peleus, dear to the gods above all other men from birth, to whom they gave a goddess for wife – a splendid paradigm of mortal happiness, but overshadowed by sorrow: the goddess was unwilling, and their only son foredoomed. The story became, with variants and elaboration, a favourite subject of art and poetry. The last Greek poet of consequence to make use of it was Apollonius, whose *Argonautica* Catullus studied with care, taking from it whatever he could use for his own poem. The form, or idea, of 64 is due ultimately to Callimachus, much in its content and manner, however, to Apollonius. Callimachus' epyllion, the *Hecale*, ends with an αἴτιον, as, presumably, did the *Zmyrna* and the *Io*; but Catullus' epyllion has none, at the end or elsewhere. (The suicide of Aegeus offered an opportunity; but that would have been merely a distraction.) For this singular lack Catullus had a double precedent: Callimachus' story of Acontius and Cydippe has no αἴτιον, though it seems to invite one, nor does Apollonius' story of Jason and Medea, though Books 1, 2, and 4 of the *Argonautica* are replete with such.[3]

> sed quid ego a primo digressus carmine plura
> commemorem...? (116–17)

But why should I digress from the first of my song to recount more...?

Catullus is referring not to the marriage of Peleus and Thetis, as the reader might, for a blurred moment, suppose, but to the story of Theseus and Ariadne (52–75). Now, after embroidering as much of it as pleased him – Ariadne's fearful emotions as she watches Theseus struggling with her brute half-brother, the simile of the storm-felled tree (in both of which passages Catullus is indebted to Apollonius) – Catullus breaks off, in the manner of Apollonius:

> ἀλλὰ τί μύθους
> Αἰθαλίδεω χρειώ με διηνεκέως ἀγορεύειν; (1.648–9)

But why should I tell the tales about Aethalides straight through?

Thus Catullus underlines his own adroit description of the labyrinth and, in so doing, prepares for Ariadne's entrance and great speech (132–201).

[1] Compare 132–3: *Aen.* 4.305–6; 141: 4.316; 154: 4.365–7; 171–2: 4.657–8; 175–6: 4.10; 181–2: 4.21; 201: 4.629. Allowing for the scale and decorum of epic, *Aen.* 4 may be read as an epyllion.
[2] Dated 'about 570 B.C.' by Beazley (1951) 26–9; also depicted on it are Theseus and Ariadne.
[3] Fraser (1972) 1 726–7, 627.

It has been objected that the inflated role of Ariadne impairs the economy of the poem. The incidental story or digression[1] from the main story – if it was that for Catullus – is longer than any other of its kind, and does seem excessive; but so do other features, small as well as large, of this strained and oddly personal poem. The two stories are inversely parallel: the voyage of Peleus ends in love and marriage (in the normal version Peleus is married before the voyage begins), the voyage of Theseus and Ariadne in forgetfulness of love, betrayal, and separation – themes that haunted Catullus' imagination.[2] A happy marriage with a suggestion of sorrow to come: an unhappy marriage (so to speak), with an unexpectedly joyous conclusion; the mortal Peleus in love with the immortal Thetis: the immortal Bacchus in love with the mortal (as then she was) Ariadne – all this Catullus contrived, and wished his reader to notice. Notice, for example, the obvious similarity of the references to Peleus and Bacchus in love:

> tum Thetidis Peleus incensus fertur amore... (19)

Then Peleus is said to have been aflame with love of Thetis...

> te quaerens, Ariadna, tuoque incensus amore... (253)

seeking you, Ariadne, and aflame with love of you...

Ornate, purposeful description of a work of art is a very old device of poetry, as old as Homer's description of the shield of Achilles (*Il.* 18.478–608); and has a long history.

> What men or gods are these? What maidens loth?
> What mad pursuit? What struggle to escape?
> What pipes and timbrels? What wild ecstasy?

Inanimate scenes and figures are stirred briefly to life by the poet's voice; then left to quietness.

> O Attic shape! Fair attitude! with brede
> Of marble men and maidens overwrought...

> talibus amplifice uestis decorata figuris
> puluinar complexa suo uelabat amictu. (265–6)

With such figures richly wrought, the tapestry covered the bed, embracing it in its folds.

Thus, with quiet formality,[3] the turbulent episode of Ariadne concludes.

---

[1] Or ἔκφρασις, the technical term; Friedländer (1912) 1–23.
[2] The forgetfulness of Theseus had become proverbial (Theocr. 2.45–6, where the scholiast puts the blame on Dionysus), but Catullus stresses it as a personal fault leading to his father's death: lines 58, 123, 134–5, 148, 208, 209, 231, 248.
[3] Bühler (1960) 108.

Catullus knew several examples of such description in Hellenistic poetry. In Apollonius 1.721–67: Jason's elaborately figured mantle. In Moschus 2.43–62: Europa's golden flower-basket; in this poem, for the first time, an intimate relationship is established between the ἔκφρασις (the story of Io) and the main story. And, especially, in Theocritus 1.27–56: the goatherd's promised gift to Thyrsis for a song. (Catullus seems to have modelled his song of the Parcae – the deliberate irregularity of the refrain, to suggest in hexameters the form of a song, and the shape of the refrain itself – after the song of Thyrsis.[1]) The gift is a deep wooden cup, washed with sweet wax, two-handled, newly made, still smelling of the knife; and handsomely chased without and within. Within are three scenes. A woman, a divine creature, and two suitors hollow-eyed from love, passionately arguing in turn – but their complaints (unlike Ariadne's) go unheard; the woman is unconcerned, now smiling upon one, now shifting her attention to the other. Hard by, an old fisherman on a sea-cliff, eagerly gathering his great net for a cast with all the sinewy strength of youth. A little apart, a fine vineyard laden with purplish clusters, a boy sitting on a dry-wall to guard, and two foxes, one busily ravaging the ripe grapes, the other eyeing the boy's wallet; meanwhile the boy – careless sentinel – is plaiting a pretty cricket-cage of rush and asphodel. Through reading and studying such lavish, self-delighting passages Catullus was enabled to depict the variety and movement of the wedding reception at Pharsalus (267–302), the wild canorous rout on the isle of Dia (251–64).

A tapestry as a vehicle of the story of Theseus and Ariadne may have been suggested to Catullus by Apollonius, 4.421–34: the murder of Medea's brother Apsyrtus – in Apollonius a grown man who has tracked down the fugitive pair. They lure him to his death with gifts of specious friendship, among them Hypsipyle's crimson robe, fashioned by the very Graces on sea-girt Dia for Dionysus, who gave it to Thoas, and he to Hypsipyle, and she to Jason:

> τοῦ δὲ καὶ ἀμβροσίη ὀδμὴ πέλεν ἐξέτι κείνου
> ἐξ οὗ ἄναξ αὐτὸς Νυσήιος ἐγκατέλεκτο
> ἀκροχάλιξ οἴνῳ καὶ νέκταρι, καλὰ μεμαρπώς
> στήθεα παρθενικῆς Μινωίδος, ἥν ποτε Θησεύς
> Κνωσσόθεν ἑσπομένην Δίῃ ἔνι κάλλιπε νήσῳ.   (4.430–4)

And out of it came forth ambrosial sweetness, after the time Nysa's lord himself lay down upon it, high with wine and nectar, and clasped the lovely breast of Minos' virgin daughter; her Theseus once (for she followed him from Cnossus) left behind on Dia's isle.

Earlier, in Colchis, Jason had told Medea of Ariadne, of how she saved Theseus in his hour of peril; and hinted (for he badly needed Medea's magical aid) that she might elope with him.

[1] Gow (1952) II 16; Wilamowitz (1924) II 303.

ἀλλ' ἡ μὲν καὶ νηός, ἐπεὶ χόλον εὔνασε Μίνως,
σὺν τῷ ἐφεζομένη πάτρην λίπε · τὴν δὲ καὶ αὐτοὶ
ἀθάνατοι φίλαντο, μέσῳ δέ οἱ αἰθέρι τέκμωρ
ἀστερόεις στέφανος, τόν τε κλείουσ' Ἀριάδνης,
πάννυχος οὐρανίοις ἐνελίσσεται εἰδώλοισιν.   (3.1000–4)

But she, when Minos' wrath was lulled, boarded ship with Theseus, and left her country. Even the gods loved her, and in mid-sky a sign, a starry crown that men call Ariadne's, wheels all night among the heavenly figures.

A seductive paradigm, with a considerable adjustment and a significant omission. The wrath of Minos remained vigilant and unsleeping,[1] nor is there a word about the forsaken Ariadne. The gods loved her...Apollonius' version (or perversion) of the story is a poet's: Jason persuades the foreign girl with his sweet Hellenic speech.

Perhaps Catullus was emboldened by the example of Apollonius. All other accounts agree:[2] Thetis was a most reluctant bride. (In a fit of rage she left Peleus soon after the birth of Achilles: Apollonius 4.865–79 – an inconvenient detail and so omitted by Catullus.) But Catullus twice insists to the contrary, with all the force and elegance of rhetoric at his command:

> tum Thetidis Peleus incensus fertur amore,
> tum Thetis humanos non despexit hymenaeos,
> tum Thetidi pater ipse iugandum Pelea sensit.   (19–21)

Then Peleus is said to have been aflame with love of Thetis, then Thetis did not scorn a human marriage, then the father himself of the gods deemed that Peleus should be joined to Thetis.

And again, in the wedding song:

> nulla domus tales umquam contexit amores,
> nullus amor tali coniunxit foedere amantis,
> qualis adest Thetidi, qualis concordia Peleo.   (334–6)

No house ever sheltered such love, no love ever joined lovers in such a compact, such a harmonious compact as that of Thetis, of Peleus.

Why did Catullus make so drastic a 'correction' in so venerable a story? In part, his reason must have been that of Apollonius, a poet's: to satisfy the logic of his poem as he conceived it; for Catullus is an uncompromising artist. But the peculiar emphasis can be related only to the intensity of his own awareness and desire.

For Catullus, then and now, *quondam* and *nunc*, were starkly opposed – an

---

[1] Clausen (1976b).
[2] With the curious exception of Alcaeus 42 (Lobel–Page), a poem that Catullus could hardly have known.

ideal past and the present, void of innocence and miserable. This emotional perspective recurs in the poems to or about Lesbia, in 8, 11, 58, 68.67–76, 72, 76.

> Miser Catulle, desinas ineptire,
> et quod uides perisse perditum ducas.
> fulsere *quondam* candidi tibi soles... (8.1–3)

Poor Catullus, stop playing the fool, and what you see is lost, consider lost. Bright suns once shone upon you...

> fulsere uere candidi tibi soles.
> *nunc* iam illa non uolt... (8.8–9)

Bright suns truly shone upon you. Now she no longer wants it...

In the luminous, mythical world Catullus envisions, the felicity of Peleus must be pure and undisturbed:

> talia praefantes quondam felicia Pelei
> carmina diuino cecinerunt pectore Parcae. (382–3)

With such glad and solemn song the Parcae sang for Peleus once from their divining hearts.

Now earth is imbrued with crime and guilt, horrible desecrations of kinship, faith, love. A reference to Hesiod (*Works and Days* 177–201) will not suffice to explain the powerful, dark conclusion of this poem.[1] Few poets can have felt so painfully the pollution and remorse of time. *Peliaco quondam*: at the beginning *quondam* is traditional, at the end it is personal as well. The poem is both.

3. 'CATVLLI VERONENSIS LIBER'[2]

> Cui dono lepidum nouum libellum
> arida modo pumice expolitum?
> Corneli, tibi; namque tu solebas
> meas esse aliquid putare nugas
> iam tum, cum ausus es unus Italorum
> omne aeuum tribus explicare cartis
> doctis, Iuppiter, et laboriosis.
> quare habe tibi quidquid hoc libelli,
> qualecumque quod, o patrona uirgo,
> plus uno maneat perenne saeclo.

To whom shall I give this pretty new book, just polished with dry pumice-stone? Cornelius, to you; for you thought my trifles worth something even then, when you

---

[1] As Wilamowitz understood (1924) II 304: 'In der Seele des Dichters nicht in seiner Hand-bibliothek ist die Antwort zu suchen.'

[2] This section appeared originally in *Class. Philology* 71 (1976), and is reprinted in a somewhat revised form by kind permission of the University of Chicago Press.

dared, alone of Italians, to unfold all the world's history in three volumes – learned volumes! and laborious! So have this for yours, this little book; and such as it is, may it, o patron Muse, last more than one age.

With this brief and unobtrusive poem, for which almost no precedent exists, Catullus introduces himself and his book. Commentators cite Meleager:

Μοῦσα φίλα, τίνι τάνδε φέρεις πάγκαρπον ἀοιδάν,
ἢ τίς ὁ καὶ τεύξας ὑμνοθετᾶν στέφανον;
ἄνυσε μὲν Μελέαγρος, ἀριζάλῳ δὲ Διοκλεῖ
μναμόσυνον ταύταν ἐξεπόνησε χάριν... (*Anth. Pal.* 4.1.1–4)

Dear Muse, to whom do you bring this rich harvest of song? or who was it arranged this garland of poets? It was Meleager, and he fashioned this present as a keepsake for glorious Diocles.

The Muse, the poet and his book, and a receptive friend: there is a similarity, apparent and superficial. Catullus knew Meleager's poem, and may even have had it in mind as he was composing his own. But what, finally, has the studied simplicity of Catullus to do with Meleager's long and implicated conceit? Catullus' poem is personal and Roman. Publication of Nepos' *Chronica* furnished the pretext. Not that Catullus feigned a gratitude he did not feel, rather his gratitude cannot have been altogether literary. Cornelius Nepos was a fellow-Transpadane, considerably older than Catullus, with important friends in Rome, notably Cicero and Atticus; and, as an established author, had bestowed words of praise or encouragement on the younger man. It is not likely that Catullus admired so unreservedly the chronological survey Nepos had compiled, or that he much valued his literary judgement. Some twenty years later Nepos was to maintain that L. Julius Calidus (it is perhaps suggestive that Nepos gives the name in full) was by far the most elegant poet the age had produced after the death of Lucretius and Catullus: *L. Iulium Calidum, quem post Lucretii Catullique mortem multo elegantissumum poetam nostram tulisse aetatem uere uideor posse contendere.*[1] Had Nepos forgotten Catullus' friends Calvus and Cinna? Was he too old to appreciate Cornelius Gallus or Virgil, whose *Eclogues* had just been published? Only one conclusion is probable: like his friend Cicero, Nepos did not care for the *cantores Euphorionis*. But, like Calidus and other worthies, he was an amateur of verse, risqué verse according to Pliny, *Epist.* 5.3.6; fit recipient therefore of a small book of short poems, mostly in hendecasyllables, in which there was little or nothing overtly neoteric.

Was this *libellus* – a papyrus roll – substantially the same as the *liber* – a *codex* or book in the modern sense – that miraculously appeared in Verona towards the end of the thirteenth century? No doubt there is a delicate irony in Catullus' disparagement of his own book; but no *libellus* would contain so many

---

[1] *Att.* 12.4, a biography begun about 35 B.C. and finished after the death of Atticus in 32 B.C.

lines of poetry, nor could the long poems be described, even playfully, as *nugae*, in particular not *Peliaco quondam*, which must originally have formed a *libellus* by itself, like the *Culex* (of about the same length) or the *Ciris* (somewhat longer), or the *Zmyrna* or the *Io*.

Any effort, however subtle or elaborate, to prove that *The Book of Catullus of Verona* is an artistic whole, arranged and published by the poet himself, founders on an obvious hard fact: the physical limitation of the ancient papyrus roll. And for Catullus, as for writers before and after him until the supervention of the *codex*, the papyrus roll was the only 'book'. Too much is now known about the Greek roll, and too much can be inferred about the Latin, to leave room for doubt or special pleading. Book 5 of Lucretius, although shorter than Catullus' putative book by a thousand lines or so, is still extraordinarily long (some 1,457 lines). An ordinary roll would contain a book of Virgil's *Aeneid*, of Ovid's *Amores* or *Ars amatoria*, of Statius' *Thebaid*, of Juvenal, of Martial; a roll, on average, of between 700 and 900 lines.[1]

What, then, did the *libellus* dedicated to Nepos contain? No precise answer can be given; but a poem by Martial, a frequent imitator of Catullus, and the dedicatory poem itself indicate an answer.

'Tis the season to be jolly, the Saturnalia. Martial invites Silius Italicus, serious epic poet and constant imitator of Virgil, to unbend and read the poetry he has sent him, books of it 'steeped with racy jests':

> nec torua lege fronte, sed remissa
> lasciuis madidos iocis libellos.
> sic forsan tener ausus est Catullus
> magno mittere Passerem Maroni. (4.14.11–14)

So mayhap sweet Catullus dared to send
His 'Sparrow' book to Virgil, his great friend.

So mayhap sweet Catullus...A fancy highly agreeable to both parties. It is clear from the context that Martial refers to a book like his own (a *libellus* of 680 lines, not allowing for interstices) and not to a poem or two; and he does so, after the use of antiquity, by quoting the first word of the first poem – in this case, of the first poem after the dedicatory poem, which he may have regarded as belonging to the whole collection.

In metre as in manner the dedicatory poem is consonant with the poems that follow, 2–60, or more exactly, fifty-seven poems and two fragments, 2*b* and 14*b*. Of these, forty-five are in hendecasyllables, a pretty verse (6.17 *lepido...uersu*) in a pretty book, and favoured by the New Poets. In this part of the collection artistic design is discernible. Thus, two similar poems will be separated by a

---

[1] Exact figures in Birt (1882) 292–3.

21

poem dissimilar in subject or metre: 2 and 3, Lesbia's sparrow, by 2*b*; 5 and 7, Lesbia's kisses, by 6; 34 and 36, a hymn and a parody of the hymnic style (36.11–16), by 35; 37 and 39, Egnatius and his gleaming teeth, by 38. The arrangement of 37, 38, 39 and 41, 42, 43 seems especially careful. 37 and 39 are longer poems of almost the same length (20 and 21 lines) in choliambics separated by a short poem (8 lines) in hendecasyllables; both 37 and 39 end with a word of the same meaning: *urina* and *loti*. Conversely, 41 and 43 are short poems of the same length (8 lines) in hendecasyllables separated by a longer poem (24 lines) in the same metre; the three poems are attacks on prostitutes, 41 and 43 directly, 42 indirectly. Such evidence is not sufficient to prove that the *libellus* contained all the polymetric poems; but probable cause for believing that it contained most of them, and in their present order.

If Catullus did not edit his 'collected poems', who did, and when? A member of his circle, a close friend perhaps – in any case, a *homo uenustus* like himself, and shortly after his death when it would still be possible to do so. The editor (so call him) collected all the poems he could find, poems in Catullus' papers whether at Rome or Verona, poems in the hands of friends, poems...[1] How did he go about putting them together? To begin with he had the *libellus*: to it he could add any unpublished polymetric poems. An easy, mechanical decision that would not disturb the already published order. If the *libellus* ended with 50[2] – and 50 would be, for several reasons, the perfect ending – then the position of 51, which should precede 11, as 2 precedes 3 and 5 precedes 7, or at least stand closer to it, is explicable. The fourth stanza of 51 is somehow unsatisfactory, and no ingenuity of interpretation will make it seem otherwise.[3] May it be that this famed poem of passion did not quite satisfy its author? That Catullus left it out of his *libellus*; and that the editor, connecting the first line of 50 (*otiosi*) with the last stanza of 51 (*otium, otio, otium*), added it? 53 and 56 are amusing squibs, 52 and 59 less so; 57 is as elegantly obscene as 29, 58 extremely moving. Catullus may have omitted these poems (reasons why can be invented), or he may have written them after he had published his *libellus*. It need not be assumed that he died immediately thereafter, or that he gave up writing in these congenial metres. Very little can be made of 54; 55 reads like a failed metrical experiment; 58*b* must be unfinished; and 60 is a mere scrap. Would Catullus end his *libellus*, his pretty book of poems, this way? No; but the editor, more concerned to preserve than to present, would.

The second *libellus*, the editor's, begins with 61, an epithalamium, for a reason simple enough: it is in virtually the same metre as most of the poems in

---

[1] Naturally he missed a few; Mynors (1958) 106.
[2] A *libellus* of 772 lines, not allowing for the lacuna in 2*b* or 14*b* or for interstices.
[3] See below, pp. 24–5.

Catullus' *libellus*. Next, the editor put the other epithalamium (62); and next, the *Attis* in galliambics (63) to separate the two poems in hexameters, so that the epyllion (64) enjoys pride of place at the end.

At some point the editor had decided to keep all the elegiac poems, of no matter what length, together. Again, an easy, mechanical decision. (The editor must not, however, be imagined as a man without taste; an occasional artfulness of arrangement may be owing to him.) The third *libellus* begins with a suitably long elegiac poem, 65–6; perhaps the editor thought it appropriate initially because of the reference to the Muses in the opening lines:

> Etsi me adsiduo confectum cura dolore
> seuocat a doctis, Hortale, uirginibus,
> nec potis est dulcis Musarum expromere fetus
> mens animi... (65.1–4)

Although I am so wearied with constant sorrow, Hortalus, that grief keeps me from the learned maids, and my inmost soul is unable to produce the sweet fruits of the Muses...

Three rolls, *tres libelli*, the first containing poems 1–60, or 863 lines, not allowing for the lacuna in 2*b* or 14*b* or for interstices; the second, poems 61–4, or 802 lines, allowing for the lacuna in 61 but not for that in 62 or 64 or for interstices; the third, poems 65–116, or 644 lines, not allowing for the lacuna in 68 (after line 141) or 78*b* or for interstices – or 2,309 lines in all.[1]

Another consequence of the size of the roll is that collected editions of an author's work could not exist, except in the sense that the rolls containing them could be kept in the same bucket... Volumes containing the whole corpus of an author's work only became possible after the invention of the codex, and especially of the vellum codex.[2]

In late antiquity, probably in the fourth century, these three rolls, or rather rolls copied from them, were translated into a *codex* with the first poem now serving as a dedication to the whole collection. From such a *codex*, by a long and hazardous route, descends *The Book of Catullus of Verona*.[3]

---

[1] The first three books of Horace's *Odes* were published together, *tres libelli*: the first containing 876 lines; the second, 572 lines; the third, 1,004 lines – or 2,452 lines in all, not allowing for interstices.

[2] Kenyon (1951) 65.

[3] Additional documentation of this argument in Clausen (1976c).

4. LESBIA, SIRMIO, CALVUS

51

Ille mi par esse deo uidetur,
ille, si fas est, superare diuos,
qui sedens aduersus identidem te
    spectat et audit
dulce ridentem, misero quod omnis   5
eripit sensus mihi; nam simul te,
Lesbia, aspexi, nihil est super mi
    . . .
lingua sed torpet, tenuis sub artus
flamma demanat, sonitu suopte   10
tintinant aures, gemina teguntur
    lumina nocte.
otium, Catulle, tibi molestum est,
otio exsultas nimiumque gestis
otium et reges prius et beatas   15
    perdidit urbes.

He seems to me the equal of a god,
He seems, if that may be, above the gods,
Who sitting opposite looks again and again
At you and hears

Your sweet laughter – and misery strips me
Of all my senses; for once I have seen you,
Lesbia, nothing remains to me,
No voice . . .

But my tongue grows numb, a thin flame
Flows through my limbs, with their own sound
My ears ring, my eyes are covered
With double night.

Idleness, Catullus, is your trouble,
Idleness – you're wild, beyond restraint:
Idleness has ruined kings of old
And prosperous cities.

This is commonly taken as Catullus' first poem to 'Lesbia'. Catullus watches
jealously – so the scene is imagined – as another man converses with Clodia:
his senses waver, he nearly faints, he recollects an old and passionate[1] poem by
Sappho: Φαίνεταί μοι κῆνος ἴσος θέοισιν 'He seems to me the equal of the gods'.
Hence, from an altered point of view, this translation; and hence the pseudonym

---

[1] And well known, an 'anthology piece'; Russell (1964) on 10.2 and Ross (1969a) 149–50.
Catullus had not read through the *opera omnia* of Sappho.

24

Lesbia. But Lesbia no more wanted explaining than did Cynthia or Delia or the others; and she had already been introduced, in hendecasyllables, to the reader of the *libellus*, 5.1 *Viuamus, mea Lesbia, atque amemus* 'Let us live, my Lesbia, and love.' A less romantic aspect is ignored. This is indeed a first poem, the first Latin poem written in Sapphic stanzas: a bold and not altogether successful literary experiment. The Hellenistic poets, although they were given to renovating old forms, did not attempt this one; perhaps they knew better. Catullus' poem may plausibly claim to be the first Sapphic after Sappho.

It is by no means an inert translation: Catullus was concerned to modernize Sappho, to bring her poem up to date. To a close rendering of her first line he adds a second entirely his own, importing a note of Roman solemnity.[1] Lines 5 and 6 exhibit him enveloped in his own misery, *misero...mihi*; his general condition preceding a diagnosis of individual symptoms. Sappho's symptoms have been so re-ordered by Catullus that sight falls last: it was, in the first instance, the vision of Lesbia that all but unnerved him. Here in his third stanza, Catullus the New Poet has most carefully shaped and refined Sappho. There is a detail of Hellenistic technique – the postposition of *sed* – at the beginning; a verbal sophistication – *gemina...nocte* – at the end. In each line the caesura occurs at the same point, coinciding with the end of a clause; and each clause is discrete. With this stanza Catullus' direct emulation of Sappho ends (he disregards her fourth stanza); but his poem does not.

For many readers, however, it will always seem to end – as Landor maintained it did – with the beautiful cadence *lumina nocte*; a sort of premature success that Catullus cannot have intended. Sappho's 'congress of emotions' (so termed by 'Longinus': παθῶν σύνοδος) apparently concluded with a brief moralizing soliloquy: 'But all is endurable...' (The first line of a fifth, and probably final, stanza is preserved partially corrupt in 'Longinus'.) Catullus designed a similar conclusion, but with a larger reference, Roman in sensibility. At this juncture his poem fails: the added stanza is abrupt and inconsequent, and the mechanism of effect – *otium, otio, otium* – too obvious. The poet's erotic trouble appears as contingent, as hardly related to the downfall and perdition of empires.

58

Caeli, Lesbia nostra, Lesbia illa,
illa Lesbia, quam Catullus unam
plus quam se atque suos amauit omnes,
nunc in quadriuiis et angiportis
glubit magnanimi Remi nepotes.

[1] Fedeli (1972) 276; to his examples add Suet. *Div. Aug.* 98.

Caelius, my Lesbia, the Lesbia,
Lesbia, the one Catullus loved
more than himself and all his own,
now, in cross-roads and alleys,
'peels' great-souled Remus' sons.

The iteration of Lesbia's name is extremely moving. The nearest equivalent in Latin is, perhaps, the anguished cry with which Cicero begins a letter to his brother, 1.3.1 *Mi frater, mi frater, mi frater* 'My brother, my brother, my brother'; in English, David's lament for his son: 'O my son Absalom, my son, my son Absalom'. The poem consists of a single sentence of unrelenting intensity culminating in the stark juxtaposition *glubit magnanimi*: a low word, out of the gutter, and a high heroic word; with such force can Catullus – as only he, of Roman poets, can – bring the weight of the fabled past to bear on his own enormous sense of injury and disgust.

36

Annales Volusi, cacata carta

'*Annals* of Volusius...' This drastic line, the first and last of the poem,[1] defines its subject: poetry, the old and outmoded as opposed, implicitly, to the neat and new: the poetry of Catullus and Cinna and their friends, of which this poem is meant to be, as it is, an elegant specimen.[2]

Lesbia had made a naughty vow to Venus and Cupid: if Catullus should be restored to her and cease hurling his fierce 'iambs', then she would donate the choicest verse of the worst poet (meaning Catullus) to the slow-footed god of fire. Catullus assents: let her charming vow be paid, and into the fire with – the *Annals* of Volusius! Lesbia, like the inamorata of Caecilius in the poem preceding, is a *docta puella*, a witty, seductive woman whose taste in poetry and poets is impeccable. This peculiar involvement of poetry (or pedantry, as occasionally it becomes) with passion is not easy to comprehend, not even with the help of Catullus' 'explication' (68.1–40).

The amusing little comedy of Lesbia's vow serves as a pretext for Catullus' prayer to the goddess of love and the sea – an exquisite passage of literary and personal geography:

nunc, o caeruleo creata ponto,
quae sanctum Idalium Vriosque apertos,
quaeque Ancona Cnidumque harundinosam
colis quaeque Amathunta, quaeque Golgos,
quaeque Durrachium Hadriae tabernam...   (11–15)

Now, o thou created of the sky-blue sea,
that dost dwell in holy Idalium and wind-swept Urii,
in Ancona and reedy Cnidus,
in Amathus, in Golgi,
in Dyrrachium, Adria's tavern...

---

[1] Like 16.1 and 57.1, lines equally drastic.   [2] See above, p. 11.

Hadriae taberna: sailors' slang picked up by Catullus on his Bithynian tour? Here it functions to reduce the heightened tone of the invocation to the conversational level of the rest of the poem (1–10, 16–20). Idalium, Urii, Ancona,[1] Cnidus, Amathus, Golgi, Dyrrachium – all names of places where the goddess of love was worshipped, with scant ceremony, as may be surmised, at Dyrrachium.

A line in *Peliaco quondam*: *quaeque regis Golgos quaeque Idalium frondosum* 'that dost rule Golgi and leafy Idalium' (64.96) indicates that Catullus had read and remembered Theocritus: Δέσποιν', ἃ Γολγώς τε καὶ Ἰδάλιον ἐφίλησας 'Lady, that dost love Golgi and Idalium' (15.100). Catullus would have read of Cnidus too, and probably visited it on his sight-seeing cruise down the coast of Asia Minor (46.6); for it was a tourist attraction, and he seems to have gone as far south as Rhodes (4.8). Golgi, Idalium, and Amathus were towns in Cyprus – towns Catullus had never seen – and all three connected with the legend of Adonis. At Amathus, according to Pausanias 9.41.2, was an ancient sanctuary of Adonis and Aphrodite. But Amathus is not now to be found, whether in prose or poetry, before Catullus. Where did Catullus find so rare a name? Most likely in Cinna's *Zmyrna*;[2] and he employs it here as he employs *Satrachus* in 95: to flatter a poet-friend and point the contrast between the New Poetry and the old. Three names remain: Dyrrachium, Urii, Ancona – names of the three stopping-places on Catullus' voyage through the Adriatic in the spring or summer of 56 B.C.[3] From Dyrrachium he crossed over to Urii, a small harbour on the northern side of Monte Gargano, then sailed up the coast to Ancona before a following wind,[4] then into the Po (by the Padua mouth?) – and home at last to Sirmio.

31

Perhaps no poem of Catullus has been so persistently misread or, for all its brevity, so incompletely read. The subject of the poem, home-coming, is likely to occasion diffuse sentiment; but 31 is not a sentimental poem. Whatever the emotions Catullus felt as he arrived at Sirmio, they were not – not, certainly, as expressed in his poem – 'the simplest and most natural...plainly expressed' (Kroll, and others similarly). Catullus' delight is exactly reflected in the wit and complicated play, the 'happiness', of his language.

The poem commences with a flamboyant conceit, *uterque Neptunus*: Neptune

[1] That Venus had a temple at Ancona is known from another poet, Juvenal 4.40. To make poetic a place obscure or previously unsung, as here by associating it (Urii) with illustrious names, is in the Alexandrian tradition; cf. 64.35–6 (Cieros).
[2] And *Amathusia* (68.51)? Similarly, Parthenius in his *Aphrodite* (fr. 3) calls the goddess 'Acamantis' after Acamas, an obscure promontory in Cyprus. It is surely no accident that nearly all of Parthenius' fragments are preserved in geographical authors.
[3] Wiseman (1969) 42–5.
[4] Cf. 4.18–24. Dante, *Purg.* 28.19–21, heard the south wind, the scirocco, stirring among the boughs of the pine-wood at Chiassi (Ravenna), past which Catullus would have sailed.

in his either capacity, that is, sweet or salt. (A dim memory of an old Italic god of lakes and rivers may have lingered on in the region of the Po.)

> Paene insularum, Sirmio, insularumque
> ocelle, quascumque in liquentibus stagnis
> marique uasto fert uterque Neptunus... (1–3)

Gem[1] of all-but-islands and islands, Sirmio, which either Neptune bears in clear, quiet lakes and the vast sea...

Obviously, Catullus was glad to be home:

> quam te libenter quamque laetus inuiso (4)

how glad and how happy I am to see you

– a plain statement, but immediately qualified with a playfully erudite geographical allusion in the manner of Callimachus (or Parthenius):

> uix mi ipse credens Thyniam atque Bithynos
> liquisse campos... (5–6)

scarce myself believing I have left behind Thynia and the plains of Bithynia...

The Thyni and Bithyni were in fact adjacent but distinct tribes (Herod. 1.28), as Catullus would have learned in Bithynia. But he cared nothing for the ethnic differentiation, and even shows a fine indifference to the rough terrain of the province.

> o quid solutis est beatius curis,
> cum mens onus reponit ac peregrino
> labore fessi uenimus larem ad nostrum
> desideratoque acquiescimus lecto?
> hoc est quod unum est pro laboribus tantis. (7–11)

O what more blissful than cares resolved, when the mind lays down its burden, and, weary from effort abroad, we come to our own household and rest on the bed we have longed for. This, this alone makes up for efforts so great.

Again, a plain statement, ampler and occupying the centre of the poem, with only a hint of deliberate rhetoric in the contrast *peregrino/nostrum*; but again qualified, in a final exuberance of expression:

> salue, o uenusta Sirmio, atque ero gaude,
> gaudete uosque, o Lydiae lacus undae,
> ridete quidquid est domi cachinnorum. (13–15)

Hail o lovely Sirmio, and be glad for your master, and you, o Lydian waves of the lake, be glad, laugh with all the noisy laughter you own.

[1] See p. 32 n. 1.

o uenusta Sirmio: *uenustus* belongs to the same range of feeling as *ocellus* (2 *ocelle*). Only one other writer uses both these words of lovely places, Cicero – of his villas, *Att.* 16.6.2 *ocellos Italiae*, of the sea-shore at Astura (?), *Att.* 15.16*b*.1 *haec loca uenusta*. (On the language of Catullus in his polymetric poems the most informative 'commentator' by far is Cicero in his letters.) But the vocative here is unique, and all but personifies Sirmio. The tone is further heightened by the second apostrophe *o Lydiae lacus undae*; an example of enallage or 'transferred epithet', a figure appropriate to the highest style of poetry. Earlier critics therefore, persuaded that Catullus should be simpler in his shorter poems, wished to rid the line both of its figure and its too erudite allusion (by emendation, *limpidi*, *lucidae*, or the like): plainly they were reading, or fancied they were, a quite different poem.

85

> Odi et amo. quare id faciam, fortasse requiris.
> nescio sed fieri sentio et excrucior.

I hate and love. Why do that, perhaps you ask. I don't know, but I feel it happen and am tormented.

The pathos of ordinary speech: fourteen words, a poem. The reader may be strangely moved, and perhaps ask why. There is no ornament of language, no learned allusion, no very striking word. For too much, probably, has been made of *excrucior* in this context: while *excrucior* can signify the deepest distress, it is Plautine and colloquial, like *discrucior* in 66.76 or Plaut. *Cas.* 276 *ego discrucior miser amore* 'I am wretchedly distracted by love'; the metaphor is scarcely felt. The whole effect of a poem only two lines long, a couplet, must depend rather, or as well, upon the compression and exactness of its form. The hexameter is active in sense (*faciam*), the pentameter passive (*fieri*); the initial phrase of the hexameter (*od(i) et amo*) is balanced by the final phrase of the pentameter (*senti(o) et excrucior*); and the pentameter is so articulated that a rhythmic emphasis falls on *nescio* and *sentio*: I don't know, I feel. The poem defines not so much the feeling as the fact of feeling.

109

> Iucundum, mea uita, mihi proponis amorem
> hunc nostrum inter nos perpetuumque fore.
> di magni, facite ut uere promittere possit,
> atque id sincere dicat et ex animo,
> ut liceat nobis tota perducere uita
> aeternum hoc sanctae foedus amicitiae.

You promise me, my life, that this love of ours will be pleasant, and will endure. Great gods, make her able to promise truly, and say this sincerely and from her heart, so that we may extend, our whole life through, this everlasting compact of sacred friendship.

The poem rises, as it were, from the bland elegance of the first couplet through the prayerful earnestness of the second to the solemn conclusion of the third. Why, then, does the final, climactic line fall flat? Or rather, why does it seem to? Lesbia proposes love (*amor*), Catullus opposes friendship (*amicitia*): the structure of the poem, and of the last line in particular, requires that 'friendship' be the stronger, the weightier term. No English reader can hope to have a contemporary Roman's sense of *amicitia*, much less of its absolute rightness here. *Amicitia* was basically a political term, well understood and capable of accurate definition.

amicitia in politics was a responsible relationship. A man expected from his friends not only support at the polls, but aid in the perils of public life, the unending prosecutions brought from political motives by his personal enemies, his *inimici*, his rivals in the contest for office and for the manifold rewards of public life. Friendship for the man in politics was a sacred agreement.[1]

Catullus 'abuses' the phrase *foedus amicitiae* to define the unusual nature of the relationship he wants to have with Lesbia. *Aeternum hoc sanctae foedus amicitiae*: the intertwining word-order is Hellenistic,[2] the sentiment pure Roman.

The second couplet depends mainly upon adverbs for effect – more precisely, two adverbs and an adverbial phrase. Catullus remembered a passage in Terence's *Eunuchus* (a young man speaking to a prostitute):

> utinam istuc uerbum *ex animo* ac *uere* diceres
> 'potius quam te inimicum habeam'! si istuc crederem
> *sincere* dici, quiduis possem perpeti. (175–7)

How I wish you said that from your heart and truly, 'rather than have you for an enemy'! If I could believe that was said sincerely, I would be able to endure anything.

In these two passages, and in these two only, are these three adverbs combined. *Potius quam te inimicum habeam*: did *inimicus*, in this context, suggest the erotic possibilities of a political vocabulary to Catullus? However that might be, Catullus discovered this potent metaphor and made it his own; the Augustan elegists neglect it.

50

> Hesterno, Licini, die otiosi
> multum lusimus in meis tabellis,
> ut conuenerat esse delicatos:
> scribens uersiculos uterque nostrum
> ludebat numero modo hoc modo illoc,
> reddens mutua per iocum atque uinum. (1–6)

---

[1] L. R. Taylor, quoted by Ross (1969*a*) 84. On Catullus' metaphorical use of this political vocabulary – *amicitia, foedus, fides, fidus, iniuria, pietas, pius, officium, bene facere, bene uelle* – see Reitzenstein (1912); Ross (1969*a*) 80–95. Most enlightening in this regard is a letter written by Cicero to M. Licinius Crassus in 54 B.C., *Fam.* 5.8: note especially *amicitiae fides* (2), *foederis, sanctissime* (5).

[2] And for that reason objected to by Reitzenstein (1912) 28–9, who preferred to read *aeternae hoc sancte* after the Oxford MS.

Licinius, yesterday at Leisure
We in my tablets took much pleasure,
As either of us then thought fit
To Versify, and deal in Wit;
Now in this sort of verse, now that,
As Mirth and Wine indulg'd the Chat.[1]

Catullus and Calvus had passed an idle day together drinking and making extempore verses; a 'wit-combat' had been stipulated: *ut conuenerat esse delicatos*. (*Delicatus* is practically untranslatable. It is one of those words used by Catullus and, presumably, Calvus and the others – *deliciae, lepor, lepidus, illepidus, facetiae, infacetus, uenustus, inuenustus, iucundus, elegans, inelegans, ineptus, ludere*; ordinary words, frequent in Plautus and Terence, and yet, as used by the New Poets, intimating a special sensibility.) Catullus went away so fired by the charm and wit of Calvus – *tuo lepore incensus, Licini, facetiisque* (7–8) – that he could neither eat nor sleep; at last, half dead with fatigue, he made this poem as a means of quenching his ardour.

One of Cicero's letters[2] was written under similar circumstances, a brief letter to his lawyer-friend Trebatius Testa which begins: *Illuseras heri inter scyphos* 'You made fun of me yesterday over our cups'. At issue had been an abstruse point of testamentary law. On returning home 'well liquored and late', Cicero looked out the pertinent chapter, found that he had been right, and wrote to Trebatius in the morning to tell him so, closing with a graceful compliment to the younger man. Cicero's letter and Catullus' poem have this in common, that each was prompted by an occasion; but there is a crucial difference. Cicero's letter was intended for Trebatius only; Catullus' poem, though it is addressed to Calvus, was intended for publication. Calvus, after all, did not need to be told what he and Catullus had been doing only a few hours earlier, but other readers would, for the poem's sake.

The poem seems to be an effusion of sentiment; and it is – while being also, as might be expected, a meticulous composition. It is composed of three sections: six lines (1–6) on yesterday's conviviality, seven lines (7–13) on Catullus' emotional reaction, and eight lines (14–41) divided into two subsections (the form is as calculated as the term implies) of four lines each: the making of the poem (14–17), and a playful warning to Calvus:

nunc audax caue sis, precesque nostras,
oramus, caue despuas, ocelle,
ne poenas Nemesis reposcat a te.
est uehemens dea: laedere hanc caueto.   (18–21)

---

[1] An anonymous translation published in 1707: Duckett (1925) 103.
[2] *Fam.* 7.22, cited by Fraenkel (1956) 281–2.

Now don't be over-proud, and don't, I beg you, despise my prayers, dear friend,[1]
*lest Nemesis require penalties of you. She is a vehement goddess: offend her
not.*

By convention Nemesis punished any overweening speech or act, but her wrath
might be averted by spitting, preferably three times. This quaint custom is
hinted at in *despuas* (here first in this sense) and the triple caveat: *caue, caue,
caueto*, the archaic form being put last for a mock-solemn emphasis.

This poem has, finally, a unique feature: Calvus is addressed not once but
four times, once in each section and subsection of the poem. He is twice
addressed by name: *Licini* (1), *Licini* (8), and twice – to match the intensification of mood – with increasing warmth and affection: *iucunde* (16), *ocelle* (19).
So apt is Catullus' response to the passionate and fiery nature of his dearest
friend.[2]

[1] *ocelle*: a diminutive term of endearment which English is helpless to render.
[2] There is a vivid 'portrait' of Calvus in Seneca the Elder, *Contr.* 7.4.6–8.

3

LUCRETIUS

The *De rerum natura* of Lucretius represents one of the rarest of literary accomplishments, a successful didactic poem on a scientific subject. Few great poets have attempted such a work, and many critics, from Aristotle on, have argued that the contradictions which are implicit in the genre, and indeed in all didactic poetry, can never be fully reconciled. 'Didactic poetry is my abhorrence', wrote Shelley in the preface to *Prometheus Unbound*, 'nothing can be equally well expressed in prose that is not tedious and supererogatory in verse', and Mommsen dismissed the greater part of the *De rerum natura* as 'rhythmisierte Mathematik'. What, then, is the relationship between Lucretius the poet and Lucretius the philosopher? To what extent do they come together to form a successful unity? Otto Regenbogen called this the 'central question' in Lucretian criticism,[1] and in his famous essay 'Lukrez: seine Gestalt in seinem Gedicht' he attempted to answer it in three ways: by examining the background of the poem, the personality of the poet, and the structure and quality of the work itself. Most Lucretian criticism falls under one or other of these headings and it will be convenient to consider each in turn.

I. BACKGROUND

One might imagine that a didactic and moralizing work like the *De rerum natura* would have deep roots in the society which produced it. Yet there is a wide disparity of views about the purpose of the poem and the character of the audience for which it was composed. Ostensibly it was written for the poet's aristocratic patron Memmius, but, since literary convention required that a didactic poem be addressed to some particular person, we may suppose that behind Memmius stands the general reader. Both are linked, rather awkwardly, in the famous programmatic passage about the poet's mission.

> ...quoniam haec ratio plerumque uidetur
> tristior esse quibus non est tractata, retroque
> uolgus abhorret ab hac, uolui tibi suauiloquenti
> carmine Pierio rationem exponere nostram...   (1.943–6 ∼ 4.18–21)

[1] Regenbogen (1932) 2.

33

...since my philosophy often seems too bitter to those who have not tasted it, and the crowd shies away from it, I have desired to set out for you, Memmius, an explanation of our system in the sweet language of the Muses...

This passage does not explicitly state that the poem is intended for ordinary men, but it does imply a wider audience than might have been attracted by a purely technical treatise.

We should not, however, exaggerate the popular nature of the poem. There cannot have been in the first century, any more than there is today, a large number of people interested in the indivisible magnitudes of the atom or in the weaknesses in Anaxagoras' theory of *homoeomeria*. In spite of Lucretius' reference to the 'crowd', he has clearly in mind an audience which is prepared to follow a long and complex argument. Granted that the poet simplifies and that some of his arguments are addressed more to the emotions than to the intellect, the *De rerum natura* is nevertheless a serious attempt to explain the principal doctrines of Epicurean physics and it requires the reader's cooperation and concentration. This is true not only of the argument but also of the poetry itself: recent critics have rightly stressed the sophistication of the poet's literary technique and his ability, when he wished, to adopt the allusive manner of his neoteric contemporaries. That Lucretius is a distinctly 'literary' author can be seen from the long list of his debts to earlier writers, both Greek and Latin. To mention only Greek authors, and to exclude the philosophers, there is evidence that he knew Homer, Euripides, Thucydides, parts of the Hippocratic *corpus*, Callimachus, some of the writers of epigram, and probably also Hesiod, Sappho, Aeschylus and Aristophanes. The list is significant not only for its length, but also for the range of its intellectual sympathies.

It is instructive to compare the *De rerum natura* with the philosophical dialogues which Cicero was writing about the same time and with the same general aim, to make the message of Greek philosophy available to his countrymen. In Cicero the manner is less intense: he is constantly aware of his Roman audience and always ready to adapt the argument to the needs of practical men. Lucretius by contrast makes far fewer concessions, and the Roman elements in the poem are outbalanced by those which are clearly Greek. Lucretius' subject is 'the dark discoveries of the Greeks' (1.136) and Epicurus is hailed as 'the glory of the Grecian race' (3.3). The setting is frequently Greek: Book 6 begins with the praise of Athens and ends with an account of the Athenian plague. Greek place-names are ten times as common in the poem as Roman. Apart from a reference to Etruscan scrolls (6.381), to the habit of covering the head during prayer (5.1198–9) and possibly to the *parentatio* (3.51), specifically Roman religious practices are never mentioned in the poem. It is difficult to explain why one who appears so obsessed with religion should have neglected the experience of his own people. Did he consider, as Schmid suggests, that references to Roman ritual would have been out of place in a scientific poem written in the Alexandrian tradition?[1] Or did he prefer to speak indirectly to his countrymen through a polemical treatment of Greek ideas? Whatever the explanation, this apparent reluctance to deal directly with Roman religious practices says something about the audience for which Lucretius wrote.

It is against this background that we must assess Lucretius' attitude towards the events of his own time. It was an age of dangerous instability and violent factional strife. In his childhood and youth Lucretius had lived through the fierce conflict of the Social War, the reign of terror organized by Marius and Cinna and the proscriptions of Sulla. The period which followed Sulla's retirement was hardly less tense, and although the years during which the *De rerum natura* was being written were quieter by contrast with what had gone before, there was continued rioting in the streets and the danger of civil war was coming closer. All this must have had its effect on a sensitive mind and it may account for the intensity with which Lucretius condemns political ambition in the prologue to Book 2 and elsewhere in the poem. Yet he does not drive home the lesson himself, though it would have been easy to reinforce his moral strictures with examples from his own time. The nearest he comes to pointed contemporary comment is in the following lines on the subject of human greed:

> sanguine ciuili rem conflant diuitiasque
> conduplicant auidi, caedem caede accumulantes.   (3.70–1)

> *They mass a fortune through the blood of fellow citizens*
> *and greedily multiply their wealth, heaping death on death.*

Lucretius' contemporaries could hardly have read these lines without thinking of the crimes and confiscations which made the revolution profitable for the strong. But passages of this sort are rare in the poem; for the message of Lucretius was not national regeneration, but personal salvation. In adopting such an attitude he was following the orthodox teaching of his school. Yet, when Epicurus counselled his followers to avoid the political struggle, he did not intend that the state should wither away or lapse into anarchy. Epicurean political theory always implied a distinction between what is right for the philosopher and what is right for the mass of men, and in practice the good life would hardly have been possible without the stability of law.[2] Certainly there were Epicureans at Rome like C. Velleius and L. Manlius Torquatus who managed to reconcile their beliefs with an active public life. But Lucretius was not a man for compromise and his acknowledgement in the first prologue (1.41–3) that, if war comes, Memmius will have to do his duty, is doubtless not so much a statement of principle as a recognition of the inevitable.

[1] Schmid (1944) 98–9.
[2] R. Müller (1969) 63–76. See also Momigliano (1941) 149–57.

It is therefore only in a special sense that the *De rerum natura* can be called a 'tract for the times'. It is not a political poem, and there is no stress on contemporary themes. Even the account of the development of government in Book 5.1105–60 is surprisingly theoretical and it is hard to square what Lucretius says on the subject with what the Romans believed about their own constitutional history. Marxist critics in particular have overemphasized the political relevance of the poem. It is unlikely, for example, that Lucretius' attacks on religion were aimed at the wealthy and powerful whose authority rested in part upon the dignity of established custom. The last century of the Republic offered a rich field for a writer of Lucretius' satiric gifts and there was much which he could have said, had he wished, about the cynical exploitation of religion for political ends. But clearly this was not his purpose. Lily Ross Taylor puts it well: 'His poem on the Nature of Things was not directed to the common man at the mercy of the men who manipulated state cult to suit their own ends. If it had been, Lucretius would not have failed to show up the shocking religious abuses of his day.'[1]

The use which Lucretius made of his philosophical sources raises another issue about the contemporary significance of his poem. Epicureanism was the most conservative of the Hellenistic philosophies, but it was not immune to change and modification. While Lucretius was writing, Epicurean philosophers like Philodemus were busy developing the master's doctrine and attempting to answer the objections of their philosophical opponents. Yet it cannot be established that Lucretius was familiar with Philodemus or was in any way influenced by his work. More significant is the poet's relationship with contemporary Stoicism. The Stoics, along with the members of the New Academy, constituted the principal opposition to Epicureanism, but they are never mentioned in the poem. It is true that much of Lucretius' argument might be interpreted as a direct challenge to Stoic teaching; but Furley has argued convincingly that, when the poet attacks rival schools, the target is always the Presocratics, or the Platonists and Aristotelians.[2] If this is correct, it is a conclusion of some importance: not only is it a significant clue to the understanding of Lucretius' sources but it implies also a somewhat distant attitude on the part of the poet towards the philosophical controversies of his own time. Lucretius must have been aware of the relevance of many of his arguments to current debate, but he was not at pains to point it out or to insist upon his philosophical modernity.

The most crucial problem in relating the *De rerum natura* to its contemporary background concerns the attitude of the poet towards religion. The attack on *religio* is one of the central themes of the poem and it is pressed with such force that Lucretius, like Epicurus himself, has sometimes been considered an atheist.

[1] Taylor (1949) 96.
[2] Furley (1966) 13–33; for a contrary opinion see De Lacy (1948) 12–23.

This verdict cannot be correct and there is little reason to doubt his Epicurean orthodoxy. Not only does he accept the doctrine of the existence of gods in the distant spaces between the worlds, but it is clear from an interesting passage in the prologue to Book 6 about the 'tranquil images of the gods which strike the minds of men' that he was aware of the deeper side of Epicurus' religious teaching. Nevertheless, in spite of his orthodoxy in matters of doctrine, Lucretius' references to religious practice are nearly always hostile and it is difficult to decide where he would have drawn the line between what was acceptable and what was not. We know that Epicurus took pleasure in the public ceremonies and even urged his followers to participate in the sacrifices in spite of the dangers of absorbing false beliefs (Philodemus, *De piet.* 2, col. 108, 9, p. 126 Gomperz). Lucretius, on the other hand, showed little interest in such matters and, like Empedocles, he was repelled by animal sacrifice (5.1198–202).

Epicureans at Rome were often criticized for exaggerating the terrors of religion. The attack on superstition had become a commonplace of the school, and Cicero knew of 'whole books of the philosophers full of discussions of such matters' (*Tusc. disp.* 1.11). What, then, are we to say of the relevance of Lucretius' polemic? Was he flogging a dead horse and attacking beliefs which, as Cicero suggests (*Tusc. disp.* 1.48), troubled no one any longer? To this question two answers have generally been given: either that the real situation was more complex than Cicero admitted, or that Lucretius was not writing for the educated but for the men of the provinces, or even for the 'man in the street'. The second line of argument cannot be correct; for, apart from the fact that scientific epic is not the favourite reading of unsophisticated men, Lucretius makes it clear that superstitious fears affect all men, even kings:

> non populi gentesque tremunt, regesque superbi
> corripiunt diuum percussi membra timore...?   (5.1222–3)
>
> *Do not peoples and nations tremble and proud kings*
> *crouch in terror, struck by fear of the gods?*

The other response is more plausible; for it is not difficult to show that in the last years of the Roman Republic, even among the educated classes, there was a wide variety of religious beliefs and practices. Against the wavering rationalism of Cicero and the hostility of Lucretius we can set the religious conservatism of men like Appius Claudius Pulcher or the popular teaching of the Pythagorean astrologer Nigidius Figulus or the growing support of foreign cults which prompted the Senate to take action four times during the decade 58–48 B.C. Cicero's own evidence is ambivalent: his *De divinatione* was intended to combat an increasing interest in religious prophecy and it ends with an eloquent attack on superstition, which is described as 'spreading throughout the world oppressing the minds of almost everyone and seizing on the weakness of men' (2.148).

It is important to realize that the criticisms of Epicurean exaggeration refer to one topic only, the old stories about the torments of the damned. When Cicero says that legends of this sort were not generally believed, we should take his word for it. These stories are described as 'the marvels of poets and painters', that is to say, they are part of the literary tradition and belong to a different theology from that of the old Roman notion of the *di Manes*. Professor Jocelyn Toynbee, after surveying the literary and epigraphic evidence, concluded that in the late Republic and throughout the Empire, 'views on the nature of the life that awaited the soul beyond the grave were, in the main, optimistic'.[1] It follows that to rescue men from a belief in eternal torment cannot have been a serious part of Lucretius' intention. In fact, the underworld theme is not prominent in the poem, nor in the extant writings of Epicurus is there a single reference to the legends of the damned, although the topic is discussed by Democritus (DK II 207, B 297) and by later Epicurean writers. Lucretius mentions the fear of the underworld in the prologue of the poem, but the long *consolatio* about death in Book 3 is mainly about man's general fear of extinction and not about the terrors of the underworld. The legends of the damned are introduced in one section only (987–1023), but here the poet's interest is in contrasting these ancient stories with the ethical doctrines of Epicurus.

It should now be clear that Lucretius' poem is not to be interpreted simply as an attack on popular religion. If he refers sometimes to fading beliefs and old superstitions, it is as symbols of a more persistent misconception. His target is larger and more important: he is attacking a whole way of looking at the world in theological terms, of explaining its movements and its mystery as evidence of the working of a higher power. *Religio*, as Lucretius conceived it, was not just a source of vulgar superstition: it could also deceive more serious and reflective minds. It was *religio*, for example, which inspired belief in the divinity of heavenly bodies (5.110–21), a view which had impressive philosophical support and was accepted by Aristotle. What Lucretius found humiliating about the theological mode of thought was that it made men slaves. The universe, which ought to inspire wonder, became arbitrary and inexplicable, and men suffered as the victims of their own imaginings. For Lucretius the scientific materialism of Epicurus was a liberating doctrine: it made it possible to see the world as it really was, to understand not just its surface appearance, but its inner workings as well. Sellar may have exaggerated in claiming for Lucretius a 'genuine philosophic impulse and the powers of mind demanded for abstruse and systematic thinking';[2] but there is no mistaking the

---

[1] Toynbee (1971) 38.   [2] Sellar (1889) 335.

genuine excitement, the *diuina uoluptas atque horror*, which the poet feels in the understanding of nature. It is here that we should seek the clue to the meaning of the poem. The pervasive influence of Empedocles proves that Lucretius thought of his poem as belonging to the Presocratic tradition. This does not mean that he would have claimed for his work a philosophical originality – he was the first to acknowledge his debts – but in the physical doctrines of Epicurus he had found a system which gripped his imagination and satisfied his reason. It was this revelation which the poem attempts to describe, and it could not be understood by simple or unsophisticated minds.

2. POET AND PHILOSOPHER

If the central question in Lucretian criticism is the relationship between poetry and philosophy, then it is important to understand the extent to which Lucretius accurately reflects the spirit of Epicurus. The poet clearly thought of himself as an orthodox Epicurean and there can be no doubt about the intensity of his devotion to his philosophical mentor. Yet the *De rerum natura* is very different in tone and character from the writings of Epicurus. How are these differences to be accounted for? One way in which this question has commonly been answered is through an examination of the poet's personality: the *De rerum natura* differs from the writings of Epicurus because Lucretius himself was different. The biographical approach to literature is always hazardous and in the case of Lucretius it is particularly so because it is biographical criticism without a biography. Almost nothing is known about the poet's personal life and we are forced therefore to draw inferences about his personality from the poem itself. Of the external testimony the most influential is that of Jerome. In the additions which he made to Eusebius' *Chronicle* he noted under the year 94 or 93 B.C.: *T. Lucretius poeta nascitur; qui postea amatorio poculo in furorem uersus, cum aliquot libros per interualla insaniae conscripsisset, quos postea Cicero emendauit, propria se manu interfecit anno aetatis XLIIII.* (Titus Lucretius, poet, is born; afterwards, he was driven mad by a love potion, and when, in the intervals between bouts of madness, he had written several books, which Cicero later corrected, he died by his own hand in the forty-fourth year of his age.) Every detail in this sensational sentence has been contested: the dates can hardly be right (see Appendix); Cicero's editorship has been denied on account of his hostility to Epicureanism and defended because of his interest in literature; love potions are not likely to have produced the dire medical consequences which Jerome's statement suggests, though some ancient doctors believed that they did;[1] and the story of madness and suicide, unsupported by any other ancient testimony, may be the result of historical confusion or Christ-

---

[1] See, e.g., Caelius Aurelianus, *Chronic diseases* 1.5.147 (Drabkin).

ian malice. Nevertheless, brief and controversial though it may be, Jerome's statement has done much to set the mould of Lucretian criticism.

Those who have stressed the temperamental differences between Lucretius and Epicurus have often sought confirmation of their view in the poet's pessimism. 'The Epicurean comedy of Nature', wrote Giussani, 'almost changes into tragedy in Lucretius.' The whole question of the poet's pessimism has been discussed at enormous length and widely different verdicts have been reached, ranging from gentle melancholy to morbid depression. It is unlikely that the subject would have bulked so large in Lucretian criticism if Jerome had not written about the poet's madness and suicide and thus challenged critics to find in the poem evidence of mental instability. Such an approach has no doubt been encouraged by the poet's own interest in medical and psychological matters. He is the most Freudian of Latin poets: not only does he discuss, as his subject demanded, the working of the human mind, but he concerns himself also with the explanation of dreams, human sexuality and the psychological effects of fear and insecurity. For all of these interests he could claim respectable Epicurean precedents, but the emphasis which he places on psychological factors is his own. In discussing dreams, for example (4.962–1036), he first makes the orthodox and commonplace point that dreams reflect the pattern of one's waking life, but then he proceeds to discuss sex dreams and wish-fulfilment dreams which cannot be so readily accounted for on the theory which he has presented. Such interest in psychological matters is typical, but in none of the relevant passages is it easy to find evidence of a mind in conflict with itself. The attitude throughout is scientific and rational, not morbid or obsessive. One must be on one's guard therefore against overemphasizing the darker side of Lucretius' personality. It is true that there are sombre pages in the *De rerum natura* and that Lucretius never softens the tragedy of human suffering or human ignorance, but to compare him with Leopardi or to write, as Sellar does, of the 'grandeur of desolation' is to go beyond the evidence of the poem. Moreover the bleaker passages do not necessarily reflect a bias in the man himself. As Seneca recognized (*Vita beata* 13.1), there was an austere side to Epicureanism, and much of what has been interpreted in Lucretius as pessimism is in fact orthodox doctrine.

The same may be said about the internal conflicts which some have seen in the poem. Here too we should look first at the poet's sources. The view of Lucretius as a man divided against himself received its classic statement in the essay which Patin published in 1868. Patin's thesis of an 'Antilucrèce chez Lucrèce' is no longer so influential as it once was, but in various modified forms it has become embedded in the tradition of Lucretian criticism.[1] It rests on the belief that there are contradictions within the *De rerum natura*, and that

---

[1] Patin (1883) I 117–37.

these can be explained only by supposing that in the deepest parts of his nature Lucretius was unconvinced by the doctrine which he expounded. There may be some truth in this assessment, but before one presses it too far, it should be recognized that Epicureanism itself had its own contradictions – between freedom and law, for example, and between detachment and involvement[1] – and it is not easy to reconcile the optimism of its ethics with the neutrality of the atomic world. Such conflicts are implicit in the system itself and it is natural that they should have left their mark on Lucretius' poem. There is another, and more important, factor to be taken into account. Lucretius was not simply summarizing Epicurean physics: he was writing a poem, and poetry sharpens and intensifies the emotional impact of a subject. Epicurus believed that the world is decaying and will one day perish, but when Lucretius (not without a hint of irony) describes the old ploughman shaking his head over the declining fertility of the earth (2.1164–7), the effect is immediate and memorable. Another example of how the emotional involvement of the poet places an essentially orthodox argument in a different light is provided by the satiric passage about love at the end of Book 4. As Kleve has shown,[2] what Lucretius says on the subject is perfectly in accord with the teaching of Epicurus so far as we can reconstruct it; yet the ironic tone of the writing and the violence of the language are likely to leave the reader with a somewhat exaggerated impression of the Epicurean position. To conceive an idea poetically is to modify its shape.

The view that poetry subtly distorts or at least transforms the thought which it expresses would have been familiar to Epicurus. There has been much discussion, especially since Giancotti published his *Il preludio di Lucrezio*,[3] about the extent of the philosopher's opposition to poetry. Giancotti believed that Epicurus wished to discourage only those kinds of poetry which were based on mythological subjects or which appealed to the passions, and that a genuine philosophical poetry would have escaped his censure. But this is not a conclusion which emerges readily from the small number of texts which bear upon the subject, and it is difficult to see how Epicurus could have held it. 'In practice the wise man will not compose poems' (Diog. Laert. 10.121) is the philosopher's unambiguous assertion and he does not modify it with any qualifying phrase. Epicurus' opposition to poetry was not a matter of taste or temperament: it was founded on a serious conviction that the proper language of truth should be free from the glitter of poetry and the exaggerations of rhetoric and related as closely as possible to the objects of sense experience. Such a view would seem to exclude philosophical poetry, though it might leave room for unpretentious forms of verse which made fewer claims upon the reader's mind. We know that Philodemus defended – and composed – poetry of this kind, but

---

[1] The point is well argued by De Lacy (1957) 114–26.
[2] Kleve (1969) 376–83.   [3] Giancotti (1959) 15–90.

he too insisted that, whatever may be the excellence of individual poems, they are not to be judged by veridical or moral standards. All the evidence suggests that the Epicureans, though they may have differed in their attitude to poetry in general, were unanimous in holding that it was not a suitable medium for philosophic thought. Epicurus and Philodemus both seem agreed on this and the Epicurean Colotes wrote a celebrated work attacking Plato's use of poetic myth. Cicero took it for granted that Epicurus could find 'no solid value' in poetry (*Fin.* 1.72) and in his own dialogues he is generally careful to avoid poetical allusions when Epicureans are speaking, though such references are relatively common elsewhere in his philosophical works.[1] There seems no means of escaping the conclusion that, when Lucretius decided to describe the physical doctrine of Epicurus in verse, he was doing something which, from the point of view of his school, was strictly unorthodox.

Almost certainly Lucretius himself was aware of the dilemma. One would not expect much discussion of the function of poetry in a poem about nature, but in fact Lucretius was very conscious of his position as a philosophic poet and there are more than a dozen references to poetry in the *De rerum natura*. From the Epicurean point of view the most striking claim which he makes for poetry is that it lends clarity to an obscure subject (1.933–4 ~ 4.8–9). The emphasis on clarity is certainly Epicurean, but the idea that this might be achieved by writing in verse would have been rejected by Epicurus and indeed by most ancient theorists. It was because of its ambiguity that Aristotle judged the poetic style of Empedocles unsuitable for scientific thought (*Rhet.* 1407a31), and when Philodemus attempted to define obscurity (*Rhet.* 1.158–9 Sudhaus), he listed among its principal causes metaphorical language, digressions and archaisms, all prominent features of Lucretian style. The confident statement therefore that poetry can shed light on dark places sounds like a direct challenge to Epicurean belief. Whether or not Lucretius intended it as such, he must surely have been aware that he was following an unorthodox and difficult course. In spite of a revival of interest in scientific poetry there was nothing in contemporary Latin literature which would have made him confident of success. Lucretius must have been aware that, if philosophy and poetry were to be brought into some kind of creative harmony, he had first to solve a number of difficult problems: in particular he had to find a satisfactory structure for his material and he had to develop a suitable style for poetic argument which would combine the clarity upon which Epicurus insisted with that special excitement of language without which there can be no poetry at all. In the remainder of this discussion we shall examine the solutions which Lucretius sought for these difficulties and we shall deal in turn with the structure, style and imagery of the poem.

[1] Jocelyn (1973) 69.

3. THE POEM

Structure

Like Virgil's *Aeneid*, the *De rerum natura* never received its final revision. But although unrevised, it is not substantially incomplete and there is no compelling reason to believe that Lucretius would have continued beyond the present ending except perhaps to add some identifying lines such as Virgil appended to the *Georgics*. We have the poet's own statement (6.92–5) that Book 6 was designed to conclude the work and its impressive final section on the Athenian plague is the longest descriptive passage in the poem and must surely have been written for its present climactic position. As it stands, the poem has a rational and satisfying structure. It is divided into three parts, each consisting of two books. The first and third parts deal with physical doctrine, the microcosm of the atom in Books 1 and 2 and the macrocosm of the universe in Books 5 and 6. Between these two outer panels the central section describes the Epicurean doctrine of the soul, the senses, the mind and the will. Each of the six books begins with a formal prologue and ends with an extended passage of particular interest or striking poetry. The first book in each pair is more systematic in argument, the second is generally more relaxed and discursive. Each book has a number of clearly articulated sections and within each section there is usually a neat pointing of the argument. This 'klare, harmonische Gliederung der Form' is considered by Büchner an archaic feature of Lucretius' style;[1] and undoubtedly the effect would be monotonous if there was not a considerable variety in the length and tone of the different sections. By means of this careful articulation of the argument, Lucretius creates an impression of logical exactness and sweeps the reader on with an imposing array of balanced proofs. To some extent this impression of a systematic progression is misleading: for if we attempt to follow the argument closely, we soon discover a number of passages where the logical connexion is elusive, and not all of these can be blamed on the inadequacies of the textual tradition or the incompleteness of the poem. But in spite of these difficulties the general impression which the work creates is of great structural simplicity and strength.

So far as we can tell, the broad plan of the *De rerum natura* is the poet's own. No known work of Epicurus appears to be exactly parallel to Lucretius' poem in the order in which the subject matter is presented. The capacity to organize material in a logical and coherent fashion was not one of Epicurus' strong points and critics in antiquity found fault with the looseness and repetitiveness of his most important work (Diog. Laert. 10.7). It is not likely, therefore, that anything which he produced would have anticipated the balanced structure of the *De rerum natura*. It may be, of course, that Lucretius' immediate source

---

[1] Büchner (1936) 15.

was not Epicurus, but his persistent claims to be treading in his master's footsteps and the closeness of many of his arguments to the surviving Greek text suggests that his main debt was to the philosopher himself.[1] If this conclusion is correct, then Lucretius must have undertaken a considerable reorganization of his philosophical material. The problem which he faced was not simply that of the expositor who must present his argument in the most logical manner possible. As a poet he needed also to create a feeling of unity and to direct and condition the reader's response. To achieve this larger purpose, Lucretius concentrated on the anti-theological elements in Epicurean thought and put them in the forefront of his poem. The process begins in the opening prologue. This contains two programmatic passages separated by about seventy lines which between them summarize the contents of the work. The first (54–61) mentions the atoms and the working of the heavens and the second (127–35) stresses the nature of the soul. Some commentators have thought that these two passages represent different stages in the composition of the prologue and this may be so; but in fact both are necessary to indicate the scope of the poem. The *De rerum natura*, as Lucretius presents it, is a work about the soul and about the heavens. It is significant that Aristotle traced the origin of belief in the gods to these same two factors, τὰ περὶ ψυχήν and τὰ μετέωρα, 'the experiences of the soul' and 'celestial phenomena' (fr. 10 Rose). This is the clue to the structure of Lucretius' poem; after the first two books have laid the necessary theoretical foundation, Books 3 and 4 deal with the soul and the senses and Books 5 and 6 with the heavens and the gods. The whole concept of the poem is determined by its theological position. Once this is clear, not only the general outline of the work but also some of its details fall into place. For example Book 4, after the brilliant satiric passage about the nature of love, ends rather quietly with two paragraphs, the first on sterility and the second about the unattractive woman. At first reading they may appear something of an anti-climax; but there is nothing arbitrary or makeshift about them. In the first Lucretius shows that sterility is not caused by the gods and that prayers to heaven will be of no avail. The second passage is designed to show that improbable unions are not the work of heaven and that the shafts of Venus have nothing to do with the matter. Both are part of the anti-theological argument of the poem.

This preoccupation with religion may correspond to something deep in Lucretius' nature. It is possible to argue, as many have done, that the attack on superstition was the main motivation for the poem. But the critic should also be aware of the importance of the religious polemic as an organizing device. It is this which holds the argument together and gives it its emotional force. One may suspect that Lucretius sometimes exaggerated this aspect of Epicurean

---

[1] On Lucretius' sources see Giussani (1896) 1–17.

teaching. The prologues, for example, often draw attention to theological issues which are subsequently lost sight of or passed over without emphasis in the text which follows. The opening of Book 4 is particularly revealing. In the syllabus we are told that one of the main themes of the book will be false beliefs in the ghosts of the dead. This subject was first announced in the preface to Book 1 and is recalled near the beginning of Book 5. With such widespread advertisement one might imagine that belief in ghosts would occupy a major section of the poem. In fact, Lucretius devotes to the subject only a single short paragraph (4.757–67). It is true that these lines could not be understood if separated from the longer discussion of dreams and visions. But that discussion is carried on in a purely scientific manner and is not related particularly to the ghosts of the dead. What this suggests is that in the prologues Lucretius is deliberately directing the attention of his readers to the theological implications of his work even when his own interests lay elsewhere. By stressing this element in Epicurean doctrine, he is guiding and conditioning the reader's emotional response and giving to his scientific account of the world a far-ranging and profound human interest. It was a brilliant solution to the problem of unity.

Style

Something must now be said about style, though in a brief survey it is not possible to do more than touch on a few of the more important points. We may begin with the problem of vocabulary. Three times in the poem Lucretius complains of the poverty of the Latin language, always in relation to the translation of unfamiliar ideas, and he was clearly aware of his pioneering role in the development of a philosophical vocabulary. There was no difficulty with simple concepts like the 'void' which could be turned directly into Latin; but where there was no obvious Latin equivalent or where a more complex idea had to be expressed, it was necessary to adapt an existing word to a new context or invent a new term on the analogy of the Greek original. One solution which Lucretius rejected was simply to transliterate the Greek term. A few Greek words for scientific notions are to be found in the poem, particularly in botanical and astronomical contexts, but it is probable that many of these had already been naturalized in the Latin language. When it came to translating unfamiliar concepts, Lucretius almost never used a Greek word: *harmonia* and *homoeomeria* are two exceptions, but both are used ironically to dismiss an opponent's theory. Lucretius is often credited, along with Cicero, with the invention of a philosophical vocabulary for the Latin language and there is some truth in the claim. But if we follow the poet's innovations through the later history of the language, it is surprising how few of them survived. Words like *clinamen* (for the Greek παρέγκλισις 'swerve') and *adopinari* (for προσδοξάȝεσθαι 'to add to evidence by conjecture') have no subsequent history in philosophical Latin. The fact is that Lucretius managed to operate to a remarkable extent without a technical vocabulary. It is instructive to compare his account of the Athenian plague with that of Thucydides. Both deal with the medical symptoms in some detail, but whereas Thucydides in a single chapter (2.49) uses almost seventy words which are either technical medical terms or are commonly found in medical authors, Lucretius manages very largely with the regular vocabulary of epic poetry. There is obviously some loss of precision in such a method and scientific discussion can hardly proceed without accepted definitions and a technical vocabulary. But the Latin of Lucretius' day lacked such resources and the poet had to grapple with the problem as best he could. Paradoxically the absence of a philosophical language may have helped him as a writer; for he was compelled to adopt a more concrete mode of expression. What the philosopher lost in precision, the poet gained in clarity and vividness of style.

Didactic poetry always involves compromise. Lucretius' aim was to be both impressive and intelligible, to do justice to the *maiestas rerum* while preserving the lively spirit of a philosophical debate. For this purpose he combined the dignified language of Roman epic with the spirited manner of the popular diatribe and both traditions affected his style. The influence of epic can be seen in the Ennian diction, in the frequency of alliteration and assonance, and above all in a pervasive archaism, both in metre and language, which admirably suited the antique dignity which he wished to impart to his theme. The popular tradition contributed other features to his style, a tone of biting irony, the occasional use of a more colloquial language, and a habit of dramatizing the argument. The result of this combination is a highly individual style which cannot be mistaken for anything else. Its principal characteristic is a feeling of energy, a quality which Baudelaire called 'la grâce littéraire suprême'. There is a robust vigour in the very sound of his verse, which, though it lacks Virgil's metrical subtlety, had a wider range of verbal effects than Augustan taste found acceptable. The piling up of arguments, the use of doublets, a sentence structure which seems to tumble over itself in its eagerness to reach a conclusion, a fondness for word-play ranging from simple locutions like *innumero numero* to complex puns, all helped to produce that feeling of exuberance which is so characteristic of his style. Only an artist of great self-confidence would have attempted to create a unity out of such varied elements.

The peculiar texture of Lucretius' writing is in part the consequence of his fondness for repetition. No other major Latin poet repeats himself so frequently. Phrases, sentences, and indeed whole passages recur, sometimes more than once. In a seventeen-line paragraph about the origin of the world (5.416–31) not a single verse is wholly new and several are borrowed without alteration from earlier parts of the poem. The function of these repetitions has been much discussed. 'What is right may well be said twice', wrote Empedocles (DK 1 322, B 25), and doubtless part of Lucretius' purpose was to drive home his message with repeated emphasis. This explanation will account for the repetition of such key passages as that on the conservation of matter, which appears four times in the poem (1.670–1 ~ 792–3, 2.753–4, 3.519–20). But it will not explain the repetition of unimportant and incomplete sentences or of decorative passages which have no significance for the argument. The longest of all the repeated passages in the poem is the brilliant prologue to Book 4 which first appears in an almost identical form at the end of Book 1 (926–50). Editors generally suppose that one of these two passages would have been removed in the final revision and they are probably right; but with Lucretius one cannot be certain because of his willingness to repeat passages of memorable poetry. Pedagogical considerations may have been a factor in the poet's use of repeated phrases, but the main explanation is almost certainly stylistic. The nearest parallels are in Homer and Empedocles and these are among the poet's principal literary models.

Every reader of the *De rerum natura* is aware of a considerable difference in the level of poetic excitement between the great set pieces and the passages of technical argument. The former contain some of the finest poetry in Latin, while the latter are marked by a deliberate prosiness which serves to underline the didactic purpose. The existence of such contrasts has given rise to the doctrine of 'two styles' in Lucretius, but perhaps it would be better to think of 'differences of tone' rather than 'differences of style', since the disparity which the reader feels is less the result of any significant change in the basic ingredients of Lucretius' language than in the intensification of emotion and the concentration of imagery. In fact it would be impossible to draw a sharp line between what is poetic in the poem and what is expository. Lucretius' aim is to 'touch all with the charm of the Muses' (1.934), and when he describes his poetry as honey on the lip of the cup, he is not thinking of the purple patches only. It is a mistake, therefore, in attempting to understand the poet, to concentrate too much upon the 'poetic' passages; for the total effect of the *De rerum natura* depends upon the balance of its lyrical and expository elements. For the same reason it is difficult to demonstrate Lucretius' quality as a writer from a single extract; but perhaps the following lines, which fall somewhere between the grand manner of the prologues and the austere writing of the more technical sections, will illustrate some of the points which have already been made about the poet's style.

> quod superest, ne te in promissis plura moremur,
> principio maria ac terras caelumque tuere;
> quorum naturam triplicem, tria corpora, Memmi,
> tris species tam dissimilis, tria talia texta,

una dies dabit exitio, multosque per annos
sustentata ruet moles et machina mundi.
nec me animi fallit quam res noua miraque menti
accidat exitium caeli terraeque futurum,
et quam difficile id mihi sit peruincere dictis;
ut fit ubi insolitam rem apportes auribus ante
nec tamen hanc possis oculorum subdere uisu
nec iacere indu manus, uia qua munita fidei
proxima fert humanum in pectus templaque mentis.
sed tamen effabor. dictis dabit ipsa fidem res
forsitan et grauiter terrarum motibus ortis
omnia conquassari in paruo tempore cernes.
quod procul a nobis flectat fortuna gubernans,
et ratio potius quam res persuadeat ipsa
succidere horrisono posse omnia uicta fragore.　　　　(5.91–109)

To proceed and not to put you off with promises,
first look upon the seas, the lands, the heavens:
their threefold nature, Memmius, their three bodies,
three forms so different in appearance, three such varied textures,
a single day will destroy, and the immense contrivance of the world,
upheld for many years, will collapse in ruin.
I am not unaware how strange and novel
is this doctrine of the future disappearance of earth and sky
and how hard it is to prove my proposition in words;
it is always thus when one brings to men's ears some unfamiliar fact
which cannot be set before the eyes
or touched with the hand (for touch is a paved road
which leads directly to the human heart and the precincts of the mind).
But yet I shall speak forth. Perhaps the event itself
will bring belief to my words and shortly amid the shock of earthquake
you will see everything shattered.
May guiding fortune pilot this fate from us
and may reason, rather than experience, convince us
that the whole world may fail and fall with a dread-sounding crash.

These lines, which impressed Ovid so deeply that he cites them no less than four times, follow immediately upon the long prelude to Book 5. They introduce the first important argument of the book, but the supporting proof does not begin until line 235, since Lucretius characteristically 'suspends the thought' and inserts a long polemical passage to show that the universe is not divine (110–234). In spite of the length of this insertion there is no loss of momentum or confusion of thought because the 'digression' is closely related to the main subject of the book, and both it and the basic argument have been anticipated in the prologue. This feeling of unity is further assisted by Lucretius' typically formular style: nearly a dozen phrases in this short paragraph are repeated elsewhere in the work and some, like the brisk opening formula, appear several times. The passage is simple in structure and the writing is direct and straight-forward. There is little of that interweaving of words and phrases which Augustan writers employed to add tension to their verse. Enjambment is kept to a minimum and in general the thought is accommodated to the units of the hexameter verse. This is not Lucretius' invariable way of writing: there are passages, for example in the prologues, where he creates a strong sense of forward movement by allowing the thought to spill over from one line to another (over a quarter of the lines in the poem are enjambed); but here an important statement is enunciated in measured phrases and the shape of the verse adds clarity and point to the argument.

Many of the formal features of Lucretius' style can be seen in these lines: archaism (*indu*), periphrasis (*oculorum uisu*), dignified poetic diction (*effabor*), the occasional telling use of a compound adjective (*horrisono*), and most obviously, alliteration and assonance. But what makes the passage impressive is the energy and fullness of the writing. Much of that energy resides in the use and placing of the verbs (*sustentata ruet, conquassari*). Although the *De rerum natura* is a great descriptive poem, it depends far more for its effect upon the choice of verbs and participles than upon picturesque adjectives or decora-tive epithets. Lucretius' style is above all functional and the commonest adjectives in the poem are colourless quantitative words like *magnus* and *paruus*. In fact Lucretius is seldom content simply to describe: he wants to explain what is happening behind the surface appearances of things and for this words of action are needed. They impart to his style a tremendous vigour and strength. Alliteration contributes to the same result. Grammarians warned against its over-use and sometimes Lucretius, like the older poets whom he imitated, may be guilty of excess. But the device is effective when it is employed, as here, to point a striking phrase like *machina mundi* or to draw attention to a new and important subject. It can also underline and punctuate the meaning: the first sentence, for example, divides into three parts of approximately equal length and each is marked off with its own alliterative sequence. The musical effect of alliteration is particularly pleasing when it involves the blending of different sounds: lines 104–5 provide a good example with their interweaving of the consonants *d*, *t*, and *f* and their strong assonantal pattern, *ta- -tīs -tan -ter ter- -ti- -tīs*. In trying to account for the characteristic energy and amplitude of Lucretius' style, one should also mention his use of doublets (*noua miraque*) and his habit of piling up nouns within a single verse (*principio maria ac terras caelumque tuere*, 92). Like Milton, Lucretius is fond of such 'catalogue lines' and employs them with a wide range of effects: impressiveness and majesty in 5.115: *terras et solem et caelum, mare, sidera, lunam* 'lands and sun and sky, sea, stars and moon'; lyrical beauty in 5.1190: *luna dies et nox et noctis signa seuera* 'moon, day and night and the night's solemn constellations'; and irony in 4.1132: *pocula crebra, unguenta, coronae serta parantur* 'cups in abundance, perfume, crowns, garlands are made ready' (note in this last example how the mocking tone is supported by the rhythm: in all six feet there is coincidence of ictus and accent).

But there are hazards in this manner of writing; for amplitude can easily degenerate into bombast. At first sight lines 93–4 may seem an excessively ponderous way of making the simple point that earth, sea and sky are three bodies which differ in appearance and texture. Yet the sentence is not mere padding; for 'appearance' and 'texture' are key themes in the poem. The reference to texture in these lines recalls a passage in Book 1 (238–49) in which Lucretius argues that it is on account of their different textures that the objects of our experience do not suddenly disintegrate at a single stroke. Here by contrast a more sinister point is being made: that in the final cataclysm the varied textures of sea, earth and sky will not prevent their simultaneous destruction. The emphasis on the complex texture of the world is not, therefore, simply rhetorical: it is part of the argument itself. This is typical of the best of Lucretius' writing; his success as a didactic poet lies in his total absorption, both emotionally and intellectually, in the message of his poem. The passage which we have been examining is a good example of this capacity to transmute argument into poetry. Clearly the Epicurean doctrine of the eventual destruction of the world captured the poet's imagination, as it captured that of Ovid, and inspired him to a solemn and impressive statement. Such an emphatic manner of writing would not have suited more tender or commonplace writers, but it was admirable for Lucretius' purpose. For him the majesty of his theme demanded and justified an impressive rhetoric. This does not mean that he is uniformly solemn. He could turn an epic phrase to mock-heroic effect, as when he describes a goose as *Romulidarum arcis seruator candidus anser* 'the white goose, saviour of the citadel of the children of Romulus' (4.683), and he could stand back and smile at the very force and vigour of his own dialectic (see, e.g., 1.410–17).

Image and symbol

One important feature of Lucretius' style which has been neglected in this analysis is his use of imagery. According to Epicurean theory all knowledge is ultimately based upon the evidence of the senses and what cannot be known from direct observation must be inferred by analogy from observed fact. This stress upon the importance of visual experience was grist to Lucretius' mill and it may help to explain the astonishing richness and vitality of his imagery. Few Latin poets can rival him in this and none can equal his range. Like Empedocles, he extended the field of imagery beyond the traditionally 'poetic' subjects: not only did he borrow from arts and crafts, but also from war, politics, law, and public ceremonial. There is nothing like this in the writings of Epicurus; in spite of the philosopher's insistence on the value of the senses, he rarely attempted to clarify an argument with an apt illustration. Other philosophers, both inside and outside the Atomic school, were less austere, and some of Lucretius' most celebrated pictures are derived from the philosophical tradition: the motes in the sunbeam go back at least to Democritus (Aristotle, *De anima* 404a1–6); the torch race and the famous image of honey on the lip of the cup are both anticipated by Plato in the *Laws* (776b and 659e); the illustration of the worn ring was used by Melissus of Samos (DK 1 274, B 8.3); the image of the road in the passage which we have just discussed is derived from Empedocles (DK 1 365, B 133); and the important comparison of the atoms to the letters of the alphabet appears in two passages of Aristotle which deal with the atomic theory of Leucippus and Democritus (*Metaph.* 985b15–19 and *De gen. et corr.* 315b9–15).

Illustrations of this sort are part of the dialectic of the poem. They are employed not simply to add a decorative veneer, but to clarify the argument or to provide the evidence on which it is based. But 'the function of imagery in poetry is never that of mere illustration'.[1] A good image should do more than engage the reader's mind through the aptness of the comparison: there should be some element of surprise, something to stir the imagination. In fact the more logical and exact an illustration may be, the less effectively will it work as poetry. What is impressive about Lucretius' use of imagery is the skill with which he goes beyond mere illustration or analogy. Even a commonplace picture like that of drying clothes (a favourite with Lucretius) can be changed into poetry: a crack of thunder is compared to the flapping of clothes in a fresh breeze (6.114–15) and the sea, evaporating into the air, is like washing spread out on the green (6.617–19). In these examples the image does more than bolster the argument: it also adds a touch of imagination and quickens science into poetry. Much of the special feeling of the *De rerum natura* is generated by its imagery. There is a characteristic sensuousness about the column of air which 'brushes through the pupil of the eye' (4.249); and there is wit in the description of cosmetics as the 'backstage business of life' (4.1186) or of the cock 'chasing the night off the stage with the applause of his wings' (4.710). Above all, it is through imagery that Lucretius heightens and intensifies the emotional quality of his writing. Sometimes this concentration is achieved by boldly mixing metaphors, as in the magnificent lines about the insatiability of love:

> . . .quoniam medio de fonte leporum
> surgit amari aliquid quod in ipsis floribus angat. . .   (4.1133–4)

> . . .*since from the centre of the fountain of enchantment*
> *bitterness rises up to choke delight even amid the flowers*. . .

[1] Brooks and Warren (1960) 556.

Is it possible to go further and see in the poet's imagery some clue to the larger meaning of the poem? It is easy enough to recognize the obvious symbolism in Lucretius' equation of darkness and light with ignorance and truth, if only because such secondary meanings are implicit in the language itself. But other cases are not so plain, and because of the Epicurean insistence on clear and simple language it is hazardous to impose upon Lucretius' text a conscious and complex symbolism. The most difficult passages to interpret are the great set pieces and the mythological parts of the poem. The very existence of myth in an Epicurean poem is itself surprising, and in the treatment of such passages, if anywhere, one might expect some concessions to the traditions of epic poetry in order to enlarge and deepen the meaning of the poem. The problem of interpretation is complex and it is not possible to do more than illustrate its complexity by examining briefly two passages, those which close and open the poem.

The account of the Athenian plague at the end of Book 6 is introduced ostensibly as an example of the sort of pestilence which Lucretius has explained in the previous lines. The illustration serves no purpose in clarifying the argument and in fact little is said about the causes of the disaster. The passage is elaborated beyond the immediate needs of the context and it brings the poem to a stark and dramatic conclusion. It is natural to suppose that such a passage in such a position must have some special significance for the poem as a whole. Lucretius' emphasis throughout on the psychological effects of the disaster, and the frequent use in the poem of the imagery of disease in reference to moral sickness both suggest that the poet saw the plague as a symbol of man's tragic predicament. But such an interpretation, attractive though it is, involves an uncomfortable corollary. For the plague, as Lucretius describes it, knows no cure. It is true that some of its victims recovered (though this fact is barely hinted at), but recovery was as unpredictable as the onset of the disease. Medicine could do nothing but 'mutter with silent dread'. The plague at Athens, sudden in its attack and undiscriminating in its victims, is not a satisfactory symbol for the moral degeneracy which Lucretius saw around him, and if it were, it would be a strange point on which to conclude a poem which proclaims the victory of man over fear and circumstance. Surely we cannot imagine that, as Lucretius approached the conclusion of his great task, he suddenly lost his nerve and chose to end in a mood of uncertainty and gloom. The victory of Epicurus dominates the poem and must guide our understanding of its final pages. We shall distort the poet's meaning if we insist on reading his account of the plague as a coded statement about man's spiritual blindness. But if the passage is not to be interpreted symbolically, it is nevertheless at a deeper and more emotional level an entirely satisfactory ending to the poem. What was needed was a passage which would suit the subject matter of Book 6 and which would at the same time produce an effective cadence to a long and emotional poem. The poet has found a solution which satisfies both of these requirements. The account of the Athenian plague, which depends heavily on material set out earlier in the work, forms a fitting climax to a book which deals with striking natural events; and the tragic story is told in such a way as to recapitulate some of the principal themes of the poem: the bitter consequences of ignorance, the almost universal fear of death, man's crippling anxiety and his hopeless dependence on divine powers. In this long description of a terrible disaster Lucretius appears once again in his characteristic role as the scientific observer of natural causes, the ironic critic of man's folly and the sympathetic poet of human misery.

Let us turn, in conclusion, to the prologue to Book 1, perhaps the most difficult passage in the poem. Here there can be no question of a literal interpretation; for, although Epicurean theology conceded the possibility of some form of communion with the gods, the sort of prayer which Lucretius addresses to Venus, that she endow his poem with 'undying grace' and bring peace to Rome by clasping Mars in her arms, goes far beyond the decent limits of Epicurean piety. Clearly the poet had something else in mind and we naturally look for some secondary meaning in his words. But what? The difficulty here is not so much to find some suitable equation for Lucretius' goddess as to know where to stop, how to determine the limits of the poet's symbolic imagination. Is Venus here simply the power of love or the generative force of nature? Or is the main emphasis on the concept of peace? Or should she be interpreted at a more philosophical level and equated with one or other of the two types of pleasure which Epicurus defined in his ethics? As Bignone has shown, there is ample precedent among Greek writers for this sort of philosophical allegory.[1] The idea of introducing the old Homeric myth of Venus and Mars may in fact have come to Lucretius from Empedocles, who is said to have used it for the two great forces of love and strife which control the Empedoclean universe.[2] The world which Lucretius describes, though it differs from that of Empedocles, is also dominated by an unending cycle of birth and decay. Some idea of this sort may have been at the back of Lucretius' mind when he introduced the story of Mars and Venus, but this cannot be what the myth *means*. For the Mars of the Lucretian prologue is not presented as a grim symbol of destruction and decay, but as a sensual being with the instincts of the elegiac lover. Mars is not in fact a potent figure in the poem at all and after the prologue his name never reappears except as a more or less conventional synonym for war.

What then does Venus stand for in the prologue? Whatever answer is given

---

[1] Bignone (1942–50) II 434–9.
[2] Heraclitus, *Alleg. Hom.* 69; Eustathius, *ad Od.* 8.367. Cf. Empedocles, DK I 317, B 17.24.

to this question must take into account the poet's attitude to myth and allegory. The term 'allegory' is often loosely applied in Lucretian criticism in contexts where it does not properly apply. There is certainly allegory in the Magna Mater passage (2.600–60), but it should be noted that half of Lucretius' allegorical interpretations of the myth are inconsistent with his own beliefs and are clearly not intended to be taken seriously. The description of the tortures of the damned in 3.978–1023 comes close to allegory, but even here one should hesitate. What Lucretius says could be paraphrased like this: 'Nowhere is there a Tantalus numb with fear because a huge rock hangs over him; but in this life men fear the blow of fate...' This is not allegory in the strict sense. No attempt is made to reinterpret the myth or find a deeper meaning in it. Rather the purpose is to deny the validity of myth and to contrast the punishments of the underworld with realities of a more pressing and credible kind. Other mythological passages are even clearer: their function is almost always polemical and they lack that quality of reverence which genuine allegory requires. If this is correct, then we should not expect to find Lucretius saying important things about his own philosophy in mythical terms. In particular the equation of Venus with the Epicurean concept of 'static pleasure' is not likely to be right. Nor does so sophisticated a notion emerge readily from what Lucretius actually says. A complex symbol of this sort, if it is to be understood, needs a context and the opening of a poem has no context.

A good poem always means more than it says. It would be wrong therefore to limit in too arbitrary a fashion one's response to so complex a piece of writing as the prelude to Lucretius' poem. One should, however, be clear where the main emphasis is to be placed, and for this the poet has given us the help we need. The first two words of the poem, *Aeneadum genetrix*, echo the *Annals* of Ennius and the phrase which follows, *hominum diuumque uoluptas*, is used again in Book 6 in an address to Calliope. Lucretius could hardly have made it plainer that we are here in the realm of the imagination rather than of truth and that Venus is being invoked as the poet's Muse. In this context the reader is likely to think of a different range of symbols from those we have been considering before. As Classen has pointed out, Venus and Aphrodite and ἡδονή, the Greek equivalent of the Latin *uoluptas*, are all associated in the literary tradition with grace and ease of style.[1] Lucretius' prayer to Venus is for *lepos*, for beauty of words and persuasiveness of speech; and Venus is invoked as the embodiment of that beauty which manifests itself throughout the whole Nature of Things. In the opening prayer Lucretius is careful not to reveal the scope and purpose of his poem. We are still in the world of poetry and have not yet been told what the real subject of the poem will be. To seek in such a passage for a complex network of philosophical symbols is to approach

[1] Classen (1968) 103–5.

poetry in too cerebral a manner. The main function of the prologue is to
indicate the beauty and majesty of the world and the magnitude of Lucretius'
task. As C. S. Lewis says of the opening of *Paradise Lost*: 'The ostensible
philosophical purpose of the poem...is here of secondary importance. The
real function of these...lines is to give us the sensation *that some great thing
is now about to begin.*'[1]

One final observation about the prologue will bring us back to the question
which we posed at the start. If we compare the manner in which Lucretius
begins with the opening of Empedocles' poem *On nature* (so far as it can be
reconstructed from its fragmentary remains), we become aware of an important
difference of tone. Although Empedocles had the reputation in antiquity of
being a braggart and there is a strain of dogmatism in his work, he began his
poem rather tentatively, stressing the shortness of life, the limitations of human
knowledge and the dangers of presumption and he called on his white-armed
Muse only for 'such knowledge as it is lawful for creatures of a day to hear'.
Where Empedocles is tentative, Lucretius is full of confidence and joy. The
colour and excitement of the long opening sentence underline the magnificence
of the subject and the importance of the message. Lucretius never doubts that
reason will prevail if only the right words can be found. It is the poet's task to
set forth the *diuina ratio* in the most persuasive language possible. The difficulties – both of convincing the timid and of mastering a difficult literary
form – are not to be concealed; but the ultimate message is of victory and hope
and joy. It is the poet's confidence that the doctrine of Epicurus can explain the
whole of life and set the mind at peace which makes the task possible. For
Lucretius the philosophy of Epicurus was something which could be conceived both intellectually and emotionally, that is to say, it was something
which could be conceived poetically. The problem of matching poetry and
philosophy was on its way to being solved.

[1] Lewis (1942) 40.

4

CICERO AND THE RELATIONSHIP OF ORATORY TO LITERATURE

1. CICERO'S ATTITUDE TO CULTURE

Marcus Tullius Cicero (106–43 B.C.) has been endlessly studied as a character and as a politician, and certainly these aspects of him are of absorbing interest; but his chief historical importance is as a man of letters. Deeply conscious of the philistinism of most Romans, this 'new man' with no ancestors adopted as his spiritual ancestors the younger Scipio and his friends of the second century, the disseminators, under the guidance of the Stoic Panaetius, of Hellenism, who were also exemplars of Roman patriotism, *decorum* and *humanitas*. 'I am more than others a philhellene and known to be', he says to Atticus, though his admiration was for the literature, philosophy and art of the great Greeks of the past rather than for the shifty modern 'Greeklings' (*Q. Fr.* 1.2.2). In his dialogues, composed in the beautifully situated villas he had acquired at Tusculum (above Frascati) and down the west coast of Italy, which he sometimes also used as their *mise en scène*, he seems concerned to portray a particularly courteous society (like Shakespeare in *The Merchant of Venice*): no one is allowed to be rude, unlike some of the Sophists in Plato. His characters have that tolerance which is one of his own characteristics.

When he was eighteen Philo of Larissa, head of the 'New' Academy at Athens, visited Rome and made a deep impression on him. Philo stood for hearing every side in a debate before making up one's mind. Holding that nothing could be known for certain, he deplored dogmatism and insisted that all conclusions were provisional. So when Cicero later visited Athens to study, he chose to join the Academy.[1] His own philosophy of life was eclectic and unsystematic, adapted to his temperament. He was no real philosopher, and knew it, though fascinated by philosophy. He welcomed criticism, and claimed the right to change his mind. In a passage in the prologue to his dialogue *On the nature of the gods* (1.10) that won Voltaire's admiration he deplored the Pytha-

---

[1] Now under Antiochus of Ascalon, however, it had become eclectic rather than sceptical – drawing ideas from Peripatetics and Stoics as well as Academics; but Cicero remains true to Philo's undogmatic spirit of discussion. Philo had also introduced courses in rhetoric, alongside those in philosophy, which would attract Cicero.

gorean formula 'The Master said...' (*Ipse dixit*): 'Those who ask what I think myself are unnecessarily curious. In a discussion what is to be sought is not so much weight of authority as force of argument. Indeed the authority of professed teachers is often a positive hindrance to would-be learners.'

Such openmindedness was also encouraged by the rhetorical exercise, recommended by Aristotle, of arguing both sides of a question. How deeply this conditioned Cicero's way of thinking is shown by a letter he wrote to Atticus in his agony of indecision two months after Caesar crossed the Rubicon in 49 (*Att.* 9.4). He says he has been debating a series of 'theses' (discussions of general principles) relevant to the situation, first in Greek and then in Latin, and proceeds to list the topics in Greek. He says he is doing this partly to distract his mind, partly to give relevance to his exercise.

The prologues to his dialogues and treatises form collectively an interesting corpus of intellectual autobiography, in which the defence of cultural studies as an occupation for an ex-consul consonant with '*otium cum dignitate*' is a recurrent theme. (He makes the Muse Urania praise him for this in his poem on his consulship: *Div.* 1.17.) Deploring utilitarian values, he remarks sarcastically in the *Brutus* (257) that, while no doubt it was more important for the Athenians to have watertight roofs over their heads than to possess that ivory statue of Athena, he would rather be Phidias than a master-roofer. In his famous Dream of Scipio (see p. 261), at a time when he was in eclipse as a statesman, he made Africanus reveal that there is a place in heaven reserved for benefactors of their country, including not only men of action but (remarkable for a Roman) others who have devoted their genius to divine pursuits (*Rep.* 6.19). The debate that began among Aristotle's followers as to whether the life of contemplation was better than the life of action was continued intermittently in Cicero's soul. Normally the life of action prevailed.

Naturally he was drawn to men who needed no conversion to culture; to Atticus, with his hospitable library, his propagation of books and his historical interests, who bought works of art for him at Athens; to Cato and Brutus, who, even if at times he did not see eye to eye with them, were likewise lifelong students of philosophy; even to Caesar, politically his arch-enemy, whose keen critical interest in literature and language provided them with safe topics of discourse. But he aimed at reaching a wider circle, with special hopes of influencing the rising generation. All his life he was concerned to promote humane education. It was unthinkable at Rome that higher education should be anything but rhetorical in basis; but in the *De oratore* (55 B.C.) he put forward the view that the perfect orator should be a 'full man', and propounded accordingly an unprecedented scheme of liberal education, *politior humanitas* (*humanus*, a word embracing both culture and human-kindness, meant something like our 'civilized' as applied to people). His letters provide ample evidence that he was himself a 'full man', well versed in Greek and Latin literature, and in philosophy, history and law. (It must not however be assumed that quotation by Cicero from a Greek poem means that he had read it. Some of his quotations in his philosophical works seem to have been lifted from his sources; some, there and elsewhere, may have been commonplaces in conversation; and he makes tell-tale slips.[1])

In philosophy he was a moralist with hankerings for the transcendental. He therefore went back to 'that god of mine Plato', whose statue stood on the lawn of his town house. Of the Hellenistic philosophies Stoicism attracted him most, again as a moralist: he encountered Posidonius at Rhodes, and the domestic philosopher he kept was a Stoic, Diodotus. Epicurus he praised as a good man. He appealed to Memmius to preserve his ruined house at Athens (*Fam.* 13.1), and Jerome says he 'corrected' (*emendauit*) the *De rerum natura* of Lucretius. But he dismissed the hedonistic Epicurean philosophy with a contempt softened only by indulgence for some of its practitioners.

Books meant a great deal to him. He begs Atticus not to resell a library he has bought, in the hope that he himself will find the resources to buy it for his new Tusculan villa. 'Now that Tyrannio has arranged my books', he says after returning from exile to his wrecked property, 'my house seems to have acquired a soul.' We find him reading books relevant to his situation, and using Aristotle's library, which Sulla had brought to Italy. When his public life was shattered, he wrote to Varro: 'I must tell you that...I have made it up with those old friends of mine, my books...They have forgiven me, and invited me to resume our former intercourse' (*Fam.* 9.1.2). Even in his speeches he quotes sometimes from the old Latin poets (as did some of his contemporaries), especially in the period during which he composed the *De oratore*. Usually it was from plays which might be familiar to his audience from stage revivals. In the *Pro Caelio* (37–8) he adroitly solicits tolerance for the young man's peccadilloes by contrasting an unattractively stern father in Caecilius with an attractively lenient one in Terence. But he was careful not to alienate his hearers by transcending their ignorances and prejudices.

His historical sense was also exceptional: 'to be ignorant of history is like remaining a child for life'. He tried to see not only external events but himself also in its perspective: just as, when appealing to Caesar the Dictator for Marcellus, he urged him to think what posterity would say about him, so he was concerned about what people would be saying about his own conduct a thousand years hence. His *Brutus* and Book 2 of his *De re publica* are notable pieces of historiography, his account of himself at *Brutus* 313–36 a landmark in the history of autobiography. And in other dialogues besides the *Brutus* he makes the continuity of Roman history felt. Cato in the *De senectute*, whose dramatic

[1] Jocelyn (1973) 77ff.

date is 150 B.C., had known Duillius, commander in the First Punic War (260) and met people who remembered the war against Pyrrhus before that. He was talking there to the younger Scipio, who in the *De re publica* transmits Roman and family tradition to the younger generation, including the sons-in-law of his friend Laelius. In the *De amicitia*, set in the same year (129), Laelius in turn is entertaining his sons-in-law; while in the *De oratore* Crassus, initially in the presence of Laelius' son in-law, the now aged Scaevola the Augur, is represented as discoursing in 91 to a distinguished gathering, one of whom, Cotta, could be represented by Cicero as later describing the occasion to himself.[1] In the Prologue to *De finibus* 5 (1–8) he recalls his youthful explorations of Athens with his brother, his cousin, Atticus and another friend: 'wherever we step, we are treading on history'.

It must be admitted however that Cicero sometimes compromised with his principles. In politics he was bad at seeing opponents' points of view and dogmatic in formulating his own. He was capable of soliciting Lucceius to waive the strict veracities of history when he came to deal with his own consulship (*Fam.* 5.12). With specious chauvinism he even once asserted that the Latin language, far from being poor, as was popularly supposed, was richer than the Greek (*Fin.* 1.3.10). He was as ready in his speeches as any other advocate, if it suited his brief, to disparage the law and lawyers, laugh at Stoics, insinuate that an Epicurean must be a libertine, suggest that you could not trust a Greek or a Gaul, and call Judaism a barbarous superstition (see p. 78). Only in defending the Greek poet Archias, where there was little case to answer, did he feel he could speak out in court for culture. His studies, highly though he valued them, were in truth a second best to political activity: 'I see nothing else I can do now.' He suggested that Scipio, the philosophic man of action, had the edge over Socrates and Plato. Writing after Caesar's murder, when he was once more at the helm, to his son, then a student of philosophy at Athens, he said, 'one should know what the philosophers recommend, but live as a man of the world (*ciuiliter*)'.[2] However, as with Seneca, it is the ideals he so eloquently proclaimed, not the extent to which he lived up to them, that have mattered in the cultural history of the world.

2. ORATORICAL THEORY AND PRACTICE AS CICERO FOUND IT

Not only higher education but literature in general at Rome was founded on oratory. For its early history we have to rely on Cicero's account in his *Brutus*. Though he shapes this in such a way that it culminates in himself, there is no evidence, at least in our fragments of previous speeches,[3] to gainsay him.

---

[1] Rambaud (1953) 104–7.   [2] Lactantius, *De fals. sap.* 3.14.
[3] Assembled by H. (= E.) Malcovati (1955).

Tradition, represented by Ennius, celebrated the eloquence of Appius Claudius the Blind, who persuaded the Senate not to compromise with Pyrrhus, and of M. Cornelius Cethegus in the Hannibalic War; but the first real figure in the story was the elder Cato (234–149 B.C.). Before his time the scope for rhetoric was limited. Apart from funeral orations (buried in family archives) there were speeches to the Senate; but its decisions would often have been pre-empted behind the scenes by groups of noble families. A magistrate would sometimes address the popular assembly, a general exhort his troops. But there was none of the 'epideictic' (display) oratory of Hellenistic Greece; and the 'formulaic' system of the praetorian law courts lent itself more to argumentation and cross-examination.

Things changed in the second century with the establishment of larger juries, as in the centumviral court and the standing tribunals (*quaestiones perpetuae*). Henceforward the chief theatre of eloquence was to be the law courts, where many of the cases tried were really political. Trials were held publicly, in the Forum or an adjoining basilica, and amid a ring (*corona*) of bystanders. At the same time the revolutionary activities of tribunes such as the Gracchi were furthered by rhetorical harangues to the inflammable popular assembly. (Mark Antony's in *Julius Caesar* plausibly conveys the effect.)[1]

Coincidental with these changes of circumstance was the influx of Greeks and Greek ideas. Under the Hellenistic monarchies eloquence had had less political scope than in such milieus as democratic Athens of the fourth century. It concentrated on display, and at the same time established a scholastic discipline of definition and classification, on Aristotelian principles, which was inculcated into the young by catechism and repetition in unison. In Roman pupils the Greeks found at last a political outlet for their skills; conversely the Romans were captivated by the rhetorical virtuosity of Greek embassies, increasingly frequent as the empire grew, notably that of the three philosophers from Athens in 156–155, which so excited the young and incensed Cato. Expelled by the Senate in 161, the Greek rhetoricians crept back, first perhaps as tutors in private houses. One difference the Greeks will have found at Rome was the persuasive power of *auctoritas*, the prestige of the speaker. Advocacy was much more personal: your advocate was called your *patronus*, and he might say more about himself than about you.

Romans were predisposed in two quite different ways in their attitude to rhetoric. On the one hand the image of themselves cultivated by Romans favoured a pithy, laconic, unadorned directness. In this they were abetted by the Stoics, to whom any oratorical device was meretricious and the only permissible rhetoric was dialectic – argument aimed at persuading by truth. The most famous example was that of P. Rutilius Rufus (consul 105), condemned on a

[1] Kennedy (1972) 7–21.

trumped up charge because, according to Cicero, he declined the help of the most eloquent advocates of the time: 'Why, none of his defenders even stamped his foot, for fear, I suppose, that the Stoics might hear it.' On the other hand the Italian character could be highly emotional, witness Cicero's own letters. Aristotle had emphasized the importance of emotion in rhetoric; and Cicero was clear that it was by moving, more than by pleasing or convincing, the jury that verdicts were obtained. *Flectere uictoriae est.* Hence he preferred to speak last of the several advocates who were retained. Servius Sulpicius Galba (consul 144), when vigorously impeached by the elder Cato for cruelty and treachery to the Lusitanians, obtained a monstrous acquittal by producing his weeping children in court and commending them, with added tears of his own, to the protection of the Roman people. The dullness of his speeches when read after publication was in itself testimony to the emotional power of his performances. He was also the first Latin orator consciously to employ the resources of rhetoric, seeking to charm and to move his hearers and enlarging on his theme with exaggeration, generalization and ornamental digressions.

But the pivotal figure was the elder Cato. He was the first to publish his speeches, and Cicero unearthed more than 150 of them. Some displayed schemata of rhetoric such as 'rhetorical question' and anaphora. The one 'On his own expenditure' contained a most elaborate exploitation of the figure *praeteritio* (mentioning things by saying you will not mention them). He certainly owed more in general to Greek influence than he pretended, but whether or not in rhetoric is a moot point.[1] All rhetorical schemata are systematizations of nature. Yet although anaphora (repetition of a word or words at the beginning of successive clauses), for instance, might seem a spontaneous feature, it is noteworthy that it is almost completely absent from Homer, the few instances seeming intended for expressive effect. Its use in literature becomes much more marked after the formulation of rhetorical schemata by Gorgias. Though Cato's own encyclopaedia contained a section on rhetoric (Quint. *Inst.* 3.1.19), if the famous dictum *rem tene, uerba sequentur* ('stick to the matter and the words will follow') came from it, it may have been a sort of anti-Rhetorica. What he lacked that he could have learned from the Greeks was *concinnitas* – the elegance of clarity, smoothness, artistic weighting and disposition of clauses (*membra*), and the quantitative rhythm conspicuous at cadences, in fact the art of the rounded Isocratean 'period'. The first Roman to display the Isocratean virtues, the '*stilus artifex*', was M. Aemilius Lepidus Porcina (consul 137); but the first to equal the Greeks, in Cicero's opinion, were the leading orators of his youth, L. Crassus and M. Antonius. Crassus was careful of euphony; and his periods, though he preferred to break them into smaller members, were rhythmical.

[1] Norden (1898) held the former view (1 165f.), Leo (1913) the latter (1 286). Clarke (1953) 40–2.

Hellenistic criticism recognized three styles, the grand, middle and plain. Cicero in the *Orator* (69) associated these with the three aims of oratory, to move, to please and to convince respectively. The grand style was forceful, weighty, spacious, emotional and ornate, carrying men away: it was what we understand by 'rhetorical'. Galba was its first notable practitioner in Latin, Gaius Gracchus a gifted exponent, who strode up and down, bared his shoulder, and employed a backstage piper to keep his pitch right.[1] This style prevailed over the plain for decades, despite the inclination of Stoicism to plainness. It was akin to the 'Asianic', represented by Hortensius, leader of the Bar from Antonius' death in 87 until the young Cicero's triumphant prosecution of Verres in 70. 'Asianic' was an ambiguous, not very helpful term. As late as 46 B.C. Cicero still felt obliged to define it (*Brut.* 325; cf. 51). It covered two styles prevalent in Asia Minor; (1) the epigrammatic and brilliant (*sententiosum et argutum*), relying on neatness and charm (*concinnum et uenustum*); (2) the swift and impetuous (*uolucre et incitatum*), but lacking in Isocratean refinements. These clearly differ widely, though Cicero alleges that Hortensius excelled in both. Generally the latter seems to have been meant. A detailed comparison between Hortensius and himself forms the climax of Cicero's *Brutus* (317–30).

3. ORATORICAL THEORY AND PRACTICE IN CICERO AND HIS CONTEMPORARIES

The ambition to be an orator probably came to the boy from the hill-town of Arpinum, south-east of Rome, through his being entrusted by his father to the care of Rome's leading orator, Lucius Crassus. While still in his 'teens he embarked on the composition of a full-scale Rhetorica; but he completed only the first section, preserved for us under the title of *De inventione*. Some idea of what the whole would have been like may be obtained from the anonymous *Rhetorica ad Herennium*, composed about the same time, possibly with the help of notes from the same teacher.[2] Some thirty years later, when Cicero came to compose the *De oratore*, it was partly in order 'to efface that crude, unfinished stuff that slipped out of my boyhood or adolescent notebooks'. In his oratorical, as in his philosophic, studies he favoured eclecticism, comparing the painter Zeuxis (*Inv.* 2.1–8).

Ancient criticism and pedagogic concentrated on artistry, as being susceptible of analysis; the genius of the artist, though no less essential, was not reducible to rules, so more cursorily treated. Cicero reversed the priority. He set out to describe the perfect orator, defined by his Crassus as 'a man who can speak with fulness and variety on any topic'. His spiritual ancestor was Isocrates.

[1] Plut. *Tib. G.* 2.2; Cic. *De or.* 225.
[2] Kennedy (1972) 106–11; 126–38. On Cicero's style the standard work is Laurand (1907/1936).

However much he might revere Plato, to him, as to Plato's rival, 'philosophy' meant culture, not dialectic. Philosophy was 'all knowledge of the best subjects and practice in them' (*De or.* 3.60). (Plato and Aristotle had claimed the term for dialectic, and despite Cicero they ultimately won.) Isocrates, the refiner and consummator of sophistic culture, had given his pupils a fairly wide education in the humanities, as a basis for eloquence and success in statesmanship. Cicero believed that it was his own general education that had enabled him to outshine other orators (*Brut.* 322). Further, the formal artistry which Cicero considered essential was another legacy from Isocrates, 'the father of eloquence', whose style had by 350 B.C. become the norm for Greece, though he brought to it also something of the fire of Demosthenes.

The essence of Isocrates' style was what the ancients called 'rhythm', in Latin *numerus* (with verse in mind, though prose must never fall into actual verse) – any construct of words which could somehow be measured by the ear. This covered 'length' of syllables as well as of members, and artistic disposition of members. These might, for instance, be balanced, and the balance pointed by antithesis or anaphora, or they might be arranged in threes (*tricola*) or in fours (*tetracola*), of ascending length so as to round off the period. The whole should be easily grasped, with no syntactical inconsequences or loose ends (such as we find in the speeches in Thucydides, for instance), and comfortably utterable in one breath. As to what we more narrowly distinguish as 'rhythm', the dis-position of long and short syllables, this should be controlled, certain effective combinations being reserved for the cadence (*clausula*).[1] The various figures of speech should also be suitably exploited. Further, the Isocrateans were careful of smoothness, avoiding 'jaw-breaking hiatus' (R. L. Stevenson's phrase) between final and initial vowels and tongue-twisting juxtapositions of consonants.

Peripatetic critics, developing Aristotle, *Rhetoric* 3.8–9 and Theophrastus' lost book *On speech*, analysed such refinements. Cicero gives a fuller account of them, he claims, than any predecessor.[2] He expresses surprise that early orators, when they produced a good period by accident, did not realize the effect and consciously cultivate the art; and he credits even the uneducated multitude with

[1] Lacking the modern signs for 'long' and 'short', the ancients tended to borrow from verse the terminology of 'feet'. As applied to prose this encouraged excessive schematization in criticism. Cicero's rhythm exercised scholars from about 1900 to 1930. His likes and dislikes have been diag-nosed, and compared with what occurs in prose that does not try to be rhythmic. They are naturally more marked in exordia, perorations etc., though they are characteristic of all his serious prose, even his more carefully composed letters. But he himself emphasized that he did not work strictly to rule (*Orat.* 220); and his seven favourite clausulae account for only 56·5% of his period-endings (as against 28% for their occurrence in non-rhythmical prose). The pioneer of modern investigation was Th. Zieliński (1904). See Wilkinson (1963) 156–60; and for a survey of literature on the subject, 237–42.

[2] *De or.* 3.171–98; amplified at *Orat.* 134–9; 149–236.

an instinctive feeling for rhythm. The skilled orator will organize a period as soon as he knows what to say, his mind disposing the words with lightning rapidity in appropriate order and rhythm relative to a foreseen ending.[1] But to avoid monotony there must not be excessive regularity, and the sword-sweeps of long sentences must be varied by stabs with the short dagger.

An example from the speech *Pro lege Manilia* of 66 B.C. (2) will show how quite a long sentence can be controlled and kept intelligible through balance emphasized by correlatives and anaphora. (To translate for the Latinless would be pointless here.)

Nunc cum
    et auctoritatis *in me tantum* sit
        quantum uos honoribus mandandis ēssĕ uŏlŭīstĭs,
    et ad agendum facultatis *tantum*
        quantum homini uigilanti ex forensi usu prope
        cotidiana dicendi exercitatio pŏtŭĭt ādfērrĕ,
certe
    et si quid auctoritatis in me est,
        apud *eos* utar *qui eām* mĭhĭ dĕdērŭnt,
    et si quid in dicendo consequi possum,
        iis ostendam potissimum *qui ei* quoque rei
        fructum suo iudicio tribuendum ēssĕ dūxērŭnt.

We note how *nunc cum* and *certe* mark off the subordinate and main clauses, how nearly the two parts are parallel in the length of their corresponding members, and how this parallelism is emphasized even by corresponding clausulae of types that Cicero favoured.[2]

In chapter 43 of the same speech (a speech which Cicero himself chose to exemplify the *middle* style at *Orat.* 103) the grand, impetuous manner, throbbing with emotive words, is in full swing:

Quod igitur nomen unquam in orbe terrarum clarius fuit? Cuius res gestae pares? De quo homine uos, id quod maxime facit auctoritatem, tanta et tam praeclara iudicia fecistis? An uero ullam unquam oram tam desertam putatis quo non illius diei fama peruaserit, cum uniuersus populus Romanus foro completisque omnibus templis ex quibus hic locus conspici potest unum sibi ad commune omnium gentium bellum Gnaeum Pompeium imperatorem depoposcit?

We note how the short rhetorical questions build up to the longer one, and how the period ends with a resounding *clausula*, the 'Asiatic ditrochee' ($- \cup - \cup$), which was among Cicero's favourites. (He recalled (*Orat.* 213–14) how, when

---

[1] *De or.* 3.195–8; *Orat.* 199–200.

[2] In terms of feet, the tribrach 'pŏtŭĭt' counts as a resolution of a trochee, and is thus rhythmically equivalent to 'ēssĕ'.

he was sixteen, he heard Carbo end a stirring period with *temeritas fili compro-bauit*': 'It was marvellous what a shout arose from the crowd at this ditrochee.')[1]

Such however was Roman subservience to Greek precepts that Cicero, regardless of the differences between the two languages, is found recommending some rhythms which in practice he markedly avoided. He even begins to pre-scribe that bugbear the avoidance of hiatus, but is for once pulled up by the glaring discrepancy with what happens in Latin. (He himself has just written *legendo oculus*.) For whereas in Greek the occurrence of a final long vowel before an initial vowel was avoided, in Latin such vowels were fused together by 'synaloepha', as in Italian, 'even by rustics'.[2] So he withdraws (without how-ever deleting) what he has just said, with 'But we can leave that to the Greeks: we cannot gape between vowels even if we want to.' And analysis makes it almost certain that synaloepha does in fact operate in Latin prose rhythm. Again while he despises the formalism of Greek teaching, Cicero is loth to shake it off: his *Partitiones oratoriae*, a handbook in the form of a catechism of himself by his son, is conventional school stuff.

In practice Cicero cultivated the Isocratean manner. Though he recognized that it was primarily suited to the oratory of display, he allowed that it could be used in the exordium, peroration and other heightened passages of both political and forensic speeches, provided it was not so obtrusive that the hearer suspected he was being beguiled against his better judgement. Indeed it became his normal prose style, characteristic of his discourses as well. He also tended in his speeches to the vehemence and ornament of the grand manner. Up to the age of twenty-five he declaimed throughout with voice and body at highest tension, so much so that he endangered his health. A visit to Rhodes during his peregrin-ation not only restored him but enabled him to learn restraint from a rhetorician called Molo (whom he had already met at Rome), though his style still remained what we should call 'rhetorical' and, as it seemed to others, inclined to the Asianic. He had the actor's ability to live his part and to feel for the moment the emotions he expressed: 'that supreme manipulator of men's hearts', Quintilian called him.[3] He cultivated the acquaintance of the great actors, Aesopus and Roscius, who gave him hints on dramatic delivery (Plut. *Cic.* 5). The element common to the ornate periodical and the grand emotional styles was, that both sought to appeal to irrational instincts in the hearers. Cicero's success was due to a combination of faculties, including wit and humour (he lists them in a mock-modest *praeteritio* at Brutus 322), none of them new, but exploited with such flair that the difference from his predecessors, and even his contemporaries,

---

[1] A molossus (– – –) was often the ditrochee's springboard, as here; more often a cretic (– ◡ –).

[2] Laurand (1907/1936) 124 cites a passage from the *Verrines* (4.117) in which there are 9 hiatuses in 47 words. For Latin practice in this matter see Allen (1973) 142–6.

[3] *Summus ille tractandarum animarum artifex*: *Inst.* 11.1.85; cf. 8.3.4.

amounted to one in kind, so that Caesar could flatteringly call him 'almost the pioneer and inventor of eloquence (*copia*)'.

For some twenty years after the *Verrines* he remained the undisputed master of oratory. Then began a predictable reaction, probably less coordinated than some have supposed, towards a chaster style. There were always Stoics and characters such as Brutus who were temperamentally allergic to the passionate and the ornate. When Brutus wished to publish the speech he made to the people after Caesar's murder, he submitted the text to Cicero for criticism; but Cicero had to tell Atticus he could do nothing with it, it was so dispassionate; he himself would have handled the whole thing differently.[1] (This is the speech represented by Shakespeare in *Julius Caesar* III ii; it fell flat.) Then there were the self-styled 'Atticists', led by Catullus' poet-friend Calvus (d. 47), who affected a dry, unadorned style and claimed Lysias among the fourth-century Attic orators as their master. Calvus had at least one great success, against Vatinius, celebrated in a snatch of verse by Catullus (53). About the year 50 the young Virgil, leaving Rome for Naples and the Epicurean philosopher Siro, dismissed with relief the 'futile paintpots of the gaudy rhetoricians, words inflated with un-Attic hot air'.[2] Dionysius of Halicarnassus wrote of the recent return, within a short period, everywhere save in a few cities of Asia, to the old, temperate style of oratory. This he attributed to the political influence of Imperial Rome, the chief agents being members of her ruling class, 'highly cultivated men of refined taste'.[3]

As to historical writing, Caesar, besides being rationalistic by temperament, wrote his commentaries on his campaigns in plain style because he wanted to give an impression of unvarnished truth; and Cicero himself praised them as 'naked, regular and beautiful, stripped of all oratorical ornament'. Sallust's reaction against the Ciceronian style was more positive: in emulation of Thucydides he affected an abrupt, asymmetrical, arresting style prefiguring that of Tacitus.

Cicero defended himself with spirit against the Atticists in two treatises, the *Brutus* and the *Orator*, composed in the year 46, by which time both the chief exponents of Asianism and Atticism, Hortensius and Calvus, were dead. Rightly championing the Panaetian principle of appropriateness (*decorum*), he maintained that an orator should be master of all the styles. Lysias was too narrowly plain to be a general model, and Calvus, in following him with painful scrupulosity, had become jejune and too fastidious for the common man to appreciate. The consummate Greek orator, with no less right to the title 'Attic', was

---

[1] *Att.* 15.1a.2. Brutus should not be bracketed with the Atticists, though in some respects they agreed: Portalupi (1955); Douglas (1966) xiii–xiv.

[2] *Catalepton* 5.1–2 (reading '*rhoezo* non Achaico' with K. Münscher).

[3] *De antiqu. or.*, proem 3; Rhys Roberts (1901) 34–5. Dionysius resided at Rome from about 30 to 8 B.C.

Demosthenes; and he instanced speeches of Demosthenes and of his own to illustrate the stylistic range of both, which included variation within speeches as dictated by *decorum*.[1] As for 'rhythm', no orator capable of making use of it neglected to do so.

The plainness of Lysias may have sufficed at that moment, when under Caesar's dictatorship political oratory was dumb; but Demosthenes' style came into its own again when freedom was for a few months restored, in Cicero's *Philippics*, pointedly named after his. Yet Cicero himself was not unaffected by the movement in taste. In his mature speeches the style tends to be less Asianic, less Isocratean, less elaborated with figures of speech and cluttered up with redundant synonyms, more disciplined and muscular. This can be seen even in the Ninth *Philippic*, from the last year of his life, a panegyric proposing public honours for his dead friend Servius Sulpicius. On such a subject he would, in his young days, have pulled out all his organ-stops. But he realized now that that style was at best only consonant with youth (hence the decline in the reputation of Hortensius: *Brut.* 325).

Finally, there was the question of language. The 'genius' of a language is something real, but elusive and subtle. Why, for instance, should Latin be less tolerant of compound words than Greek (see *Orat.* 164), English than German? The influx of foreigners into Rome in the second century B.C., most of them slaves, of whom many would be freed by their masters and thus automatically become citizens, inevitably affected the purity of the Latin tongue. The younger Scipio called the Roman *plebs* 'the stepchildren of Italy'. He himself and his friends spoke pure Latin by heredity. It is not surprising that people alleged they had a hand in the plays of their protégé, the African slave Terence, whom Caesar saluted in retrospect as 'lover of pure language'; for Cicero noted that no such purity was to be found in the language of two playwrights contemporary with him, Pacuvius from the 'heel' of Italy and Caecilius, an Insubrian Gaul. Equally important, there was a Roman accent and intonation. An empire of many peoples needed a common Latin (corresponding to the 'common' Greek of Alexander's empire), and Roman aristocrats were concerned that it should be that of the capital. Grammar and syntax, vocabulary and pronunciation, were all involved.[2] There had been similar movements in Greek lands in defence of pure 'Hellenism', and latterly, of pure 'Atticism'.

In the matter of grammar and syntax the purists sought to standardize: there should be a 'correct' form for every word, e.g. for 'old age' *senectus*, not *senecta*. There should also be a correct construction for each syntactical relationship. Standardization raised a question which had exercised the Greeks: should

[1] He claimed that he used the plain, middle and grand styles in the *Pro Caecina*, *Pro Lege Manilia* and *Pro Rabirio perduellionis reo* respectively, all three in the *Verrines* and *Pro Cluentio* (*Orat.* 102–3).
[2] *De or.* 3.44; on language in general, 149–70; *Brut.* 170–2. Meillet (1948) 205–17.

language be governed by rules ('analogy') or by usage ('anomaly')? The Alexandrian scholars had sought to identify underlying rules, whereas the Stoics, champions of Nature, accepted what was produced by evolution. At Rome the encyclopaedic scholar Varro (116–27 B.C.) in his partly extant *De lingua Latina*, while leaning towards analogy, made ample concessions to usage. A stricter analogist was Caesar, whose efficient and systematic mind wished to correct the language just as he corrected the calendar. His treatise *De analogia* was a scholarly work, dedicated, like most of the *De lingua Latina*, to Cicero.

Strict analogy was associated with the Atticists, and as such it comes under attack in the *Orator*. Cicero's position was a sensible compromise. Thus he did not wish to alter phrases hallowed by tradition, nor to suppress exceptional forms which Nature had introduced for the sake of euphony. Though aware that it is incorrect to introduce an *h* into certain words such as *pulcer* and *Cartago*, 'after a while – a long while – I allowed correctness to be forced out of me by what was dinned into my ears'. There were even fifty-four instances in his writings (half of them in letters) of the indicative mood in indirect question, which Caesar shunned and every modern schoolboy is taught to shun. Nevertheless he repeatedly enjoined correctness in his rhetorical works; he taunted Mark Antony in the senate with using the superlative form *piissimus*, 'a word which does not exist in Latin'; and he took both his son and his secretary to task in letters for solecisms.

As to vocabulary, the purists sought to establish a 'proper' word for every thing or idea. In public speeches it was obviously important to make your meaning clear and not to give your hearers a sense of ignorance or inferiority. It may have been in this context that Caesar gave his famous warning, 'Avoid like a reef the unfamiliar or unusual word', but his taste was certainly fastidious. He held that selection of words was the beginning of eloquence, and in the *Brutus* Cicero makes Atticus say that Caesar 'speaks purer Latin than almost any orator'.[1] That 'almost' leaves room for Cicero himself. In his speeches Cicero was careful to use only good, established words still in general use. But he also insisted that they should be select words with some body and sonority. We find no instance of anything that looks like a new coinage, and only three instances of Greek words (all in the *Verrines*, about Sicily, and all carefully explained). Even naturalized Greek words occur only in one speech, *In Pisonem*, and there with ironical nuance. Aper in Tacitus' *Dialogus* singles Cicero out as one who applied selection to language, and *Tulliana puritas* is a phrase of St Jerome.

Languages do need some defence, and Latin was particularly vulnerable in the conditions of the late Republic. Cicero remarked to Brutus, 'When you

[1] 252. Gell. 1.10.4.

became Governor of Cisalpine Gaul you must have come across words that are not familiar at Rome. These can be unlearnt and replaced. More important is the fact that our orators' pronunciation has a timbre and accent that is somehow more metropolitan (*urbanius*).[1] Archaic words had to be weeded out. Even we can tell that one like *topper* ('forthwith') would be a misfit in classical Latin. There were also rusticisms to be eradicated, like dropping final *s* and the incorrect aspiration for which Arrius was pilloried by Catullus (84). And there were vulgarisms (which must be distinguished from the colloquialisms of educated speech): Cicero criticizes two Epicurean writers for using *sermo uulgaris*. Modern composers of classical Latin prose, thumbing their dictionaries, are made aware of words which are not found in Cicero or Caesar but are common in Plautus and in late Latin (vulgarisms), or in Virgil (archaisms, traditional poeticisms, poetic licences). We are not in a position to judge how far purification was necessary for the defence of Latin. Was a language admittedly poor being further impoverished merely in the interests of snobbery? Reflection on modern parallels may well make us hesitate. The French have an official Academy to protect their language and control immigration. De Gaulle instituted a special campaign to expel foreign words from common speech. The English, more empirical, have only the unofficial *Oxford English Dictionary*, the still less official *Fowler's Modern English Usage*, and the erratic example of the British Broadcasting Corporation; while the Americans follow popular usage to a degree dismaying to the more fastidious among the English. The reaction against chaste classicism, associated with the name of Sallust, included the use of archaic and poetic words in prose as well as the deliberate flouting of the Isocratean elegances.

In his careful letters to important personages Cicero is linguistically on his best behaviour; but when addressing Atticus or other familiar friends he relaxes into colloquial Latin, perhaps consciously enjoying such truancy from the Forum. He even asks Paetus, 'What do you make of the style of my letters to you? Don't you find that I use plebeian language?' In these more intimate letters, by contrast with the speeches, he uses about 850 Greek words, especially to Atticus, who was, by choice and residence, almost an Athenian.[2] They clearly came quite naturally to him. Again, for Atticus he alludes freely to Greek literature, whereas in the cautious letters referred to above he was as chary of this as in his speeches.

When he came to philosophic writing, as a sexagenarian in 45–43 B.C., he was faced with difficulties inherent in Latin, which lacked not only the terminology

[1] *Brut.* 171. One such cisalpinism may have been *basium*, the Veronese Catullus' favourite word for 'kiss', otherwise found only in his imitator Martial. On *Latinitas, urbanitas, rusticitas* see Marouzeau (1949) 7–25.

[2] It is noteworthy that Greek words were freely admitted into Roman comedy, never into tragedy or other serious poetry. Meillet (1928/1948) 109.

but the syntactical flexibility of the Greek he found in his sources.[1] Thus lack of the definite article made it hard to deal in abstractions.[2] *Omne bonum* has to serve for *to agathon*, 'the Good'. Sometimes however a neuter adjective alone would do – *honestum, uerum*. Lack of a past participle active (except in deponent verbs) sometimes drove him to clumsy periphrasis. But terminology was a more serious problem. The Romans had not dealt much in ideas. Cicero realized that existing words in the two languages were not complete equivalents, translating *physis* sometimes as *natura*, sometimes as *ingenium*. He might use an old word in a new sense, as *decreta* for *dogmata*. *Euidens*, a word not found in the speeches, does duty for *enarges*. We find him groping for the *mot juste*. Thus *pathos* is rendered by *motus animi* or *commotio* or *perturbatio*; but the ultimate rendering *passio* that has come down to us dates only from Augustine. He did however make some lasting coinages, such as *moralis, prouidentia, qualitas, quantitas*, and perhaps *essentia*. Sometimes he tells us he is inventing; but he was inhibited by his innate respect for the Latin language. He shrank from overfeeding it with indigestible neologisms or straining it with unfamiliar constructions. Thus he could not bring himself to countenance the word *medietas* ('middle position'), only going so far as to say, 'take it *as if* I had said that'.[3] (Others coming later had no such scruple; and from their use of *medietas* came the Italian *metà* and the French *moitié*.) He even apologized for venturing *beatitudo*, though *beatus* was a good Latin word found in his speeches, and *-itudo* a recognized suffix for producing an abstract word: 'whether we call it *beatitudo* or *beatitas* (both sound utterly harsh; but we should soften words by use)'.[4] Despite this last concession he seems never to have used either again. It is going too far to say that he created a supple philosophical language: he strove, as far as his fastidiousness would allow him, to enlarge his meagre linguistic patrimony, and to make philosophy comprehensible to the common reader;[5] in his own words, 'to teach Philosophy Latin and confer Roman Citizenship on her' (*Fin.* 3.40).

One means of enrichment to which he did have recourse was metaphor, which he rightly held to be a natural factor in the evolution of languages (*De or.* 3.155). A letter to Atticus gives us a glimpse of his workshop. Taking a hint from Lucilius, he had used *sustinere* to represent Carneades' Greek word for suspending judgement. Atticus had suggested instead *inhibere*, a metaphor from rowing. But now Cicero writes: 'I thought that sailors, when ordered *inhibere*,

[1] We possess translations by him which enable us to appreciate his problems: of a large part of Plato's *Timaeus*, and passages from his *Phaedrus* embedded in the *De oratore* and *De republica*. Unfortunately his translations of Aeschines' speech *In Ctesiphontem* and Demosthenes' *De corona* are lost; we have only the introduction, which goes by the name of *De optimo genere oratorum*. His translation of Plato's *Protagoras* (*Fin.* 1.7) is also lost.
[2] For 'the conquest of the abstract' in Latin see Marouzeau (1949) ch. v.
[3] *Tim.* 7.23. For Cicero's philosophic language see Meillet (1928/1948) 215–17. Glossary and discussion of renderings of technical terms in Lişcu (1937).
[4] *De nat. deor.* 1.95.   [5] Poncelet (1957); conclusions, 363–75.

rested on their oars; but yesterday, when a ship put in at my villa, I found this was not so: they don't rest on their oars, they back water. So *inhibere* involves action of a fairly strenuous kind.' He therefore asks Atticus to restore *sustinere* in the master-copy of the *Academica* he has for copying.

But while realizing that metaphor was in this respect a function, not an ornament, of speech, he also appreciated that it could be a transcendent ornament. His discussion of the subject at *De oratore* 3.155–70 is of exceptional interest. Here, as elsewhere, we may note that he considers language largely with poetry in mind, as his illustrative quotations show, forgetting the puritanism of his theory and practice as regards oratorical prose.

Latin has two outstanding qualities, sonorous gravity and conciseness. One of Cicero's great services was to reveal, following precursors such as Ennius, the possibilities of the former. Though he could also be admirably concise, it remained for Sallust, for Horace in his *Odes*, and finally for Tacitus, to exploit the latter to the full.

4. VERSE

According to Plutarch (*Cic.* 2) Cicero was considered the best poet as well as the best orator of his time, and his poetry was now neglected only because many superior poets had since appeared. This statement is less surprising when we recollect that there was a sag in Roman poetry before the emergence, roughly in the years 60–55 B.C., of Catullus and the other 'Neoterics' and of Lucretius. He may well have surpassed Hortensius in poetry as well as oratory, let alone such poetasters as Volusius, whose *Annals* Catullus derided. Even schoolboys down the ages have been taught by Quintilian and Juvenal to laugh at his line

O fortunatam natam me consule Romam

O Rome most blest, established in my consulship!

By Quintilian's time the historical context may have faded from memory; it was rather the jingles, one may suspect, that offended ears refined by Virgil and the rhetoricians. Whether or not they should so offend, is a matter of taste. After all, another master of verbal sound-effects, Tennyson, began a poem to Queen Victoria with

O loyal to the royal in yourself...

Cicero's verse is full of alliteration and assonance, a feature inherited from earlier Roman poetry which Virgil and his successors were to reserve for special purposes. The lines of Ennius that evoked his enthusiastic outburst, 'O excellent poet!' at *Tusc.* 3.44 are remarkable for this:

haec omnia uidi inflammari,
Priami ui uitam euitari,
Iouis aram sanguine turpari.

71

Better to forget that controversial line, remember historical perspective, and re-examine the surviving fragments, which at least testify that his poems were still remembered by some people centuries after his death.

What we can gather of his early poems (*Halcyones, Pontius Glaucus, Uxorius, Nilus*), varied in metre and subject, suggests an experimental precursor of the Neoterics; and it is significant that he chose for translation Aratus, the third-century astronomical poet whose *Phaenomena* and *Weather-signs* aroused among the Callimacheans of Alexandria and their Roman followers an enthusiasm that is hard for us to understand, even granted that they were nearer to people who regulated their life by the stars. But here, as elsewhere, his impulse to Latinize Greek works had an element of patriotism; and he also celebrated, likewise in hexameters, the hero of his native Arpinum, Marius the saviour of Rome.[1] His chief original poems were in this epic-panegyric hexameter tradition derived from his favourite Ennius. Others had written autobiographical apologias in prose; but it was a novelty when Cicero, disappointed in his hopes of a panegyric from his protégé the Greek poet Archias (for whose services there was a queue of nobles), composed one in Latin hexameters *On his consulship*, followed after his exile by one *On his experiences* (*tempora*). Of the former we possess a 78-line piece because he quoted it, as well as a dozen lines of his *Marius*, in the *De divinatione*.

The first thing that strikes one about his hexameters is that the position of caesuras and the limitation of metrical word-forms at the end of lines are already practically regularized as we find them in Virgil.[2] This is far from being the case in the extant fragments of his predecessors or in Lucretius. What Virgil and his successors approved (probably for reasons concerned with adapting quantitative Greek metres to the un-Greek accent of Latin[3]), it is not for us to criticize; and it may well have been the master of Latin prose rhythm himself who realized and regularized what had been only a half-conscious tendency in Ennius. But we should also be struck by the fact that the master of Latin prose *period* did not appreciate (as Virgil was to do) how his art could here also be applied to verse; for he falls into monotony. The lines are largely self-contained units of sense: the varied enjambment which imparts infinite variety and expressiveness to Virgil's verse is no more found in Cicero's than in the *Peleus and Thetis* of Catullus. There are also, as in Catullus, too many lines built round a word of three long syllables following a 'strong' caesura, such as

Principio aetherio   flammatus Iuppiter igni.

---

[1] The *Marius* was probably written after his return from exile in 57: Malcovati (1943); Büchner (1964) 302.

[2] For a detailed analysis of Cicero's versification see Ewbank (1933), introduction 40–74.

[3] For exposition of this theory, and criticism of other ones, see Wilkinson (1963), chapter 4 and appendix I. For general discussion of the reading of Latin hexameters see Allen (1973) appendix.

Lines of similar structure too often occur in close proximity; and in that long piece from the *De consulatu suo* 18 out of 19 successive lines (47–65) end in a trisyllable or quasi-trisyllable.

In celebrating his own deeds Cicero followed the ancient convention of sticking to the tradition of the genre. He incongruously adopted the whole epic paraphernalia of Ennius. Ennius had told of the apotheosis of Romulus, received into the Council of the Gods. Cicero apparently described the *Dichter-weihe* of Cicero, welcomed to Olympus by Jupiter and taught the arts by Minerva. Further, he adopted the grand manner we have seen to be charac-teristic of at least his earlier oratory, along with archaisms of language which are also features of his verse translations. Ancient critical opinion was in any case inclined to consider grandiloquence, the *os magnum*, an essential of real poetry (e.g. Horace, *Sat.* 1.4.44). The passage referred to above, put into the mouth of the Muse Urania, is monotonously 'rhetorical', and we may suspect that the rest was similarly inflated. Post-Virgilian critics who belittled him as a poet may not have been mistaken absolutely, though they may not have realized the advance he represented as a versifier. All his life he wrote verse as a gentleman's pastime, like other contemporaries, including his brother Quintus, who while serving in Britain polished off four tragedies in sixteen days. Under Caesar's dictatorship he 'amused himself', Plutarch says (*Cic.* 40), by sometimes composing up to five hundred lines in a night. Clearly he lacked that respect for poetry as an art which led the neoteric Cinna to spend nine years over his short epic *Zmyrna* and Virgil seven years over his *Georgics*. Yet he produced not a few fine lines; and his incidental verse translations of Homer and Greek tragedy in his philosophical works are at least dignified (they include a precious 28-line passage from the lost *Prometheus unbound* of Aeschylus: *Tusc.* 2.23–5).

It is worth comparing Aratus' text with Cicero's free translation, of which we possess 581 lines, half as much as the original. This youthful work, occasionally archaic in metre as in vocabulary, has some errors; but it exhibits, in Munro's words, 'much spirit and vivacity of language'. In the *Weather-signs* we may detect touches not in Aratus – rhetorical intensification, 'onomatopoeic' expressiveness, hints of personal observation, and the ascription of human feelings to animals and of animation to the inanimate, all of which presage, if they did not actually prompt, the Virgil of the *Georgics*.[1]

5. LETTERS

The letter became a literary-rhetorical form in the Hellenistic age. Timotheus employed Isocrates to compose his despatches on campaign. Artemo published Alexander's letters. Epicurus, following Plato, used letter form and Isocratean

[1] Malcovati (1943) 248–9; G. B. Townend in Dorey (1965) 113–16.

style to embody philosophy. In rhetorical schools models of socially useful letters were purveyed, and imaginary ones from mythical or historical personages composed. Rhetoric came naturally to educated letter-writers.[1] St Paul's impassioned appeal for charity in his First Epistle to the Corinthians (13) teems with its figures.

Book 13 of Cicero's letters *Ad familiares* consists entirely of seventy-nine letters of recommendation. Most of the people recommended are mere names: his secretary Tiro, or whoever arranged the corpus after his death for publication, clearly envisaged these letters as serving as models. Cicero had been at pains to vary them to suit the recipient; thus a short one to Caesar (15) contains six quotations from Greek poets, and concludes, 'I have used a new style of letter to you, to convey that this is no ordinary recommendation.' Book 4 consists mainly of letters of condolence (*consolationes*), and includes the famous one he received from Servius Sulpicius on the death of his daughter Tullia (5). He recognized three kinds of letter, the serious, the informative, and the gossipy (*familiare et iocosum*). One of his complaints against Antony was that he had violated the etiquette of social intercourse by publicizing what he had said in a private letter.[2]

Some of his letters he did however expect to be read by more than the addressee. Thus he was glad to hear that an important one he had addressed to Caesar had got around, having himself allowed several people to make copies of it: he wanted his view of the political situation to go on record (*Att.* 8.9.1). The seventy letters or more he was hoping, three months after Caesar's murder, to revise for publication (*Att.* 16.5.5) were probably selected political ones, though possibly the collection of recommendations (*Fam.* 13). How carefully he composed his serious ones can be seen in the collection of those to Lentulus Spinther, which Tiro put in the forefront of Book 1.[3] They abound in periods which would not have sounded out of place in a formal speech. The very first sentence is an elaborate antithesis:

> Ego omni officio ac potius pietate erga te
> ceteris satisfacio omnibus,
> mihi ipsi nunquam satisfacio;
> tanta enim magnitudo est tuorum erga me meritorum ut,
> quod tu nisi perfecta re de me non conquiesti,
> ego quia non idem in tua causa efficio,
> uitam mihi ēss(e) ăcērbām pŭtĕm.

---

[1] For letter-writing at Rome see Peter (1901); pp. 38–100 are on Cicero. Many of his letters are lost, including most of the collection *Ad Brutum* and all of those to Octavian, the future Augustus. (Nor have we any *from* Atticus.) Most of those that survive date from the last nine years of his life.

[2] *Fam.* 2.4; *Flacc.* 37; *Phil.* 2.7.

[3] Significantly, his letters from exile show much less care. He admits himself that his grief has bereft him of *huius generis facultatem* (*Att.* 3.7.3).

In letter no. 9, long enough to be a political manifesto, the clausulae of his rhetoric are ubiquitous (the first being his hallmark *ēssĕ uĭdĕātŭr*). Take section 5. The first sentence contains a balanced antithesis, *aut occulta nonnullorum odia aut obscura in me studia*, the second is reminiscent in its construction of the opening period of the *Pro Archia*, famous for its elegance; the third again contains balanced clauses; and all three end with a clausula from among Cicero's favourites. In 7 there is a miniature 'tricolon crescendo' with anaphora: *de ui, de auspiciis, de donatiōnĕ rēgnōrŭm*. A comparison with portrait-painting occurs in 15 and is elegantly expressed, with enough variation for relief and with a favourite clausula to each member:

> nunc
>> *ut Apelles Veneris caput* et summa pectoris politissima
>> ārtĕ pērfēcĭt,
>>> *reliquam partem corporis* incohatām *rĕlīquĭt,*
>> *sic quidam homines in capite meo* solum ēlăbōrănt,
>>> *reliquum corpus* imperfectum ac rŭdĕ *rĕlīquērŭnt.*

In 19 six lines are quoted from Terence's *Eunuchus*.

Letters of this kind are literature. So are Cicero's letter to Marcus Marius consoling him for missing Pompey's games, and that to Lucceius asking for his own consulship to be given special treatment in his history, which he himself described as 'a very pretty piece of work (*ualde bella*)'.[1]

But the great collection of letters to Atticus is wholly spontaneous, with only so much of rhetoric as Cicero had in his blood. Clearly he never intended that these outpourings, full of indiscretions, should be published, and they appear not to have become available until Nero's reign, though the historian Cornelius Nepos, who was privileged to see eleven volumes of them in 34 B.C., realized that anyone who read them would have a practically continuous history of those times by a man whom he credited with uncanny foresight (*Life of Atticus* 16). These letters show us how educated Romans talked. Some of those to his brother Quintus and to other friends with whom he was wholly at ease, to Papirius Paetus in *Fam.* 9, for instance, have the same quality. But they were to have no true parallel in general until quite modern times, and are one of the greatest legacies of Latin writing – a record of the experiences, in unusually stirring times, of a remarkable personality who was in the thick of things, and who was fortunately also exceptionally witty and a spontaneous master of literary expression.

[1] *Fam.* 7.1; 5.12; *Att.* 4.6.4.

6. SPEECHES

It is primarily on his speeches, perhaps, that the literary reputation of Cicero has depended in recent times, though to the present generation the style of '*o tempora! o mores!*' seems fustian and we are more stimulated by the unguarded self-revelation of the letters. He himself could joke to Atticus about his own pomposity: 'You know those paintpots of mine', and again, 'You know how I can thunder on about all that; it was so loud you probably heard it over there in Greece.'[1] But how did the spoken word become literature?

Although shorthand writers might operate when a speech was delivered in court, the Romans were well aware that the published speeches they read were not verbatim records. It was exceptional when Hortensius, who had a remarkable memory, delivered one in a state fit for publication, or when Cicero read out a speech, *Post reditum in senatu*, for the record. We know from Quintilian that Cicero normally wrote out beforehand the exordium, peroration and other vital passages (which incidentally show special care for rhythm) and learned them by heart, the rest being preconceived in outline only, though apparently he used notes (10.7.30–1). Everyone knew that his second *Actio* against Verres, published in five books, had never been delivered because the opposing counsel, Hortensius, threw up his brief after the first one and Verres went into voluntary exile; that the *Pro Milone* as delivered fell far short of the polished form in which we have it because he lost his nerve under heckling from Clodius' gangsters, whom the presence of Pompey's soldiers did not intimidate; and that the *Second Philippic* was not delivered on the ostensible occasion, with Antony menacingly present in Rome, but published some weeks later, after he had left, as a gauntlet thrown down. The *Catilinarians*, published more than two years after the events concerned, betray by their defensiveness (Book 4 especially) his anxiety now that he was under attack for having put Roman citizens to death without trial. (Not that publication was normally so long delayed, as is indicated by signs of haste in some other speeches; for instance, too many apparently redundant passages are left in, such as might have been helpful to hearers but are tiresome to readers.) Nor would two long passages in the *Pro Sestio* on the true nature of 'Optimates' (96–105; 136–43), a politician's apologia, have been relevant enough for even a Roman speech in court.[2] It has also been shown, from a reconstruction of Roman legal procedure, that Cicero's forensic speeches, published in the form most effective as literature, could not have been delivered in that form in court.[3] They are essentially pamphlets.

[1] For Cicero's speeches see, besides Laurand (1907/1936) and Büchner (1964), Clarke (1953) chh. VI and VII, R. G. M. Nisbet's chapter in Dorey (1965), and Kennedy (1972).
[2] Nisbet in Dorey (1965) 66.
[3] Humbert (1925); Douglas (1968) 14–15.

We may surmise however that the nature of Roman legal procedure did promote Cicero's oratorical development; for it differed from that of Athens in that the set speeches were delivered before, not after, the calling of witnesses. (The normal difference is highlit by the *Pro Milone* of 52 B.C., whose organization does approximate to that recommended by Greek handbooks because Pompey's emergency rules, designed to limit the effect of pathetic oratory as well as judicial bribery, had assimilated Roman procedure to Greek.) This meant that the speaker was more free to range, expatiating on generalities and personalities and indulging in excursuses and extended narrative; and more important, that he was less tempted to rely, with Roman deference, on the prescriptions of Greek handbooks, whose arrangement would not tally. So we find Cicero tailoring his speeches to suit the needs of the occasion. Thus in the *Verrines* he forwent the preliminary speech, since the defence was playing for delay and an adjournment till the next year, when its leader Hortensius would be consul, and went straight to the revelation of his devastating evidence. He thus sacrificed to winning his case a seductive opportunity for competitive oratorical display. Again, Greek forensic speeches were composed 'in character' to be delivered by the litigant. At Rome the advocate's own personality and prestige counted for much, and he could speak of and for himself as well as his client. In his early speeches Cicero sought to win sympathy as a courageous young man, and a 'new' man at that, in his later ones, to impress with his consular prestige (*auctoritas*). We know of 139 speeches of his out of a doubtless much larger number (speeches in civil suits were generally not thought worth publishing, Cicero's *Pro Caecina* being an exception). He won 74 of these cases and lost 16, the result of the remaining 49 being unknown.[1]

Of the 58 speeches of his which survive whole or in part the most famous are probably the *Verrines* (70), the *Catilinarians* (63) and the *Philippics* (44–43). The *Verrines* have come to life again particularly wherever there has been resistance to an oppressor of provincials or colonials, the *Catilinarians* in times of privy conspiracy and rebellion, the *Philippics* where republican freedom has been threatened by autocracy. Together they have created a rather one-sided impression of Ciceronian oratory. They are all vehement, not to say ranting, whereas many of the other speeches are relaxed. Thus the *Pro Murena*, composed amid the *Catilinarians* in the year of Cicero's consulship, has amusing passages at the expense of Sulpicius' legalism and Cato's philosophy (all the judges laughed, and even Cato forced a wry smile). Not that the invective characteristic of the *Verrines*, *Catilinarians* and *Philippics* is absent elsewhere: we meet it in the *In Pisonem*, which was soon being studied in the rhetorical schools as a model, and counter-attack was often the better part of defence. It was regarded as an art form (Ovid's *Ibis* is a counterpart in verse). No holds

[1] Granrud (1913) 241.

were barred. A man might be mocked for his banausic origins or his physical features. We have all heard of modern briefs marked 'no case: abuse plaintiff'. Brutus indeed deprecated the unbridled abuse of Antony by Cicero in *Philippic* 2. Professing however to prefer defending to prosecuting, Cicero maintained it was wrong to prosecute a man you thought innocent, though not wrong to defend someone who *might* be guilty, unless he was otherwise vicious.

Patriotic he certainly was, and courageous too as a young man attacking the powerful, and when in those supreme crises he nerved his naturally hesitant will; but it is distressing to see him tamed after his return from exile, putting his unique talents at the service of Caesar or Pompey. And while it may be too sweeping to say that 'he championed unworthy causes for short-term results in front of audiences he despised',[1] it is certainly true that, while we may admire from outside the way he handled his briefs and sometimes made political capital out of them, it is rarely that we can identify ourselves whole-heartedly with his cause, as we can in the *Verrines*, the *Catilinarians*, and (some would say) the *Philippics*. And it is disturbing to learn from a letter to Atticus (1.2.2) that he even thought of defending Catiline when they were rivals for the consulship, reasoning that, if he were acquitted, Catiline might feel obliged to pull his punches, and if condemned, he would be out of the way. But even Panaetius held that, while it is the business of the judge to find out the truth, it is sometimes the business of the advocate to maintain what is plausible even if it is not strictly true (Cic. *Off.* 2.51). In the rhetorical schools you were advised, if need be, to 'pepper your case with fibs' (*causam mendaciunculis aspergere*: ib. 59). In the *Pro Cluentio*, highly praised in antiquity and considered by the younger Pliny to be Cicero's masterpiece, he 'threw dust in the eyes of the jury', as he afterwards boasted. In this attitude to advocacy he would have had plenty of supporters, ancient and modern; but it was an awkward one to maintain in the high-minded atmosphere of philosophy, as we shall see.

A history of literature is not concerned with politics or even morality except insofar as they affect readability. But insincerity is a flaw which lowers our response from the level of sympathetic interest to that of cynical appraisal. In this respect our reaction may be the opposite of Petrarch's when he rediscovered the letters to Atticus in 1345. Petrarch was shocked to find that the philosophic master he had envisaged was a man of human weaknesses; whereas we can take a sympathetic interest in the self-revealing man while we can give only grudging admiration to the accomplished hypocrite. The most interested readers of Cicero's speeches in modern times are likely to be historians, for whom they provide a mass of sidelights on Roman life and institutions. This much said, we may turn to their literary qualities other than those already considered.

[1] Nisbet in Dorey (1965) 78.

Exordia, in Cicero's opinion, should be moderate and ingratiating in tone, spacious and periodic in style, but pointed with apophthegms designed to commend yourself or discredit your adversary (*Orat.* 125). He conformed to this doctrine unless he had reason to do otherwise, as in the most famous case of all when, no doubt in order to startle the Senate into a sense of crisis, he began: *Quousque tandem abutere, Catilina, patientia nostra?* 'How much longer, Catiline, are you going to abuse our patience?' Generally the impassioned climaxes would be more effective after a temperate opening.

A considerable portion of the speeches naturally consists in narrative. If Cicero had written history ('a particularly oratorical genre', as he called it), his style would no doubt have largely displayed the 'milky richness' that was attributed to Livy. But in court the first essential was clarity: the jury must grasp and remember the facts as represented. Hence in the story of Sopater of Halyciae in *Verrines* 2.68–75, extending to about 875 words, the average length of a sentence is only fourteen words. Narratives must also be unadorned, almost colloquial: they must give 'a most clever imitation of simplicity', in the words of Quintilian, who especially admired the account of Clodius' murder in the *Pro Milone*, perhaps the most perfect of Cicero's speeches:[1] 'Milo, after attending the senate on that day until the end of the sitting, went home, changed his shoes and his clothes, hung around a little while his wife got ready, the way wives do, and then set out at an hour when Clodius, if he had really wanted to get back to Rome that day, could already have been there...'

The Second *Actio* of the *Verrines*, in five books, was designed from the start to be read. Cicero must have been aware that, while he must refer to all possible crimes of Verres, there was a certain sameness about them that would pall. By the fifth book he was therefore particularly concerned to be readable. Verres had been Governor of Sicily from 73 to 70, his tenure prolonged because the serious slave revolt of Spartacus broke out on the mainland in 73, and Sicily, as the scene of previous revolts, was considered precarious. In fact it did not spread to the island, and Cicero had to anticipate that this would be credited by his opponents to the Governor's military efficiency. He marshalled all his powers of telling detail and innuendo in a devastating account that presages Tacitus (1–101). Even a summary may give some impression.

Hortensius, he says (3), would no doubt compare Verres with his predecessor Manius Aquilius, who had put down the slave rising in Sicily in 101. When he was impeached for extortion, Aquilius' counsel had dramatically secured his acquittal by tearing open his tunic before the jury and the Roman people to show the honourable scars he bore on the front of his body. (This is a time-fuse whose detonation comes only at 32: 'Are you going to ask Verres to stand up, bare his breast, and show the Roman people his scars – the records of women's lascivious love-bites?') Aquilius' measures had secured

---

[1] *Inst.* 4.2.57–9; *Mil.* 28.

that slaves were disarmed throughout Sicily. This gives occasion for a decorative story. A successor of his, Domitius, admiring a huge boar, had asked who killed it. When a proud shepherd was produced who said he had done it with a hunting spear, Domitius had him crucified for being armed. He may have been cruel, but at least he was not lax (7). This prepares for a scene in which Verres, having duly bound to the stake some slaves convicted of rebellion, suddenly released them and returned them to their master (10f.). 'I will not ask', says Cicero, 'how much money changed hands.' No less surprisingly, Verres had suddenly released, after eighteen months of imprisonment, a rich Sicilian whose slave foreman had got up a revolt. 'I have no ready cash', the poor man had pleaded as he was haled off at his trial.

As to military tours of inspection, laborious but essential, Verres made admirable arrangements (26ff.). He chose Syracuse for his headquarters because of its mild climate and spent his winters there, the short days in feasting, the long nights in sexual indulgence, rarely seen out of doors, or even out of bed. When the appearance of roses on his table informed him that spring had come, he began his tour. On horseback? No. Like the old kings of Bithynia, he rode in a litter with eight bearers, resting on a delicate Maltese pillow stuffed with rose petals. On arrival at any assize town he went straight to bed, where he heard and decided cases for an hour or two before devoting the rest of his visit to Venus and Bacchus. The wives of local notables were entertained, the more brazen at dinner, the discreet at later assignations. His dinner parties were riots; for although he never obeyed the laws of Rome, he scrupulously observed the rules of drinking-parties (26–8).

At midsummer, when the inspection of harvest labourers and corn-threshing, so important for Governors of Sicily, fell due, Verres left the old palace of King Hiero and set up summer headquarters with his cronies in marquees in the loveliest part of Syracuse, at the mouth of the harbour, where he and his young son received only those connected with their pleasures, including his favourite mistress Tertia, whose presence (since she was the daughter of a ballet-dancer whom Verres had enticed away from her Rhodian fluteplayer) was resented by the higher-class wives who shared his favours with her. The law-courts were deserted – but in this case that was a mercy (29–31).

If Hortensius really tried to present Verres as a military commander, baring those scars, Cicero would be obliged to reveal his previous exploits. This introduces an elaborate extended metaphor, the campaigns of love (later dear to elegists like Ovid). It is true that no slave rising occurred. Did he then also put down piracy? Here come in (42) his relations with the city of Messana, the only one that had sent a deputation to eulogize him at his trial. He had publicly received from it a fine cargo vessel for his private use, to bring home his plunder, for which the town was a convenient depot – or was it to remove it later, when he was sent into the exile he must anticipate? In return he exempted Messana not only from the corn levy but also from providing a warship. Its eulogy was thus worthless. Verres also altered the practice by which pay for the fleet was channelled through commanders. Channelling it through himself, he pocketed not only the bribes from the men he exempted but also the pay they would have got. The pirates were well aware of this. One pirate ship was indeed brought in. It proved to be full of silver, fabrics and attractive young people. Verres, though drunk when told, was not too drunk to leave his women and hurry down to it.

He executed all the prisoners who were not goodlooking, and distributed the remaining loot to his friends and hangers-on, sending six musicians to a friend at Rome. But nothing was seen again of the pirate captain. Would-be spectators of his being led in chains and beheaded were fobbed off. A man who was presumably a substitute was kept, not in the famous Syracusan quarries, where the imposture would have been detected, but in comfortable circumstances in an inland town which had never seen any sort of pirate but Verres' agent. Meanwhile he did have others beheaded, not all together (since he knew there were Syracusans who would count them) but in driblets. Yet some did keep a count, and demanded to see the rest of them. So Verres substituted some Roman citizens he had casually imprisoned on trumped up charges. Their friends recognized them though they were hooded, and protested in vain. But provoked in court, Verres lost his head: he admitted he had not beheaded all the pirate captains, but had kept two imprisoned in his own house – *because* he knew he would be charged with receiving bribes for not having executed the real pirate captain. No one doubted that he had in fact been so bribed, and that these two were in reserve in case that other substitute died or escaped (32–79).

Cicero now returns to the lunch parties at those summer quarters by the bay. Verres and his young son were the only men present – if you could call them men – except that his freedman Timarchides was occasionally invited. Apart from Tertia, the women were all wives of Syracusans. Among them was Nike, wife of Cleomenes, said to be very goodlooking. Even Verres would have felt uncomfortable if her husband had been around; so he put this Syracusan Greek in command of Roman naval forces, though there were plenty of Romans, up to the rank of quaestor, on his staff. And why, when so many Sicilian cities had always been loyal, choose a citizen of Syracuse, so suspect a city that ever since its capture by Marcellus no citizen had been allowed to live on its strategic island of Ortygia? Cleomenes' squadron of seven vessels set sail with skeleton crews only, most of the sailors having paid Verres for immunity from service. The Governor, unseen for days past, turned out to watch it, in a purple Greek cloak and a long, skirted tunic, leaning on a woman's arm. After four days at sea the ships put in at Pachynus because he had kept them so short of provisions; and while Cleomenes enjoyed himself in Verrine fashion, the sailors were reduced to grubbing up the roots of palm trees to eat. News then reached the inebriated captain that there were pirates at Odyssea. He had hoped to fill up the crews from the land garrison, but that too proved to have been depleted by Verrine exemptions. His flagship, far superior for action to those of the pirates, was the fastest, and got away. The last two ships were picked off, and the rest, having put in at Helorus following him, were burnt by the pirates when darkness fell (80–91).

Verres meanwhile had returned to the palace with his train of women. So strict was his discipline, that his orders that no one should disturb him were obeyed even in this crisis, while poor Cleomenes found no wife at home to comfort him in his troubles. Alerted however, not by any official beacon but by the glare of the burning ships, a fiercely hostile crowd gathered. Finding the Governor himself obviously dazed and only half awake, they encouraged each other to arm themselves and occupy the forum and island. The pirates, anxious no doubt to take their only chance of viewing Syracuse and its splendid fortifications, put to sea again next day and with their four ships entered the Grand Harbour, the heart of the city, passing Verres' deserted pleasure-camp; and it was only after, not frightened but sated, they had sailed out again that people began to ask themselves what was responsible for such a disaster (92–101).

Cicero was famous for his wit, which sparkles through his letters to Atticus. He complained that everyone's sallies were attributed to him – even those of Sestius; but he was flattered when he heard that Caesar not only collected his *bons mots* but claimed to be able to distinguish the spurious from the authentic.[1] Three books of them were published after his death by the faithful Tiro. In *De oratore* 2 he makes Caesar Strabo, after mocking the idea of classifying humour, proceed to do so for seventy-five chapters (216–90), a repertoire of jokes which throws considerable light on Roman mentality.[2] Wit and humour were naturally characteristic of the plain style, which eschewed emotion,[3] but they were also valuable in the middle style, which sought especially to please. Cicero's command of them was one of the things that enabled him to speak effectively, as he claimed, in whatever style was appropriate to his subject.

In his own speeches we may note a progress from the rather crude puns and sarcasms of the earlier ones, not completely outgrown even in the *Verrines*, to the more delicate irony of his maturity in the *Pro Murena*, *Pro Caelio* and *Pro Ligario*. The climax of his defence of Caelius was a brilliant piece of ridicule, of the implausible story of how one Licinius, allegedly sent by Caelius to deliver a casket of poison to Clodia's treacherous slaves at the Senian Baths, of all places, gave the slip to her agents, who lay in wait to catch him in the act (61–9). Even if there were something in the story, what the jury would retain would be an impression of farce. Indeed Cicero himself had suggested to them that it was more like a Mime than a play with a coherent plot.

7. DIALOGUES AND TREATISES

Cicero had always hoped, so he says, that after his consulship he would be free to enjoy leisure and esteem and to devote himself to literary pursuits. Instead he had to endure six years of trouble and anxiety, and it was only the leisure with greatly diminished esteem forced upon him by the Triumvirs in 56, after he had tried to take an independent line in politics, that brought him to embark, as a compensation, on two manifestos he had always wanted to write, about the things that mattered to him most, the *De oratore* on his oratorical ideals and the *De republica* on his political ideals. He was consciously setting out to inaugurate for Rome something she lacked, a prose literature worthy of the Latin tongue.

[1] Sen. *Contr.* 7.3.9; Quint. *Inst.* 6.3.5; Cic. *Fam.* 7.32.1.
[2] His own irony and humour have been exhaustively catalogued and analysed by Haury (1955).
[3] Grant (1924).

As his primary form he chose dialogue – not the Platonic dialogue in which conclusions emerge from discussion (the *Symposium* is exceptional), but the Aristotelian,[1] more congenial to an orator, in which the various characters express, in speeches that may be lengthy, opinions already formed. Indeed the speeches may be complementary, as they mainly are in the *De oratore*, which therefore approximates to a treatise; or they may express differing views, as in the *De natura deorum*, to encourage the reader, in the spirit of Philo, to make up his mind for himself (1.10). In either case he would be able incidentally to portray humane intercourse. We are spoiled by Plato's excellence; but anyone who belittles Cicero's skill in the dialogue should read Varro's *Res rusticae*.

The *De oratore* was begun in 55 and completed next year. For its dramatic occasion Cicero chose three days during a crisis over the Italian allies in September of 91 B.C., when the Senate had adjourned for the Roman Festival. The setting is the villa at Tusculum of that Lucius Crassus who had been his mentor in boyhood. Another of Cicero's old mentors is present at first, Scaevola the Augur, now old and infirm. Cicero is, in fact, escaping into his youth, and though he could hardly introduce himself, as a boy of fifteen, into that company, he probably remembered that house. One feels his involvement. In the prologue to Book 3 he tells his brother that he has wanted to do for Crassus what Plato did for Socrates, and indeed Plato is never far from his thoughts. Scaevola plays the part of Cephalus, the old man who is present for a while at the beginning of Plato's *Republic*. A fine plane tree reminds him of the one at the beginning of the *Phaedrus*, and he suggests they sit under it. And as Socrates at the end of the *Phaedrus* prophesies a great future for the young Isocrates without mentioning Plato, so Crassus at the end of the *De oratore* prophesies a great future for the young Hortensius, who in that year made his debut as an orator, without mentioning Cicero – a graceful compliment whose irony however would not be lost on the reader. As in the *Phaedo*, the occasion is described to the author by a survivor. But it is the *Gorgias* that haunts the dialogue, as we shall see. In the prologue to Book 3 Cicero bitterly recalls how within four years, of those seven courteous participants, Crassus and Scaevola had soon died, both after brave resistance to threatened tyranny, Catulus had killed himself, and Antonius, Caesar Strabo and Sulpicius had been murdered, either by Marians or Sullans. Only Cotta survived to tell the tale. The heads of those three had been spiked on the Rostra, including, to Cicero's especial horror, that of the orator Marcus Antonius, whom he admired almost as much as Crassus. For us there is an added poignancy in the thought that twelve years later his own head and hands were to be displayed there by Antonius' grandson and namesake.

---

[1] Aristotle's 'exoteric' works, admired in antiquity for their 'golden eloquence', are unfortunately lost (*Acad.* 2.119; Quint. *Inst.* 10.1.83).

The main theme is *paideia*, cultural education, or more widely, *humanitas*. Cicero claimed that he owed his oratory to the spacious Academy, not to the rhetoricians' workshops (*Orat.* 12). Crassus, who in general represents Cicero's views, deplores narrow specialization and the utilitarian approach, claiming that the ideal orator must be highly educated in all subjects, able to speak with fullness and variety on any topic. That, we remember, was what Gorgias claimed to teach; and throughout the dialogue Cicero is haunted by the spirit of the Platonic Socrates.[1] For if Socrates was right, oratory was a mere knack, morally neutral at best and potentially pernicious, and he himself has been living all along 'the unexamined life'. Right at the beginning Crassus mentions the *Gorgias* only to dismiss it with a quibble (cf. Catulus at 3.29), and he castigates people who gibe at orators, *ut ille in Gorgia Socrates* (3.129). In effect Cicero is tacitly renewing the great debate between Isocrates the pupil of Gorgias and Plato the pupil of Socrates; and as we saw (p. 63) he is, for all his veneration of Plato, an Isocratean. He was bound to be: his own life of practical politics conducted through the influence of oratory, the source of his fame and self-respect, committed him irrevocably to that camp. His clever and plausible defence, perhaps suggested by a thesis of Posidonius, consists in reproaching Socrates with having split the *logos*, divorced thought from speech, philosophy from rhetoric, the contemplative life from the active, so that some have even come to exalt the former above the latter (as Aristotle did at the end of his *Ethics*). He puts into Catulus' mouth at 3.126–30 an encomium of the *paideia* of the old Greek Sophists, whom he calls 'orators', and defines the ideal orator in such wide terms that he might seem to have stolen the thunder of the Platonic philosopher. In contrasting this 'full man' with the narrow rhetoricians he is choosing ground on which Plato and Isocrates were united, and thus avoiding a head-on collision. The fact that he is so much *engagé* imparts to the work an intensity of intellectual passion. It is his *apologia pro vita sua*. The greatest heir of the Sophists is grappling in his soul with the spirit of Socrates.

Into this, his first literary work, he pours all the riches of his own fullness. His remarkable grasp of cultural history, his sense of period and his fund of anecdotes and quotations enable him to diversify the work with such passages as Caesar Strabo's disquisition on wit (2.216–90). Book 3 alone contains passages on correct Latin speech (43–6), on the relation between philosophy and oratory down the ages (56–73), on the actor Roscius' voice-control (101–2), on metaphor (155–69), on artistic functionalism (178–80), on the sensitivity of Roman audiences to style and rhythm (195–8), and on delivery (the orator as the actor of real life; 215–27).

[1] The inevitability of this conflict had been recognized by his brother (if indeed he was the author) when he said to him, in the brochure of advice on electioneering (*Comm. Pet.* 46), with reference to the necessity of time-serving, 'But it will probably be rather hard to persuade a Platonist like you of this.'

Yet the *De oratore* is in some ways an exasperating work. The great issue is repeatedly sidestepped. Scaevola at the outset suggests that oratory may have done more harm than good and puts forensic eloquence in a cynical light (35–41), but no one takes up the challenge. We are fobbed off with 'it's all a matter of nomenclature' (1.47; 3.142–3); as if it made no difference whether *philosophia* denoted dialectic or cultural knowledge! There is too much repetition. Nor is there any real tension of argument: for Antonius, the purely utilitarian orator, after acting as a foil to Crassus in Book 1, is made to confess next day that he was only arguing for the sake of arguing (2.40), and thereafter is merely complementary to him. Moreover Cicero tries to do too many things at once. In his eagerness to portray Crassus, whom he considers to be misconceived by his contemporaries, he blurs the distinction between him as speaking in character and as mouthpiece of himself (compare Plato and Socrates). Books 2 and 3 are a '*technologia*', as he himself calls it, to supersede the *De inventione* (*Att.* 4.16.3). Sending a copy to Lentulus, he says he hopes it will be helpful to his son (*Fam.* 1.9.34). It is true that, by a salutary innovation, *ars* is subordinated to *artifex*; also that the textbook is camouflaged as literary *sermo*, the underlying subdivisions being disguised (compare Horace's *Ars poetica*), and the *disiecta membra* wrapped up in words of philosophic discourse. Yet the bones do sometimes obtrude. Thus Antonius, after saying that panegyric needs no rules, proceeds to give some (2.44ff.); Caesar Strabo ridicules the idea of analysing wit, then analyses it (2.217–18; 235ff.): and strangest of all, in Book 3 Crassus is constrained to do what all along he has protested against doing – to go into technical details of style of the most scholastic kind (200ff.) (Cicero himself would never have belittled the importance of style; and in the *Orator* he made amends nine years later for what he must have felt to be inadequate treatment.) Like other Romans, Cicero could not shake off the framework of the rhetoricians with their pigeon-holes, Graeculi whom he represents his Crassus as despising.[1] He does not start from his own experience, any more than Horace does in the *Ars poetica*.

In the summer of 54 we find Cicero deep in a dialogue on his other interest, politics, which he thought would be well worth all the labour involved, if he could bring it off. The prologue to *De re publica* 1 movingly expresses his bitterness at what has given him leisure to write, his being excluded from active participation after all his services to the state. For the dramatic occasion he chose the Latin Festival of the winter of 129, and as his spokesman the younger Scipio. As in the *De oratore*, the conversation purports to have been retailed by a survivor: Cicero reminds his brother, the dedicatee, how on their youthful tour they heard about it at Smyrna from the exiled Rutilius Rufus. The choice of a

[1] Clarke (1953) ch. v gives a fair critique of the *De oratore*.

moment when Scipio, like Crassus in the *De oratore*, was shortly to meet his death may have been suggested by the situation of Socrates in Plato's *Phaedo*, for again Plato was much in his mind, though Aristotle also had written a *Republic* in dialogue form. A friend nearly persuaded him to downdate the occasion and take the leading part himself, as Aristotle had done; but he reverted to his original plan, partly because he wanted to depict the period which seemed to him to show the Republic at its best, partly to avoid giving offence to living people (notably, of course, the Triumvirs).[1] Contemporaries could draw their own conclusions.

The *De re publica* was a broader and better organized work than the *De oratore*, but unfortunately it has come down to us only in fragments, though these were greatly increased in 1822, when Cardinal Mai published what may amount to nearly a third of the whole, which he had discovered in a Vatican palimpsest. Of the six books every other one had an external prologue. Book 1 conceives of the state as based on common interest and common rights (39). It reviews, as Greeks had done ever since Plato's *Republic*, the three constitutions of democracy, aristocracy and monarchy, and like Polybius (6.3–18) favours the composite, best seen in the Roman Republic (1.70). Book 2 traces Rome's early development towards the attainment of this equilibrium, *optima re publica*, in the second century. In 3 Philus consents to play devil's advocate, arguing that justice depends on expediency, and Laelius replies as a Stoic (his eloquent eulogy in 33 of Natural Law, god-given, above all man-made laws, is famous), Scipio reinforcing his opinions. 4, very fragmentary, was apparently on education, moral and physical as well as intellectual, probably with emphasis on the family, and on culture in general in the context of the community. 5 and 6, on the ideal statesman and his reward, are also very fragmentary except for the celebrated conclusion, the Dream of Scipio, preserved with the Neoplatonic commentary of Macrobius (*c.* A.D. 400).

Remarking that it would be easier to show how the Roman Republic came about than to invent an imaginary state like Plato's Republic, Cicero makes Scipio give (2.1–63) an account of her early history (the first indeed that has come down to us). Though the nearest approach to a political theorist that Rome produced, he is an empiricist: he follows Cato in believing that the Roman constitution is superior because it was evolved, not created.[2] The virtue of composite states was supposed to be stability, a subject highly relevant for Romans talking in 129, when Tiberius Gracchus, Scipio's own brother-in-law, had just broken it. Cicero's ideal was not an equilibrium of forces, of tensions, but a concord like harmony in music (and one thinks at once of the concord of

[1] *Q.Fr.* 2.12; 3.5.1–2. For a full discussion of the *De re publica* see the introduction to Sabine and Smith's translation (1929). Boyancé (1970) 180–96 gives a critical survey of work done on it down to 1964.

[2] 1.45; 69.2.41–3; 57.3.41.

Senate and Equites which he secured in the Catilinarian crisis and wanted to perpetuate).

The *De re publica* is naturally of great interest to historians. In it Greek ideas of the ideal state encounter the practical wisdom of the Roman *mos maiorum*. Thus Book 3 broaches the question of the basic justice or injustice of the Roman empire. The Romans had long recognized, with their Foreign Praetor and their Law of Nations, that justice transcended national boundaries. The meeting of this practical tradition with Greek (Stoic) ideas of the brotherhood of man and of Natural Law gave impetus to both.

Cicero's Scipio flirts in Book 1 with the idea of monarchy as an element in his composite state. (Plato's philosopher-king would be in mind.) There has been endless discussion as to whether the '*rector*' or '*moderator*' or '*princeps*' of Books 5 and 6 is envisaged as a particular person – Scipio as he might have been if he had not been murdered (see 6.12), or Pompey, or even Cicero; or, as seems more likely, an ideal *politicus* like that of Plato or Aristotle holding no constitutional position of autarchy. Again, did this dialogue in any way mould or colour the Augustan image of the *princeps*?[1] For us there is a pathetic irony, parallel to that we noted in the *De oratore*, in the thought that among the last of the young men Cicero was so eager to influence was one who was to consent to his proscription, the future Augustus.

The relevance of the *De re publica* to its time lay in its insistence that all men had a duty to serve their country, that no one should put his personal *dignitas* before her interests, and that private morality was applicable to public affairs. We can imagine the impact of this widely read work on the Rome of 52–1, which had just seen, amid Epicurean apathy on the part of many who should have been leaders, rioting between the rival gangs of Clodius and Milo, and a state of emergency such that Pompey had had to be made sole consul. And Cicero meant what he said. In a moral crisis for him soon after, when, as Governor of Cilicia, he decided not to countenance financial oppression of Cypriots by his friend Brutus, he commented to Atticus: 'I prefer to be on good terms with my conscience, especially now that I have given bail for my conduct in the shape of six volumes' (*Att.* 6.1.8).

As literature, what matters in the remains of the *De re publica* is Scipio's dream (see p. 231). To match the Myth of Er at the end of Plato's *Republic* Cicero invented an effective climax. Scipio tells his friends how, as a young man, he stayed with the Numidian king Massinissa, who was devoted to the memory of Scipio Africanus and talked of him far into the night. Africanus had then appeared in a dream to his adoptive grandson and had unfolded to him, from a heavenly vantage-point in the Milky Way, a (mainly Platonic) view of the universe, a presage of Anchises' revelation to Aeneas in

[1] On these debates see Boyancé (1970) ch. IX.

Aeneid 6.[1] 'The starry spheres far surpassed the earth in size. Indeed the earth itself now seemed so small to me that I was disappointed with our empire, no bigger than a spot, as it were, on the surface' (16). The message is, that while you are on earth it is your duty to serve your country, but that human glory is transient *sub specie aeternitatis*; you should set your affection on things above, for there is a reward of immortality in heaven, amid the harmony of the spheres; and that not only for men of action, but for all who have already caught that harmony and reproduced it for mankind. *Mens cuiusque is est quisque* 'the mind is the true man', and that mind is immortal. Nothing in Cicero was to prove more congenial to Christians down the centuries than this vision.

If the *De oratore* is Cicero's *apologia*, the *De re publica* is his *consolatio*. He planned the *De legibus* to follow it. This again was on the analogy of Plato; but whereas Plato in his *Laws* was creating a construct unrelated to the *Republic*, Cicero gives, after a discussion of the nature of law, an account of the actual laws of Rome, with only occasional, if sometimes important, amendments, an appendix in fact to the *De re publica*.[2] The setting is idyllic, and again intentionally reminiscent of Plato's *Phaedrus*. Cicero and his brother, at their native Arpinum in the hills, are talking to Atticus on his first visit there, walking along the bank of the Liris till they come to an island that splits the cold, swift Fibrenus before it plunges into the larger river. There are interesting discussions in Book 3, which deal with magistrates, of the institution of the tribunate (19–26), and of whether voting should be open or secret (33–9). But the dialogue form is purely *pro forma*: indeed the brothers make a joke about this (3.26). The composition of the work was interrupted by Cicero's governorship and the subsequent civil war, and it may not have been published in his lifetime. Out of at least five books only the first three, and they with gaps, have survived.

In 46, when, after the defeat of the Pompeians, Cicero had been finally allowed by the Dictator Caesar to return to Rome, he reverted to the subject of oratory, apparently in reaction to growing criticisms of his style (see p. 66). In the treatise *Orator* he depicted the perfect orator, and also elaborated the rather hurried precepts his Crassus had deigned to vouchsafe in *De oratore* 3; and in the dialogue *Brutus* he traced the history of oratory at Rome up to its culmination in himself. Both are dedicated to Brutus, most promising of the young friends he sought to mould. The following year, 45, was one of great misery for him. He had divorced his wife Terentia after thirty years of marriage, he had for some time been estranged from his much loved brother, and worst of all,

[1] For Cicero's sources and originality see Harder (1929).
[2] His tenor is reactionary. On religion in Book 2 he seems concerned to re-establish even the obsolete, on politics in 3 to reinforce the nobles, priests and censors. Rawson (1973) 342–55.

his daughter Tullia, the apple of his eye, died that February. In an attempt to assuage his grief for her he composed a *Consolatio*, novel in being addressed to himself. Then, encouraged by Brutus and Matius, he conceived the idea of seeking an anodyne in philosophical writing, in presenting Greek philosophy to Latin readers. The result was momentous for Europe. All his life, though more keenly when he was excluded from politics, he had, as he insisted (*Nat. deor.* 1.6–7), been interested in philosophy. This was uncommon at Rome; indeed at one time, he says, there was no statesman apart from Cato who shared this interest with him. He defended it in the prologue to his *De finibus*. Some were against it altogether; some thought it should be studied only in moderation; some could see no point in translating what any interested person could read in Greek. Cicero replied, that not all could read Greek who pretended they could; that if tragedy was worth translating, so was philosophy; and that in any case he did not merely translate, but arranged and criticized the arguments. He wanted to convert people to philosophy. His lost protreptic dialogue was named after a participant who had been in need of such conversion, Hortensius (d. 50). Particularly he hoped to convert young people who might become influential in the state (*Div.* 2.4–5).

We know a good deal about his motives, programme and progress from his letters and his prologues. In most of these works he makes himself a participant. Not being greatly interested, as a practical Roman, in metaphysics, he dealt mainly with ethics. The philosophers whose views he reproduced were mainly Hellenistic ones interested in the soul of man who was no longer primarily citizen of a *polis*; but his claim (*Acad.* 2.3) to go back to Socrates was justified, in view of his sceptical method of enquiry and his emphasis on ethics.[1] His scheme may be described in his own words, from the prologue to *De divinatione* 2, completed shortly after Caesar's murder:

In my *Hortensius* I exhorted my fellow citizens as earnestly as I could to the study of philosophy, and in the four books of my *Academics* I expounded the philosophical system I thought least arrogant and most consistent and refined.[2] And since philosophy rests on the determination of the ultimate good and evil, I clarified that topic in five books (*De finibus bonorum et malorum*), so that readers might understand how the various philosophers had argued against each other. There followed, also in five books, the *Tusculan disputations*, dealing with the essentials of the happy life, the first on despising death, the second on bearing pain, the third on relieving sickness, the fourth on psychological disturbances, and the fifth on the crown of all philosophy, the (Stoic) contention that virtue is in itself sufficient for the happy life. Thereafter I completed

[1] A. E. Douglas, in his sympathetic account in Dorey (1965) 137.

[2] The attempt of Hunt (1954) to show that Cicero's philosophical works are a critical edition in logical order of the lectures he had heard Antiochus (see p. 56) give at the Academy is interesting, but there are too many pieces that do not fit in. The best introduction to these philosophical works is that of Süss (1965).

three books *On the nature of the gods*, comprising all the arguments on that topic, followed by these two books *On divination*; and if, as I intend, I add a work *On fate*, I shall have fully treated this branch of study.

Of the *Hortensius*, which changed Augustine's life and turned him to God (*Conf.* 3.4–7), we have only fragments (about 100). The *Academica*, on the epistemology of the Academy, appeared in two versions, in two and four books respectively. We possess Book 2 of the '*Priora*' and part of Book 1 of the '*Posteriora*'. Cicero also mentions the *De senectute* or *Cato maior*, on old age, and the eulogy (lost) of the younger Cato; but not the lost *De gloria*, in two books, nor the *De legibus*; nor the *De amicitia* or *Laelius* on friendship, and the *De officiis*, which were yet to come. The *De senectute* and *De amicitia*, imaginary discourses by Cato and Laelius rather than dialogue, both short and both dedicated to Atticus, enshrine the quintessence of Ciceronian humanism, and with the *De officiis* were chiefly to represent Cicero for such readers as he had in the Dark and Middle Ages.

Cicero wrote by night and day, since he could not sleep (*Att.* 13.26.2). In twenty months he composed five or more major and several minor philosophical works. Naturally these, apart from the *De senectute* and *De amicitia*, have not the degree of originality, springing from personal experience, of the *De oratore* and *De re publica*, and Cicero is more scrupulous than most ancients in acknowledging his debts. But they are far from being mere compilations from the Greek; without years of meditation behind him he could never have mastered the material so quickly. Their success appears to have been immediate: there were so many other souls at this time who longed to escape into a spiritual world. As philosophy they deal with problems that still beset human beings, even if they have ceased to preoccupy philosophers except perhaps for the post-Aristotelian problem of freewill and that of cognition. But Cicero cannot be said to interest historians of philosophy so much as original thinkers like Plato and Aristotle do.

There is however historical interest in the *De natura deorum* and *De divinatione*, for example, where religion is no more exempt than any other subject from the Academic practice of hearing all sides. Cicero's mentor Scaevola the Pontiff had pragmatically distinguished three kinds of religion, that of the poets, the statesmen and the philosophers. In his poems Cicero introduced that of the poets, in his *De legibus* that of the statesmen, in these later works that of the philosophers. In spite of the cloak of dialogue in some, his views do emerge. Thus in *De divinatione* 2 this augur appropriates to himself, in answer to his brother, the role of demolishing, with Lucretian relish, superstitions he treated with solemn respect in *De legibus* 2. 'But we are alone' he says to his brother, 'so we can search for the truth freely' (*sine inuidia*, 2.28). Augustine commented that what he proclaimed so eloquently in this discussion he would not have dared to breathe in a public speech (*Civ. Dei* 2.30). Cotta in the *De natura deorum* is a pontiff who adheres scrupulously in public to the traditional cults but is largely sceptical about them in private (1.61) – like some Renaissance Pope, and no doubt like Cicero himself. Nevertheless Cicero was careful to distinguish between superstition and true religion (*Div.* 2.148). Again, at the end of the *De natura deorum*, despite his disclaimer at 1.10 (see p. 56), he briefly intimates *in propria persona* that he himself considers the Stoic view put by Balbus in Book 2 'most like the semblance of truth'. Yet he has reservations: although 'the argument from design' convinces him of the existence of a providential deity (indeed outright atheists were very few in antiquity), and he takes his conscience as evidence that the soul is divine and comprehends the divine law (though 'no one has ever owed his virtue to god'), he rejects the (inconsistent) Stoic doctrines of divine interference and determinism because of his predisposition to believe in freewill and the reality of moral choice.[1] The *Tusculans* in particular, though ostensibly a detached exposition of various views, betray by their tone his own commitment to belief in the immortality of the soul. Books 1 and 5 are really emotional declamations. Pain and death were particularly topical subjects at that time.

As literature these works are perhaps not exciting by modern standards. Their significance lies in their having become the medium by which the substance of Greek philosophy was transmitted to the West and kept alive until Greek works were studied in the original again. They are enhanced by the illustrations, literary, historical and anecdotal, that came so readily to Cicero's pen, and by the mastery of language that never failed however fast he wrote. His last and most influential work, astonishing considering that he was now in the forefront of the struggle with Mark Antony, was not a dialogue but a treatise ostensibly addressed to his student son, the *De officiis* (*On moral obligations*). This has therefore a special status as representing his own views, though the first two books are avowedly based on Panaetius; and for once he deviates into dogmatism. Though he incidentally criticizes Caesar (without sparing Pompey), approves of his assassination, and deplores the flouting of the republic by Antony, that is not sufficient reason for supposing the work to have been politically motivated. It carries on from the *De finibus*. Books 1 and 2, somewhat encumbered by repetitions but relieved by Cicero's perennial abundance of illustrations, deal with right (*honestum*) and expediency (*utile*) respectively. Book 3 examines cases of apparent conflict between the two. (There could be no real conflict, for the advantages of expediency are short-term; by doing wrong you harm your own soul.) Book 1 introduces, *à propos* the cardinal virtue of

---

[1] In the partially extant *De fato* (31ff.). The extant *Paradoxa Stoicorum* shows his interest in Stoicism. It is a rhetorical elaboration of the paradoxes, composed in the spring of 46, probably as an intellectual exercise, and dedicated to Brutus.

temperance, the interesting moral-aesthetic Panaetian doctrine of 'propriety' (*decorum*). Doing what was appropriate to nature in every sphere of life included being true to your own individual nature, insofar as that did not conflict with universal natural morality, and acting consonantly with your own age and status (107–51). The subject of Book 3, casuistry, had for some reason been left aside by Panaetius, but Cicero finds other Hellenistic philosophers to exploit. Though it is less carefully composed, and the problems sometimes recall the fantastic ones beloved of the rhetorical schools, it has a certain interest in airing ancient ideas about many of the practical problems of daily life, such as business ethics.

From the philosophic point of view the work rests on insecure foundations.[1] Nature is assumed to be good. The conflict between the springs of altruism and self-regard is superficially assumed to be easily reconcilable (as in the case of private property and common interest: 1.92). Nevertheless, in its independence of external sanctions for morality, it foreshadows modern ideas of evolutionary ethics; and from the practical point of view its emphasis on strict morality must have been as salutary in its age as it has been since. Cicero proclaims a very high standard based on the brotherhood of man. The *De officiis* laid the foundations of liberal humanism for Europe and the world.

8. LITERARY INFLUENCE IN ANTIQUITY

In dedicating the *De officiis* to his son Cicero said:

As to the subject matter, use your own judgement (I will not impede you). But by reading my writings you will certainly extend the range of your Latin... So I earnestly urge you to read not only my speeches but also my philosophical works, which are now almost as extensive; for while the former have a more forceful style, yet this equable and restrained style is also to be cultivated. (1.2–3)

Nothing could illustrate better how much greater relative importance the ancients attached to style than we do; and historically it has been primarily by his manner that Cicero has won readers, and through this that he has then obtained a hearing for his matter.

Livy advised his son to read Cicero and Demosthenes first and then the authors nearest to them – presumably to form his oratorical style. Though the Augustan poets do not mention Cicero, his memory, as of the opponent and victim of Augustus' last enemy, was allowed to survive in the rhetorical schools. His style too was still admired by some, including the elder Seneca, but not by the *avant-garde*, probably the majority, who preferred the terse and epigrammatic manner which came to be associated with the name of Seneca. The debate

---

[1] For severe critiques see Hunt (1954) 163–78, and Süss (1965) 351–69.

features in Tacitus' *Dialogue on orators*, Ciceronian in form, at the end of the first century A.D. (Messalla *vs*. Afer). Quintilian could say at that time that Cicero was popularly thought to be '*durus et ineruditus*' (? dry and unsophisticated, unadventurous in language), whereas to him he was '*perfectus*' and 'no longer the name of a man but a synonym for eloquence'. It was his advocacy that established Cicero as the model for Latin prose.[1] The letters also won admirers, such as the younger Pliny and Marcus Aurelius' mentor Fronto. His rehabilitation was permanent but his influence patchy, now in one department, now in another. The great educational ideals embodied in the *De oratore* and Quintilian's *Institutio oratoria* were too ambitious for human weakness. Ironically, it was the *De inventione*, which Cicero had repudiated, and the *Rhetorica ad Herennium*, falsely attributed to him until 1492 ('*Rhetorica prima et secunda*') that kept his reputation as a rhetorician alive in the schools. Between A.D. 800 and 1500 these occur 148 times in extant library catalogues, the *De oratore* only 12 times.[2] By his example however Cicero greatly influenced the style of some of the Christian Fathers, notably Lactantius, whose *Divinae institutiones* (304–13) were called by Jerome 'a river of Ciceronian eloquence', and whom Pico was to dub 'The Christian Cicero'.

[1] *Inst.* 8 *praef.* 26; 10.1.105–12; 2.25; 12.10.45–8.
[2] Bolgar (1954) 396, summarizing M. Manitius' researches.

5

SALLUST

Of Sallust's early life, education, and allegiances we know nothing, except that he embarked on a political career. Limited information becomes available for the years 52–45 B.C., when he was in the thick of the tumults of the period. He appears first in 52 B.C. as a tribune bent on trouble-making. He may already have been an adherent of Caesar. Certainly, when he was expelled from the Senate in 50 B.C. on moral grounds (a convenient pretext for settling political scores), it was to Caesar he turned and whom he served, with little success until 46 B.C., when he distinguished himself in organizing supplies for the African campaign. He was appointed the first governor of Caesar's new African province. There, it is alleged, he speedily acquired a vast fortune, and, on his return to Rome, faced charges of extortion, but, thanks to bribery or connivance, was never brought to trial. In 45 B.C. or not much later he withdrew from public life, and, desiring to occupy his leisure in a befitting way, set about writing history. In his first work he claims that he abandoned politics in disgust at the wholesale corruption in which he had been enmeshed (*Cat.* 3.3–4.2). In all his three works he passes stern and lofty judgements upon standards of conduct. His detractors were not slow to remark on the apparent hypocrisy of an adulterer and peculator transmuted into a custodian of public and private morality (e.g. Varro *apud* Gell. 17.18, *Invect. in Sall. passim*, Suet. *Gramm.* p. 112 R). The discrepancy still troubles a few modern critics. Others, the majority, dismiss the matter one way or another. The stories about Sallust, some say, are wholly unreliable, nothing more than echoes of the virulent personal abuse conventionally exchanged between politicians of his time. Again, we are told, even if the stories are true, they are immaterial: a man whose own behaviour is deplorable may yet make an excellent observer and moralist. Witness Francis Bacon. These arguments have their force, but do not expunge all doubts. Can we brush aside the allegations against Sallust, insecure though they are, when we enquire into his honesty as a historian?

Sallust's first two works, which survive entire, are monographs concerned with limited themes of special interest. His own statements (*Cat.* 4.2–3) suggest that he had written nothing of moment before the *Bellum Catilinae* (commonly known as the 'Catiline'), published after Caesar's death and probably after Cicero's. The *Bellum Iugurthinum* (commonly known as the 'Iugurtha') followed within about two years, if we assume slow but consistent progress in writing. Then Sallust moved to history on a larger scale, starting his narrative in 78 B.C. He had reached 67 B.C. by Book 5, which remained incomplete at his death. The loss of his *Histories* is grievous indeed, but enough fragments have come down to us, including speeches, letters, and important parts of the prooemium, to permit a reasonable understanding of the work's scope and character.

Evidence of the lively interest which Sallust provoked is afforded by three spurious writings, all concocted in the rhetorical schools a generation or two later. The *Invective against Cicero*, like its companion piece against Sallust, ascribed to Cicero, is a clumsy imposture, designed to make schoolboys titter, but the *Epistles to the aged Caesar on the state*[1] are quite accomplished fabrications. The author (or authors) made a tolerable, if imperfect, attempt to catch Sallust's historical style, forgetting that no one with the slightest taste would have used this style in letters. The *Epistles* have some slender interest as sources for the political thought of the early Principate, and they contain some pointedly expressed maxims of statecraft, still occasionally quoted, but otherwise they are only worth perusal as exercises in imitation. Surprisingly some scholars of repute have considered them genuine.

Sallust was the first recognized classic amongst Roman historians, avidly read, admired and abused, immensely influential on many diverse writers, and cited more often than any Latin prose author, Cicero alone excepted. But he was not in any obvious sense a pioneer. Romans had been writing history for over a century, and the main types were firmly established. Annalists, like Gellius and Piso, had long since begun to put flesh on the bare bones of tradition. A few at least, for instance Valerius Antias, were not punctilious about the truth, if lies would better reinforce a case or divert the reader. These men took Rome's whole history for their subject, as did Livy who used and antiquated them. Others chose particular topics, notably Coelius Antipater, who wrote of the second Punic War, or, like Rutilius Rufus and Cornelius Sisenna, related contemporary events and their own experiences. An appreciable range of interests is evident from the start, for Cato the Elder, the father of Latin historiography, accommodated in his *Origins* both speculation about the remote past and outspoken comment on recent history. Altogether there are few areas into which Sallust's predecessors had not boldly ventured. And they did not write casually. Even that bare, repetitive, and seemingly artless phraseology found in fragments of the earlier annalists may have been cultivated as appro-

---

[1] This title is incredible in itself, but, being of uncertain date, cannot be used as an argument against authenticity.

priate to the dignity of theme and narrator. Others, notably Coelius and Sisenna, preferred distinct and colourful styles. Sisenna, for whom Sallust has some regard (*Iug.* 95.2), was an innovator in language (he clearly fascinated the grammarians) and perhaps no mean historian. Sallust did not attempt to treat again the social and civil wars which Sisenna had narrated, but took up the story where he had left off. Acknowledged veneration for Cato (*Hist.* 1.4) should not obscure Sallust's likely debts to predecessors nearer in time. For adventures in expression, if for nothing else, Sisenna provided a precedent and example.

Oratory at Rome reached its maturity a generation or more before history. That simple fact largely explains why Cicero's remarks about history (*De or.* 2.51ff., *Leg.* 1.6ff., *Fam.* 5.12) are prejudiced and condescending. He sees the further development of Latin prose only as a modification of the oratory which he has perfected: hence for him history is an orator's task, and it must be couched in a style much resembling his own. In *Fam.* 5.12, anxious as always to have his consulship celebrated, Cicero outlines the attractions for a historian of a circumscribed period or topic, and explains to Lucceius how effectively a unified, varied and elaborate work may be centred upon an individual. Ironically it was Sallust, not Lucceius, who took up the challenge, displaced Cicero from the pre-eminent importance in the Catilinarian affair which he claimed, and devised a viable style which was utterly alien from Cicero's. In *Leg.* 1.6ff. Cicero observes that talented Romans had devoted themselves to political and forensic oratory, at the expense of history. Sallust, no modest man, was ready to redress the balance, but he still felt obliged, in his prooemia, to justify his decision. As yet historians were little esteemed.

The prooemia of Sallust's three works, together with his digression at *Iug.* 41–2, have engendered endless debate. Quintilian (*Inst.* 3.8.9) affirmed that in the *Catiline* and *Iugurtha* Sallust *nihil ad historiam pertinentibus principiis orsus est* 'began with prooemia not at all appropriate to history', in other words more suited for oratory or philosophy.[1] That is unfair. Greek historians, if not Roman, had often enough wandered into general discussion or generously sketched a background or praised history as a worthwhile avocation. Sallust may more fairly be criticized, in his *Catiline* at least, for the disproportionate bulk of introductory matter in a comparatively short composition. Whether or not the prooemia accord with any preconceived notions of the historical genre, they certainly raise some problems. Are the ideas expressed relevant to the narrative? And have these ideas any intrinsic interest, either through originality or as commonplaces which illuminate the intellectual preoccupations of Sallust's time?

We find in the prooemia a texture of loosely related themes. On the most general level Sallust assesses the value and scope of human activity, labouring

---

[1] Some consider (implausibly) that Quintilian means 'irrelevant to his narrative'.

over distinction between body and soul and physical as opposed to mental achievements. He proceeds to ask how men's talents may best be employed in the service of the state, accepting without question conventional Roman views on discipline, moderation, and honour. He leaves us in no doubt of the standards by which he will pass judgement in his narrative. But first, since he agrees with Cato that prominent men must render account even for their leisure, he must justify himself and defend the writing of history. In the *Catiline* he is still apologetic, but in the *Iugurtha* he takes an aggressive stance and dares to claim that historiography is quite as useful to the state as anything which politicians do. Of the purport of the prooemium to the *Histories* we can only speculate. It may have been cooler and more assured, though it contained some biting remarks (e.g. 1.5, 1.13). Sallust seems to be concerned with much the same matters in all three prooemia, and one theme at least, thanks to the preservation of certain fragments of *Hist.* 1, we can follow right through. It is the decadence of Rome, Sallust's obsession or (to speak more politely) the firmest nexus of his thought.

Sallust begins to talk directly of general moral decadence at *Cat.* 5.8, where something more than innate depravity is needed to explain Catiline's behaviour. He then (*Cat.* 6–13) offers a summary account of Rome's social and political history. While honour and patriotism directed the conduct of individuals, the state flourished (*Cat.* 7). Latterly, however, the Roman commonwealth, once so admirable, had become utterly corrupt (*Cat.* 10.6: cf. *Hist.* 1.16, Liv. *praef.* 7–10). Ambition, greed, and luxury (with, or resulting from foreign influences) had undermined the old virtues, and fortune, always wilful (*Cat.* 8.1), had grown positively malevolent (*Cat.* 10.1). Removal of external threats, completed by the destruction of Carthage in 146 B.C., permitted Roman degeneration to proceed unchecked (*Cat.* 10.1, *Iug.* 41.2–3). Before that turning-point there had been discipline and concord. These generalizations, even on cursory inspection, seem a little ramshackle: Sallust has thrown together, but not reconciled, several different ideas. For instance, he employs *fortuna* ('fortune', 'chance') only as a transient motif, dramatic and vague: the thought is not worked out. Again, he reflects the confusion of his sources and contemporaries when they sought to establish an exact time for the beginning of Rome's moral decline. Some authorities set it well before 146 B.C., others as late as Sulla's return from the East (cf. *Cat.* 11.4–8). We may easily perceive that all these views are over-simple and unhistorical, and perhaps Sallust began to realize the fact himself. At *Hist.* 1.11 he admits that many bitter dissensions existed from the beginning of the state, and at *Hist.* 1.7 ascribes such dissensions to a basic flaw in human nature. Very little weight can be given to fragments divorced from a context, but these fragments may show that Sallust's opinions (or sources) had changed for the better.

Many of the ideas found in Sallust's prooemia can be traced a long way back, to Plato, Xenophon, and Isocrates amongst others, but his immediate sources are not easily fixed. Several later Greeks had discussed the development and decline of states. Polybius saw in a balanced constitution the foundation of Rome's success, and foresaw what would happen if this balance were lost: disorder and a scramble for power. Sallust probably read Polybius, though he must have found Polybius' flat and colourless writing very uncongenial. Posidonius, historian, philosopher, and teacher, may well have appealed more strongly.[1] Two items particularly suggest a connexion with Posidonius, Sallust's quasi-evolutionary view of society, with idealization of primitive life (*Cat.* 2.1, 9.1), and his notion of the self-sufficiency of the mind (*Iug.* 2.3). And Sallust shares with Posidonius a belief in the salutary effect of external constraint upon Rome (cf. Diod. Sic. 34.33), as well as his generally moralistic approach (cf. Diod. Sic. 37.2). But Posidonius favoured the *optimates*: here at least Sallust parted company from him. Again, Stoic elements in his thought do not prove that Sallust was an adherent of that school, for other elements can equally well be used to suggest obligation to the Epicureans. If anything he is an eclectic, though he probably never thought about the matter. One important contemporary influence, Cicero, can too readily be neglected: antipathy does not preclude exploitation. Sallust probably knew Cicero's published writings extremely well, and Cicero must have been a major source of information for the *Catiline* and *Histories*. Again, in his *De re publica* and elsewhere, Cicero, like Sallust, touches upon the political problems immediately confronting Rome. They have some common ground: both, for instance, consider that parts of the second century B.C. were good periods, morally and politically.

As essays in historical analysis the prooemia are far from admirable. Sallust talks too much in extremes and makes many unwarranted assumptions. He is sometimes precipitate and heated in his opinions. But one must respect the forthrightness, indeed courage, of a man who, writing under the second triumvirate, castigated in scathing terms the pernicious effects of concentration of power in a few hands (*Iug.* 3). Again, while Sallust often rambles haphazardly, several ideas debated in the prooemia relate closely to the narrative. One instance is the idea that terminology, as well as standards, can be perverted (*Cat.* 12.1, 52.11, *Hist.* 1.12, 3.48.13), borrowed from Thucydides' discussion of the dissensions at Corcyra (3.82), a passage by which Sallust was deeply fascinated. Another is provided by Sallust's incessant concern to define and appraise virtue. At *Cat.* 7.5 *uirtus omnia domuerat* 'virtue had conquered all' summarizes the idealized picture of early Rome which Sallust too unquestioningly accepted. Where, he wants to know, may such qualities be found in

[1] We should, here as elsewhere, equally resist the current tendency to discount Posidonius' influence and the earlier tendency to magnify it.

recent history? An answer is supplied at *Cat.* 53, where Sallust compares Caesar and Cato, the two statesmen whom alone of their contemporaries he regarded as cast in heroic mould. Others then, including Cicero, fell short. The same question is posed repeatedly in the *Iugurtha*, and more searchingly debated. The nobles had counted honour and esteem as their inherited perquisites, but Marius' achievements had finally shattered the illusion: only individual virtue could secure pre-eminence.

At the outset (*Cat.* 4.2) Sallust planned to write *carptim* 'selectively', rather than attempt continuous history. It is not his declared aim to look for new facts. Indeed *Cat.* 4.3–4 may be taken to suggest that he was avid to redeploy familiar and, in particular, sensational material. How far his conception of his task broadened or matured is hard to assess. The *Iugurtha* certainly covers a much longer period than the *Catiline*, but the coverage is arbitrary and patchy. In his *Histories* Sallust had presumably to handle the whole history of the period, and could no longer select freely. If that is so, the change of form from the monograph reflects a different, arguably more serious approach. But the larger scope of his narrative in the *Histories*, while it brought obligations, also allowed much latitude. Sallust could embark on digressions, with good precedent (Herodotus for instance): his descriptions of places and peoples, particularly those around the Black Sea (*Hist.* 3.61–80), were celebrated and prompted imitation. Again, he seems to have coped with major and protracted stories (notably Sertorius and Mithridates) without anxiety over tight adherence to an annalistic framework based on the consular year at Rome.

Sempronius Asellio (fr. 1 P) had long since asserted that mere narration is not enough: a historian must lay bare causes and motives. Cicero elaborated the same point (*De or.* 2.63), adding that much attention must also be paid to personality. Sallust tries to meet those requirements. He wants to know the truth, he is alert, trenchant, and spiteful, and, like his model and inspiration Thucydides, he is interested in the realities, not the façades, of political history, in underlying as well as immediate explanations. But a resolve to probe and question is in itself of little use: insight and penetration are essential. Sallust is but modestly endowed with these qualities, and detachment, the best of Thucydides' virtues, he can hardly claim at all. The Roman critics were not wholly misguided in making a comparison between the two historians, but they failed to draw a just conclusion, unfavourable to Sallust, from it.

Some modern writers regard Sallust as primarily a literary artist. They argue, for instance, that he conceived of the *Catiline* as a tragedy: it presents the inevitable fall of a man of heroic calibre, vitiated by a moral flaw, who bravely sustains a hopeless cause to the end. The work admits such interpretation, but we cannot appraise it in these terms alone. Indeed Sallust himself prescribes the terms in which he must be judged, as a historian who solemnly declares that he will try to tell the truth (*Cat.* 4.3). At *Iug.* 95.2 he says that Sisenna, for all his merits, did not speak freely. Does Sallust then speak without bias, prejudice, or distortion? Does he represent men and events honestly?

It has been alleged that Sallust's picture of the late Republic is gravely distorted, in selection and treatment of material, by intense bias against the *optimates*. Others go further and maintain that the *Catiline* is a partisan tract, designed to exonerate Caesar from complicity in the Catilinarian affair and generally to show him in a good light. Others again believe that the *Catiline* is a riposte to Cicero's *De consiliis suis* 'On his courses of action', released after the author's death. In this work Cicero may have revealed embarrassing ramifications of Catiline's conspiracy which he had for long been obliged to suppress, but Sallust would not leave Cicero's account unchallenged. In reply to these and other criticisms Sallust's defenders assert that he is fair and impartial, or that, if he is biased, bias is not the same as falsification or an intention to mislead, or again that incompetence rather than bias is the charge properly to be directed against him.

That Sallust is hostile to the majority of *optimates* cannot be denied: he commonly describes them as arrogant, venal, and useless. Further, he appears to consider the whole political system utterly rotten. Men strove for their own selfish ends, not the good of the state. Sallust does not applaud or whitewash any party, but looks for merit in individuals, of whatever affiliations. We need not give great weight to the virulent attacks on the ruling oligarchy found in certain speeches, notably those of Lepidus and Macer (*Hist.* 1.55 and 3.48). They are aptly contrived for the speakers and occasions, like the letter of Mithridates (*Hist.* 4.69). Sallust could not draw a sharp and consistent distinction between corrupt *optimates* and virtuous *populares*, since several major figures would simply not fit any such scheme, amongst them Cicero, Caesar, and Cato. Cicero showed that talent could still find a way to the top, and Sallust notes (*Cat.* 23.5–6) that, though the nobility loathed new men, they had to back this one in a time of crisis. But Cicero's sympathies were or became optimate, and to many who held other views he was a *bête noire*. Nevertheless Sallust treats him perfectly fairly, without warmth indeed (Cicero's self-praise quenched that), but with all due acknowledgement of his services. Sallust may seem to disregard Cicero's speeches against Catiline, but for this there is a special reason. The speeches were available and well known (cf. *Cat.* 31.6) and could not appropriately have been adjusted to the fabric and compass of Sallust's monograph. Caesar obtains special prominence at *Cat.* 49 and in the senatorial debate which Sallust proceeds to record (*Cat.* 50–2), but he is not made out to be a commanding figure generally. And in the memorable comparison of Caesar and Cato which follows the debate (*Cat.* 53–4), Cato arguably comes off better. *Esse quam uideri bonus malebat* 'he preferred to be rather than to seem good' is high praise of the man whom Caesar most detested, and it would be incongruous in a work intended as an apologia for Caesar.

In chapters 18–19 of his *Catiline* Sallust sketchily records an abortive attempt at revolution two years before the main conspiracy. Catiline and various others are alleged to have been involved. As Sallust narrates it this 'first conspiracy' is a flimsy tissue of improbabilities. Straightforward interpretation of the evidence we have suggests that in 65 B.C. Catiline was still seeking power by normal, constitutional means. He resorted to force only when these means had finally failed him. If Sallust has a bias here, it is against Catiline. But that is improbable, for he presents Catiline as a man of ability and courage, albeit catastrophically misdirected. The truth is rather that he saw Catiline's career only with the narrow vision of hindsight. Catiline must play the role of villain from first to last: thus he will better point a moral and adorn a lurid tale. Gullibility, not bias, explains the inadequacies of chapters 18–19. Having no reliable material relating to an earlier conspiracy, Sallust collects some half-remembered rumours from the political warfare of the 60s and makes a patchwork of hearsay.

Chapter 25 of the *Catiline* presents no less of a problem. Why is it there at all? In 24.3–4 Sallust mentions various types of people induced to join the conspiracy, including several women of bad character. Then (in 25) he says that one of these women was Sempronia, and gives her a full-scale characterization, comparable with that of Catiline himself (5). She was high born, cultured, witty and fascinating, but also wanton, unscrupulous, and extremely dangerous. The sketch is superb, and justly admired. But Sempronia, who has not appeared in the narrative before, will only once appear again. The extraordinary oddity of this fact protrudes inescapably. We cannot well argue that Sallust wanted a female counterpart for Catiline, and count that a justification. A historian should only make use of a 'female lead' if she belongs to the story, as Tacitus, masterfully imitating Sallust's sketch (*Ann.* 13.45), accords Poppaea the prominence which she merited or may be claimed to have merited historically. There are only two reasonable explanations of Sallust's Sempronia. He may have been so enamoured of the characterization that he would not cut it out, although it impaired the unity of his monograph. Alternatively, realizing that his contemporaries would know of Sempronia's reputation and be titillated by a colourful portrait, he obligingly provided one, indifferent to the example of Thucydides who attempted to write for all time, not for the gossipmongers of his day. In a work clumsily planned as a whole Sempronia is the worst blemish.

The *Iugurtha* unfolds more simply than the *Catiline*, but still has enough complexities. In particular Sallust must simultaneously keep track of events in Africa and political developments in Rome, and explain their interrelation.

There is here much risk of confusion over chronology or between cause and effect. Again, Sallust cannot or does not entirely centre his narrative upon one person. His focus shifts and, though Iugurtha holds his interest for considerable periods, fixes in the end on Marius. Once Iugurtha has at last fallen into Roman hands, no more is said about him: we do not hear how he was dragged in the triumphal procession and then ignominiously strangled by the public executioner. That would have been a fittingly melodramatic conclusion, if he had conceived of the *Iugurtha* as a self-contained entity, a story in its own right. Since he chose to conclude with reference to the imminent peril from northern invaders and the hopes pinned on Marius, he evidently regarded his monograph as concerned with an integral segment of Roman history, to be related to the whole.

In the *Iugurtha* praise and censure are meted out equally freely. Metellus, a great aristocrat, is duly commended for his distinguished services to the state. On the other hand, Marius is by no means glorified. While his achievements obtain full recognition and we are left in no doubt that his career presages the end of the old order, he appears as brash, conceited, and selfish, a demagogue rather than a statesman. Again, when he briefly talks of the Gracchi (42), Sallust mixes criticism with approval,[1] suggesting that they were rash and over-confident, and proceeds to damn party strife generally. As far as individuals are concerned, the *Iugurtha* seems to give a dispassionate, if selective, record of a controversial period. But, when Sallust deals with wider matters, his judgement can be singularly obtuse. He supposes, for instance, that the Senate of the late second century B.C. was corrupt and venal, and finds in this venality the main reason for delay of decisive measures against Iugurtha. That view was doubtless much fostered by the *populares*. Sallust should have weighed another explanation against it. Further entanglement in Africa and the dissensions of Massinissa's dynasty would bring Rome trouble, expense, and no very certain profit. And Rome had no binding obligation to intervene. The Senate's long hesitation can be imputed to good sense and statecraft. Instead of canvassing such possibilities, Sallust opted for a crudely biased or, at least, unduly simple account. One wonders how many sources he used and suspects that they were very few.

The elder Cato excluded the names of Roman leaders from his narrative: honour and glory, he contended, belonged to the people as a whole. That view, unrealistic even in Cato's time, had been utterly antiquated by events. Those who had seen Marius and Sulla, Pompey, Caesar and Octavian could not doubt the immense importance of individuals. Naturally, then, the shift of power from an oligarchy to a succession of dynasts is directly reflected in historical writing. Detailed characterization becomes indispensable and history

---

[1] The interpretation of this passage, particularly 42.3 *sed bono...uincere*, is very problematic.

moves closer to biography. Sallust was exceptionally good at depicting character, both directly, by means of introductory sketch (cf. Sen. *Suas.* 6.21) and
supplementary comments, and indirectly, by means of speeches, report of the
opinion of others, and revealing items of behaviour included in his narrative.
But, since his approach was strongly moralistic, we sometimes find overlap,
even confusion, between description of individual traits of personality and
exemplification of the predictable qualities of certain types of men in certain
situations, be they reactionaries, liberals, or revolutionaries. Let us revert, for
illustration, to his treatment of Catiline.

Catiline is introduced (5.1–8) in a sketch of monumental gravity, abruptly
and harshly phrased, censorious in tone, brief and ponderous. Antithesis
supports and enlivens the description: great physical and mental power opposed
to depravity of disposition, greed to acquire opposed to profusion in spending,
adequate eloquence opposed to deficiency in sense, and so on. No doubt
Catiline had some or all of these characteristics, but he also represents for
Sallust a type of person allegedly to be found all too often in the aftermath of
Sulla, in that he was unprincipled, self-seeking, and insatiable. Three features
stand out in Sallust's sketch: determined courage, truculence verging on
megalomania, and acceptance of perverted values. Catiline shows conspicuous
powers of leadership, by holding together a motley following in face of great
odds, and makes a good end, in traditional Roman manner (60.7). But ferocity
and incipient dementia are recorded at the start (5.7), and the notion of madness
is developed at 15.4–5, a good instance of supplementary direct characterization.
According to Sallust, madness finally drove Catiline to desperate measures.
That is questionable: Catiline struggled long to win the consulship legitimately
(26.1), and his later conduct, desperate perhaps, was hardly mad. To the last
he claimed to stand for a cause and could calculate what might be to its advan-
tage: thus he rejected the enrolment of slaves (56.5). Sallust contradicts himself,
or at least his efforts in psychological analysis are ill attuned with his narrative.
If, as he would have us believe, Catiline is a criminal lunatic, he ought to be
shown behaving as such. No doubt Sallust drew on the stock-in-trade of political invective, which included accusations of fury and insanity, as well as lust
for regal power (5.6). But truculence is a quality which Catiline really seems
to have possessed: he displayed it before the Senate in confrontation with
Cicero (31.9) and retained it in death (61.4). As to perversion of values,
Catiline is made to assert that right is on his side, that he is a victim of
enmity and faction (35.3). Hence he feels obliged to defend his dignity and
honour. It was to dignity and honour that Caesar was later to appeal, as
justification for a greater civil war. How much better then was Caesar than
Catiline? Sallust hardly intended us to make this comparison, but it is there
to be made.

Sallust determined to forge a prose style for history unlike anything Rome had known before, and he succeeded where Sisenna, who was led by the same ambition, had failed. Wanting to be different, Sallust reacted not only against the style of Cicero, periodic, expansive, and rhythmical, but also against the movement, dominant in his day, towards standardization of vocabulary, grammar, and syntax. For such a rebel the end justifies the means. Provided he can write excitingly and colourfully, Sallust cares little what sources or devices he resorts to, except that he does not, as some have supposed, readily employ colloquialisms. Ancient critics recorded the most distinctive features of his style: archaism, brevity, abruptness, and novelty (see, e.g., Suet. *Gramm.* p. 108 R, Quint. *Inst.* 4.2.45, 8.3.29, 10.1.32, Gell. 4.15.1). One might add pure idiosyncrasy, for there is much of that. And he seems willing to admit or affect Grecisms, from which his contemporaries were shying away. Altogether he offers a daring pastiche, outlandish and grotesque, pungent and arresting.

Archaism appears not only in Sallust's choice of words, but also in variety of construction, where one construction had become normal, and in loose, paratactic sentence-structure, best paralleled in authors of the earliest period (e.g. Cato). Since Sallust is writing about recent and nearly contemporary history, he is plainly not attempting to find archaic clothing for archaic themes, as Livy may be said to do. His purpose cannot be explained simply. No doubt he seeks to enhance his expression, to lend it special dignity: the Romans believed (and we have no reason to doubt) that archaism could have that effect. Again, he wants to show that he at least will use the abundant riches of older Latin, which others were increasingly denying themselves. But above all, by employing parataxis and avoiding the rhythmical patterns beloved by orators, he would fain appear straightforward and honest, like the most artless of the old annalists. The trappings of rhetoric do not become a man who professes to tell the truth bluntly and briefly.

The brevity which Sallust pursued and often attained made a great impression on Roman readers, to judge by the numerous references to it. For this quality in particular he was thought to rival Thucydides (see, e.g., Sen. *Contr.* 9.1.13–14). Of course brevity takes several forms. There is compression of much thought into few words: Sallust, like Thucydides, can be admirably pregnant. Then there is haste to tell what has to be told, which results in selective use of material and excision of detail. In this Sallust is only too adept, but an imitator, Velleius, surpassed him in precipitancy. Again, there is economy of expression proper, which consists in omission of connectives, ellipse of auxiliary verbs, and so on. Sallust is economical, but he does not reject every superfluity. Indeed certain features of his style make for pleonasm, particularly the asyndetic lists and alliterating combinations in which he so much delights.

Many asyndeta do not effect brevity as such, but rather an impression of jerkiness and spontaneity. The words seem to pour out uncontrolled, and often an afterthought will be loosely appended. These aspects of brevity are closely allied with the abruptness of sentence-ending and switch of construction which still astonishes those who are habituated to smoothly articulated and inevitably rounded periods. Sallust clearly liked to surprise his readers and keep them wide awake: his staccato phraseology, highly conducive to point and epigram, was ideally suited for the purpose. And so too was his aversion from balanced phrases and clauses and his distaste for certain conventional terms, which he paraphrases, varies, or turns back to front. The results of his tortuous manipulations of word and phrase must have jarred horribly, as he intended, on many contemporary ears.

That Sallust should be an innovator as well as an archaizer is perfectly explicable: he claims the same freedom to develop and experiment with his medium as was exercised by the early writers. Hence he coins words, extends usage, and assimilates unfamiliar idiom. In his mixture of archaism and novelty he may be compared with Lucretius. But, while Lucretius is often compelled to experiment by his subject matter and metre, Sallust's innovations are largely a matter of free choice. He was anti-suggestible in the extreme and spurned convention. Hence his aggressive and tetchy style reflects the very nature of the man.

Sallust's outspokenness and self-will commanded the attention of contemporaries and posterity. He puts over his personality, real or assumed, very forcefully: witness the violent opening words of the *Iugurtha*. A man who writes in so striking a manner is not readily ignored, and Sallust was being blunt and provocative at a time when most people were beginning to temper their words. Again his language and style, being pointedly, indeed contemptuously, opposed to the main fashion of his age, could not fail to be exciting. He was hated by some, enthusiastically imitated by others (see Sen. *Epist.* 114.17–18). And he posed an embarrassing problem for teachers, like Quintilian, who could neither pass him by nor easily reconcile his writing with the ideals of style they tried to inculcate. Quintilian finds a convenient way out by commending Sallust for advanced pupils, but not beginners (*Inst.* 2.5.19). Most of the critical comment on Sallust which survives from antiquity relates to his expression, not his thought. But some writers, and those the weightiest, believed that he had much to say of moment. Tacitus adopted his sceptical and disenchanted view of Roman political life, and Augustine found in his observations on the nature and causes of Rome's decadence congenial material to employ in argument over the reasons for the city's final collapse. Again, Sallust has largely contributed to determining the way in which the history of the later Republic is conceived of in modern times.

Sallust has faults, some serious, some venial. His prooemia are pretentious, but for the main part barren of new ideas. In his narrative we can detect inconsistency and inaccuracies. Again, his selection of material is often wilful, occasionally inexplicable. Further, while extreme bias or partisanship may be discounted, he can fairly be convicted of lack of detachment and historical perspective. He is no Thucydides, and only Roman literary jingoists would dream of placing him in that rank. Pollio and others derided him for plagiarism (Suet. *Gramm.* p. 108 R, Quint. *Inst.* 8.3.29), a conventional jibe, but perhaps not so wide of the mark, if we consider not merely borrowing of words from Cato but also use of ideas pillaged from Greek sources. Sallust was outrageous and irrepressible, a humbug and an egotist, resolved to make his mark on Latin literature. Whatever his faults, his achievements were solid and enduring. By his fierce individualism he won a firmer place in the Roman educational tradition than the temperate and compromising Livy ever attained. He, more than anyone, prevented the style and attitudes of Cicero from becoming canonical for prose-writing in general, he enriched the Latin language at a time when it was most in danger of impoverishment, and he secured the continuation at Rome of the stern and uncompromising tradition of historiography, created by Thucydides, which rhetoricians and romantics alike would happily have discarded.

6

CAESAR

C. Julius Caesar's surviving output comprises seven books on the Gallic Wars (*Commentarii rerum gestarum*) and three on the Civil Wars. They are remarkable not only for the light which they throw on the man and on the history of the time, but as works of art.

The Commentary, as a form of literature, had a long history. Its Greek precursor was the *hypomnema* (or memoir), a term applied to official dispatches, minutes, administrative reports, private papers or even diaries. It was a narrative statement of facts for record purposes. It was distinct from History which was composed within a moralistic framework and with conscious literary art. Cicero, for instance, offered to submit *commentarii* of his consulship of 63 B.C. to L. Lucceius to turn into a history (Cicero, *Fam.* 5.12.10). The Romans, however, had a much greater interest in biography, as can be sensed from their funeral masks and inscriptions, from their portraiture and from the popularity of books dealing with historical examples of good and bad conduct; and Roman statesmen developed the Commentary into a factual account of their achievements which was to be published for their own self-justification and for the benefit of their descendants. We know of such works written in the generation before Caesar by M. Aemilius Scaurus, Q. Lutatius Catulus, P. Rutilius Rufus, and, above all, the dictator Sulla.

This is the literary background to the *Commentaries* on the Gallic Wars and on the Civil Wars. The seven books on the Gallic Wars cover the years 58 to 52 B.C., a period which witnessed Caesar's systematic subjugation of the whole of Gaul. Book 1 deals with the defeat of the Helvetii and, separately, of the German Ariovistus, 58 B.C.; Book 2 with the revolt of the Gallic tribes and his desperate encounter with the Nervii; Book 3 with the suppression of the Veneti, a coastal tribe of west Gaul; Book 4 with invasions across the Rhine and operations against rebel Gallic leaders, Indutiomarus and Ambiorix; Book 6 with continued action against Ambiorix, and Book 7 with the full-scale revolt of Vercingetorix, culminating in his siege and capitulation at Alesia in 52 B.C. The work was published some time the following year and this fact is important in understanding its nature. At that time Caesar was anxious to secure the consulship of 49 B.C. but under Roman law he was required to lay down his command before he was eligible to stand for office. During that period, however, he would no longer have been immune from prosecution, and he had many enemies anxious to foil his ambition. So in 51 B.C. he proposed to the Senate that as an exceptional measure his proconsulship should be extended to cover that period and thus shield him from attack. The publication of the *Commentaries* was timed to assert his claim on the gratitude of his fellow-countrymen and to display his *dignitas*, the Roman quality of achievement which merits recognition by high office. It will also have appealed, as did Tacitus' *Agricola*, to the imagination of an educated public fascinated by the remote and the unknown, as Gaul then was.

The work must then have been completed quickly, and we know that Caesar was a very fast writer. But it is disputed whether the whole work was composed in one year or whether it had been written year by year and was only put into final form for publication in 51 B.C. Various indications make the latter more probable, especially since one would in any case expect war-diaries and dispatches to be written up as each campaign took place. In Book 3.17–27 Caesar recounts the operations of his lieutenant, Q. Titurius Sabinus, in a way that seems based on a detailed discussion between the two men. Sabinus was killed in 54 B.C. Each of the books is self-contained, dealing with one year's action, and no book contains a forward reference to a later book. Finally, there are significant differences in style between Book 1 and Book 7, which suggests the passage of years. Word-usage changes (e.g. *ab imo* 'from the bottom' gives way to *ab infimo* (7.19.1, 73.5)), the syntax becomes less stereotyped and freer, direct speech is introduced instead of the formalized reported speech. Evidence of Caesar's editorial activity in preparing the work for publication can be found in the insertion of several digressions of a geographical kind (notably 4.1–3 on the Suebi, 5.12–14 on Britain, 6.11–28 on the Hercynian Forest). The Caesarian authorship of these has been doubted on the grounds that they contain information that was not known until after Caesar's time but this is mere speculation, and it is more likely that Caesar drew on a written scholarly source to add background information to his narrative.

The *Gallic Wars* was a statement of Caesar's achievements. That he had detractors is beyond doubt (at one point he alludes to them (*Bell. Gall.* 1.44.12); some of Catullus' poems are far from favourable, and criticism, even scandal, is preserved in Suetonius' *Life*), and Asinius Pollio alleged that Caesar had made many mis-statements in his *Commentaries*. But Caesar had no need to distort the facts to enhance his reputation: indeed he would have been too easily refuted if he had tried. So far as the actual events are concerned, his account of what happened is sober and factual. There is only one passage where a real conflict of evidence exists. In *Bell. Gall.* 1.12 Caesar described his defeat of the

Tigurini on the river Arar, making no mention of his lieutenant Labienus. Subsequently Labienus, who ultimately deserted Caesar in the Civil Wars, claimed the credit for the victory (Plutarch, *Caesar* 18.1). Scholars have attempted to find other falsifications or distortions but with more ingenuity than success. Did Caesar, for instance, cross the Thames with an elephant – a detail supplied by Polyaenus (8.23.5), but not mentioned by Caesar himself? Where there is obscurity or uncertainty, it may usually be attributed to the difficulty which Caesar will have had in finding out the facts or understanding in such a fluid type of guerrilla warfare what was actually going on. Also, it is easy to be misled by the convention, which Caesar adopted from Xenophon's *Anabasis*, of always referring to himself in the third person. This gives an air of objectivity to what is a personal, autobiographical account.

The overwhelming impression of the book is its clarity and precision, a quality which Cicero, no friend, instantly recognized when he wrote of it: *nihil est pura et inlustri breuitate dulcius* 'nothing is more pleasing than unaffected and lucid brevity' (*Brutus* 262). He had had the same literary tutors as Cicero – the perfectionist grammarian M. Antonius Gnipho (Suetonius, *Gramm.* 7) and the most famous rhetorician of his time Molon (Plutarch, *Caesar* 3). The effect is achieved in two main ways. Firstly, the style is one of great simplicity. Set phrases are used over and over again because they do their duty adequately – *certior factus est* 'he was informed', *quae cum ita essent* 'since this was so', *his rebus cognitis* 'when this had been found out', and so on. The syntax is equally clear-cut and formal. Whereas Livy enjoys variety of language, Caesar dispenses with synonyms. Thus Livy uses *gradum referre* and *pedem referre* 'to retreat' interchangeably, Caesar only uses *pedem referre*. Livy has *ad ultimum*, *ad extremum* and *ad postremum*, all in the sense of 'finally', Caesar only has *ad extremum*. There are a number of comparative expressions in Latin meaning 'as if' – *uelut* (*si*), *perinde ac* (*si*), *haud secus quam* (*si*), *tamquam si* – which Livy employs indiscriminately; only *uelut si* is found in Caesar. In the same way Caesar only writes *flumen* for 'a river', never *fluuius* or *amnis*. There is little connotative difference between the words (*amnis* may carry more power and grandeur) and Livy calls the Rhône, for instance, *flumen* thirteen times, *amnis* six times. Caesar chooses one word for one thing and adheres to it. His motive is principally simplicity, but the comparison with Livy shows that he is also influenced by concern for purity or propriety of diction. Language had always been a study of interest to him. During early 54 B.C. he had written two volumes entitled *De analogia* which were concerned with purity of diction as a counterblast to current trends, favoured by Cicero, who relished a rich and florid vocabulary. In the first volume he states a fundamental principle: 'as the sailor avoids the reef, so should you avoid the rare and obsolete word' (Aul. Gellius, *Noctes Atticae* 1.10.4). And probably at the same period he wrote his only surviving verses, on the comic poet Terence, perhaps in reply to some verses by Cicero. In them, summing the poet up as a half-Menander (*dimidiate Menander*), he praises his refined style (*puri sermonis amator*) but deplores his lack of intensity (*uis*). But it is not only rare and obsolete words which are conspicuous by their absence. Usages which are very common in Livy, such as *super* as an equivalent to *de* 'about', are not accepted by Caesar, presumably because they are loose and incorrect: it is to be noted that *super* in this sense occurs only three times in Cicero, always in letters. Adjectives followed by a genitive (e.g. *capax imperii, inops animi*, etc.) occur occasionally in Cicero, commonly in Livy, never in Caesar.

But Caesar's own simplicity, unlike Terence's, does not lack intensity. The pace of the narrative is never monotonous, always exciting. His battle-scenes are models of clear, fast-moving description with critical moments dramatically emphasized and the climax often told in breathless, clipped, staccato phrases. The outstanding example is his account of the battle against the Nervii (*Bell. Gall.* 2.18–27). First of all the battle-ground is sketched; then the Roman dispositions are described in a matter-of-fact style, suitable to a military communiqué. The first stage of the battle is told in a series of long, subordinate clauses, which convey the complexity of events until Caesar's Gallic cavalry, from the tribe of Treveri, panic. That moment is one of stark simplicity: 'they despaired of our cause and galloped for home; they reported that the Romans were routed' (*desperatis nostris rebus domum contenderunt; Romanos pulsos superatosque...renuntiauerunt*). The next word is *Caesar*, and Caesar's dramatic intervention saves the day. The account is rounded off by praise for the heroic fight which the Nervii put up, culminating in a movingly rhetorical tricolon – *ausos transire latissimum flumen, ascendere altissimas ripas, subire iniquissimum locum* 'they dared to cross a very wide river, to climb very tall banks and to approach a very impregnable position'. We do not know the quality of the writing of Caesar's predecessors, but Caesar certainly elevated the Commentary into a literary form in its own right. It was no longer merely raw material for history. Secondly, although, in line with convention, the *Commentaries* are no document of self-awareness and tell us little of Caesar's personal life but much of diplomacy and warfare, they reveal at every turn the masterful character of their author, his sharp decision, his courage in the face of daunting perplexities and disloyalties and his brilliant tactical sense. To conquer Gaul was a major undertaking whose true dimensions we only appreciate as we read the work.

The *Civil Wars* consist of three books, the first two dealing with the events of 49 B.C. and the third with 48 B.C. The time and purpose of composition are uncertain. Book 3 is formally incomplete since it does not deal with all the events of 48 B.C. and the work as a whole is more sketchy and less accurate than the *Gallic Wars*. Indeed it was criticized by the scholar Asinius Pollio a few years later for these deficiencies (Suetonius, *Iulius* 56.4). This suggests that it too was compiled in a hurry, perhaps in 47 B.C. at a time when Caesar thought that the Civil War was over and that his side of the case needed to be heard if a stable society was to be restored. The accuracy of the work can be checked much more closely because there are a number of independent witnesses to the events (notably Cicero in his letters, and authorities ultimately derived from Asinius Pollio and Livy) but it is fair-minded in the treatment of opponents (Pompey, Labienus, Domitius Ahenobarbus, etc.) and objective in the handling of fact. The style and presentation follow the pattern of the *Gallic Wars*. The same simplicity is in evidence. A fine example can be seen in the account of the emergency debate of the Senate at which Pompey tried frantically to mobilize his side (*Bell. Civ.* 1.6). Short sentences in asyndeton tumble over one another.

Both in the *Bell. Gall.* and the *Bell. Civ.* there are a few self-contained passages of more elevated writing, characterized by direct speech or general reflection, the use of the historic infinitive, unusual word-order and uncommon vocabulary. The most conspicuous is the account of Curio's campaign in *Bell. Civ.* 2.34–44, but the same phenomena can be recognized also in *Bell. Gall.* 5.26–52 (the battle for the winter quarters), 7.44–52 (Gergovia), 7.69–95 (Alesia) and *Bell. Civ.* 3.86–96 (Pharsalus). Scholars have claimed that Caesar wrote up these events, which did not reflect particular credit on his generalship, in order to distract attention from his shortcomings, but such episodes do no more than reflect the strength of Caesar's emotions. He had, for instance, great affection for Curio.

Four other works survive in the corpus attached to Caesar's name. The first (Book 8 of the *Gallic Wars*) is a completion of the history of Caesar's command written by his subordinate in Gaul, A. Hirtius (consul in 43 B.C.). The three others are brief accounts, by Roman officers, of the campaigns during the Civil Wars in Egypt, Africa and Spain. Their interest lies not only in the facts that they record but in the difference of their style from the easy command which Caesar developed. In particular the *Bellum Hispaniense* is one of the very few works written in a predominantly *un*-literary Latin, and is, therefore, a very valuable source for our knowledge of the language.

7

PROSE AND MIME

1. VARRO

Varro towered over his contemporaries: in literary output, range of achievement and posthumous influence even Cicero – who admitted as much – does not compare. He wrote some 620 books, more than any other Roman, more than most Greeks: they range from satire to theology, from etymology to navigation. Augustine marvels that he read so much yet had time to write and wrote so much as to defeat any reader.[1] This same man was a distinguished admiral and general, decorated for personal bravery at fifty; he administered rich estates, served numerous magistracies, reaching the rank of praetor, and acted both as land commissioner and as state librarian. Fate has dealt unkindly with his survival: we have a complete treatise on agriculture and six damaged books out of twenty-five 'On the Latin language'. Yet paradoxically, the loss of so much Varro constitutes a tribute to his achievement, for his systematization of so much earlier Greek and Roman scholarship made him wholly indispensable as a factual source for later writers and he has perished by absorption: from Virgil and Ovid to Ausonius, from Columella to Suetonius and Isidore of Seville his influence, not always at first-hand, was all-pervasive. One slight but characteristic example may be given: an annalist about 100 B.C. wrote about the boomerang (*cateia*) of the invading Teutones. He was in all probability excerpted by Varro, whom Virgil later consulted for learned detail in *Aeneid* 7. This boomerang-lore passed on, perhaps through Suetonius' *Prata*, to surface in Isidore of Seville and, desperately garbled, in the commentators on Virgil, as late as the ninth century A.D.[2] On a wider front, the *trivium* (grammar, rhetoric and dialectic) and *quadrivium* (geometry, arithmetic, astronomy and music) of medieval education descend ultimately from Varro's *Disciplinae*, a work of his eighties; indeed traces of Varronian systematization still lurk in modern university syllabuses.

Characteristic methods, of research and of disposition, can be detected in widely scattered areas: they serve to reveal the Roman polymath at work and

[1] *Civ. Dei* 6.2.
[2] Cf. *De gente Populi Romani* fr. 37 Fraccaro, Virg. *Aen.* 7.741 and Horsfall (1969) 297–9.

to explain how, in a full life, one man's output could be so colossal. Varro worked at speed: 'If I had had time, Fundania, I would be writing to you more agreeably what I shall now expound as I can, thinking I should hurry because, as it's said, "if a man's a bubble, an old man's more so"' is how he begins the *Res rusticae*. He never allowed didacticism to crush his markedly 'folksy' humour. Nor was he unaware of the niceties of Latin style, but in his prose-works there was rarely time to display them; if pronouns and conjunctions got postponed, relative clauses mislaid, verbs omitted and concords of number and gender violated, they were casualties of the clock. Facts and interpretations were set down as they came to hand. Varro lacks the massive elegance of Cicero because he never sought it. The arrangement of accumulated facts fell regularly into a simple pattern: people, places, periods and things (*de hominibus*; *de locis*; *de temporibus*; *de rebus*). It is discernible even in the long and delightful fragment of the Menippean satire 'You don't know what the late evening may bring' preserved by Gellius.[1] A preoccupation with numerology – under Pythagorean influence – contributed to excessive rigidity: agriculture has four divisions (*partes*) each with two subdivisions (*species*);[2] that scheme is not fully worked out, but clearly such arrangements could provide a long row of convenient pegs from which to suspend appropriate quotations and observations.

The focus of Varro's interests altered with time; periods of relatively restricted concentration assisted composition: the Menippean satires are early, the antiquarian treatises and cultural histories largely late; only the history and nature of the Latin language retained his attention throughout, from the *De antiquitate litterarum*, dedicated to the tragedian Accius in the early 80s, to *Disciplinae I*, *De grammatica*, over half a century later. Material, once accumulated, could be re-used indefinitely: the formal procedure for concluding treaties was, for instance, discussed early in the *Res humanae*, in the *De vita Populi Romani*, in the *De lingua Latina* and probably in the *Calenus*; this was a *Logistoricus*, a kind of philosophical and historical dialogue, probably not unlike Cicero's *De amicitia* and *De senectute*.

The working method may be reconstructed from internal evidence and by comparison with what we know of the elder Pliny's. From reading and from personal observation Varro made innumerable notes, with, doubtless, the help of expert *notarii*, carrying a supply of small tablets, *pugillares*. On campaign, he recorded, e.g., the statue of a lion on Mt Ida and the effects of the pirates' sack of Delos in 69 B.C.; travelling in Italy, he recorded inscriptions at Tarracina and Praeneste; on his estate at Casinum (mod. Cassino) there was evidently a magnificent library and Varro read hugely. Excerpts must somehow have been indexed, but haste shows up even in his library work;[3] study of Varro's

---

[1] *N.A.* 13.11.   [2] *Rust.* 1.5.4.
[3] Skydsgaard (1968) 64–88.

use of Theophrastus shows him reluctant to verify excerpts against a continuous text, and in consequence prone to error, to distortion and to misrepresentation of his original. Varro, one must never forget, wrote as a gentleman amateur, primarily for his peers. The *Res rusticae* is selective, muddled and at times inaccurate; it is not a practical manual for daily consultation by bailiff or overseer; depending in part on such manuals, it served rather to inform a readership of prosperous landowners, to entertain them with jokes, digressions and erudition, to charm them with precise and vivid observation,[1] to create, in effect, an agreeable illusion that there was mud on their boots.

It is particularly important not to think of Varro, with his numerous obsessions and lack of critical judgement as a scholar in anything like the modern sense. He gives five explanations for the name 'Palatine' without expressing any preference; all are now rejected. Stoic influence gave him a passion for etymology, which he used to provide evidence for his theories of Italian pre-history. Yet even here a sharp awareness is revealed that cultural and linguistic history are indivisible and the language is examined minutely for the light it can shed on the life of old Italy, which Varro loved so dearly. Social history and agricultural lore in a work on language should surprise us no more than etymologies in a work on agriculture; '*Panis* "bread" because originally they used to make it in the shape of a *panus* "cloth" '[2] is characteristic.

Varro was not an easy man: he enjoyed the friendship of Atticus and Pompey and there was a certain mutual respect between him and Caesar. But Cicero thought him strange, devious and irascible; dislike struggled with admiration.[3] A remarkable personality begins to emerge and one that was susceptible to a very wide range of influences. Varro was a romantic conservative, passionately devoted to the harsh Sabine countryside, to its simple pieties and onions-and-water life-style: 'when I was a boy I had a single adequate shirt and toga, shoes without straps, a horse without caparison, no daily bath, an occasional tub'.[4] His lifetime had witnessed vast social and political upheavals and the changes did not please him: in the Menippean satire *Sexagesis* he represents himself as a kind of Rip Van Winkle, who fell asleep for fifty years and woke about 70 B.C.; nothing was the same; piety, trust and decency, austerity and purity were all gone and Rome was a vice-ridden shambles.

In his admiration for the simple and natural life, as in his rejection of greed, luxury and intellectual pretentiousness Varro, the Roman reactionary, came unexpectedly close to the moral outlook of Hellenistic popular preaching. He was no Cynic; their rejection of social and cultural values, like the earnestness and coarse mockery of their diatribes, can only have repelled him. But he

---

[1] 2.10, for instance, on herdsmen.   [2] *Ling.* 5.105.
[3] See p. 115 for the great tribute in *Acad. Post.* 1.9.
[4] 'On the education of children', *Logistoricus Catus*, fr. xix Riese.

found in Menippus, a third-century Syrian freedman writing under Cynic influence, a model for profitable imitation and his 150 *Menippeae*, combining prose and verse, humour and moral improvement, dominated the literary output of his active public life. The Levantine exuberance of the form and the Sabine solidity of the ideas interact most successfully: Varro revels in the variety permitted; some three-quarters of the fragments are verse and in a wide range of metres (hendecasyllables, sotadeans, glyconics, limping iambi, etc.). Seneca's *Apocolocyntosis* – the only complete specimen of the genre that survives – seems almost fettered by comparison. Varro displays a remarkably wide range of characters and scenes, from Roman life and from myth. The tone is personal and vigorous, the language endlessly inventive, revelling in puns, vulgarisms, archaisms and snatches of Greek and moving rapidly through the whole scale of stylistic levels.

In the *Sesculixes*, Varro describes himself with engaging self-mockery as 'chewing over antiquities' (*ruminans antiquitates*).[1] The fully digested product, the *Antiquitates*, was his masterpiece.

Your books [wrote Cicero] have so to speak brought us home, for we were like visitors, wandering and straying in our own city; now at last we can tell who and where we are. You have revealed our country's age, the periods of its chronology, the laws of its rituals and priests, its civil and military institutions, the topography of its districts and localities, the names, divisions, duties and causes of all our affairs, both divine and human.[2]

The *Res humanae* were composed first, because divine affairs are the creation of mankind: there was an introduction and six books each on the familiar people, places, periods (i.e. the calendar) and things; Varro was concerned primarily with Rome as she actually was; Rome as she had been he described in the *De vita Populi Romani* ('On the life of the Roman People'), written at about the same date on the model of Dicaearchus' famous 'Life of Greece'. Fragments of the *Res humanae* tell us little of the work's detailed structure and content and even less of its general character.

The *Res divinae*, a central target of Christian polemic, notably St Augustine's, comes far more vividly alive. It was dedicated to Caesar as *pontifex maximus*, an office to which he attached the greatest importance, at a time when he was undoubtedly interested in religious reform. Caesar's descent from Venus through Aeneas and Iulus was being emphasized in all forms of propaganda and Varro's argument that it was useful for states that their chief men should draw inspiration for performing great deeds from a conviction, however ill-founded, of their divine ancestry, will have given parts at least of the *Res divinae* a strong contemporary relevance.

[1] *Sat. Men.* 505 Bücheler.   [2] Cic. *Acad. Post.* 1.9.

Towards the old Roman religion, Varro's attitude was complex and para-doxical: he was afraid lest the gods perish not by enemy invasion but by Roman neglect; it was his mission to save them and this would be a greater service even than that of Aeneas when he saved the Penates from the sack of Troy.[1] The cults and traditions that he described so minutely belonged to the *theologia ciuilis*, the religion of states. For Varro, it was by no means a perfect system, but he insisted that in an old city one must adhere to tradition: the populace should worship the gods, not despise them, for the growth of Rome had depended upon her religious observance. This emphasis upon the national and traditional value of the state religion was to be expected from the patriotic antiquary. But Varro's susceptibility to the influences of Antiochus of Ascalon's Platonism and Posidonius' Stoicism – not to mention his fashionable but deep-rooted acceptance of Pythagorean ideas – made him intellectually critical of the traditional pieties and it was from the standpoint of the philosophers' natural theology that he criticized Roman religion and still more the mythical theology of the poets – to conclude that in a state, religion was useful, even when untrue. Varro tried to integrate the state religion into a philosophically acceptable cosmic theory: Roman polytheism had to be explained as representing divisions (*partes*) or powers (*uirtutes*) of a universal Jupiter and the wish to reconcile the religions of Numa and Cleanthes led Varro into remarkable misrepresentations of early Roman worship. We cannot tell how far his programme for the purg-ing of religion from accretions and improprieties will have gone and indeed how Caesar reacted. But his achievements as recorder dwarf his waywardness as reformer.

2. CORNELIUS NEPOS

Nepos is an intellectual pygmy whom we find associating uneasily with the literary giants of his generation. Atticus, whom Nepos called friend and to whom he dedicated his biographies, shared jokes with Cicero at Nepos' expense. Nepos wrote a large biography of Cicero, helped publish his letters and paid eloquent posthumous tribute to Cicero's contribution to the develop-ment of Latin style and philosophy, yet declared Cicero's own favourite works not worth reading and told him bluntly that philosophy was a pernicious waste of time. Cicero's collected letters to Nepos may well have made choice reading! Catullus dedicated his *libellus* to Nepos, himself a writer of risqué short poems and a fellow Cisalpine, yet the honour was tempered by mockery, however gentle, of Nepos' pedantic learning in the *Chronica*. Varro, whom Nepos must have known through Atticus, can have found little to admire in a man of slight scholarly talents, who pursued no public career. The elder Pliny condemns Nepos' credulity; Aulus Gellius alone praises him, faintly, for his industry.

[1] Varr. *ap.* Aug. *Civ. Dei* 6.2.

Nepos' shallow learning was exercised upon fashionable topics. The *Chronica*, indebted to the renowned verse *Chronica* of the second-century Athenian scholar Apollodorus, was largely concerned with synchronisms: were, for example, the Greek poet Archilochus and the Roman king Tullus Hostilius contemporaries? The warmth of Nepos' tribute to Atticus' thorough and comprehensive *Annales*, with their accurate genealogies, suggests an acknowledgement of scholarly inferiority: one may also wonder how he stood in comparison with the great Varro's *Annales*. The moralizing didacticism of his biographies ('I'm not sure how to set out [Pelopidas'] *uirtutes*...'[1]) was to be expected from a writer who made possibly the first formal collection of moral *exempla* – the stock-in-trade of the orator and the ethical essayist; the freedman Hyginus, active as a scholar and librarian under Augustus, was soon to produce another such convenient handbook.

Nepos' sole importance to us lies in the accident of his survival as the earliest Latin biographer. In his day the genre was popular and Nepos' models for the conception and arrangement of the *De illustribus viris* are easily conjectured: Varro, Santra, Nepos and Hyginus are named by Suetonius as the founders of Latin biography. The *Imagines* or *Hebdomades* of Varro shortly preceded Nepos' work: seven hundred portraits of famous men, with explanatory text. Like Nepos' biographies, Varro's collection was international in scope, whereas Atticus' collection of portraits with appended epigrams seems to have been limited to Romans. Nepos arranged his sixteen (or more) books in pairs, non-Romans first, by fields of eminence: pairs *de imperatoribus*, *de regibus*, and *de historicis* (on generals, kings and historians) are firmly attested. A comparable arrangement seems to have prevailed in Varro's *Imagines*.

Nepos and Varro diverge sharply from the narrow traditions of Roman and familial pride, which constitute the origins of Roman biography. In Nepos' case, the purpose of his internationalism is clear: a desire to provide the materials for *synkrisis*, comparison between the eminent men of Rome and those of other nations: 'to make it possible, by comparing the deeds of both, to judge which men should be assigned pre-eminence'.[2] This desire to compare and contrast both individuals and cultures is equally evident at this time in Posidonius, in Varro and in Cicero, notably when he is writing literary history, or considering the relative virtues of Greek and Latin as languages.

Nepos has a humble notion of the status of biography: he prefaces the 'Foreign generals' by conceding that many readers will consider it a trivial (*leue*) kind of writing and unworthy of the personalities of great men and in the *Pelopidas* he is at pains to assert that he is not writing history. Nor is he writing for historians, but for the general public (*uulgus*).[3] He does not expect of his readers any real knowledge of Greek history or literature and assumes that they will be shocked

[1] 1.16.1.   [2] 23.13.4.   [3] 16.1.1.

by pederasty, sister-marriage, dancing, acting, and other non-Roman *mores* displayed by his subjects. This audience will have been not appalled but comforted by references to temples of Minerva (i.e. Athena) at Sparta and Jupiter Optimus Maximus (i.e. Baal) at Carthage, or to a Spartan senate and magistrates (i.e. gerousia and ephors)!

The 'Foreign generals' are arranged in rough chronological sequence; it seems likely that the three non-Greeks (Datames, Hannibal, Hamilcar) were added in a second edition, which will, it seems, have required a larger papyrus than any single Latin book hitherto. There is no uniformity of length or treatment; the *Agesilaus* and *Epaminondas* stand out as formal eulogies. The remainder are in the 'Peripatetic' tradition, employing anecdote as moral illustration in the manner of Aristotle's successors. Nepos cheerfully admits to irrelevant digression in the *Pelopidas*,[1] to show 'what disaster usually results from excessive confidence'.

In merit, the *Cato* and *Atticus*, which are all that survive of the 'Latin historians', clearly come highest. The *Cato* is an abbreviation of a longer life written at Atticus' request; the *Atticus*, whose manner is closer to the eulogies, displays intermittently personal knowledge and understanding. The *Alcibiades* recaptures a little of its subject's variety and energy. But it is hard to speak well of the 'Foreign generals'. Their wide and abiding popularity as a schoolbook is owed more to their morality and simplicity that to any historical value or stylistic merit. Nepos names many Greek historical authorities, but his knowledge of Greek was demonstrably poor and it is likely that much of his scholarly plumage was borrowed. To his credit, though, he did recognize the historical value of Cicero's works. Yet admiration is promptly cancelled by the grossest of Nepos' many absurd exaggerations: Cicero not only predicted events in his own lifetime but *quae nunc usu ueniunt cecinit ut uates* 'sang like a seer events that are now being experienced'.[2] Inaccuracies are startling and innumerable: Miltiades is confused with his uncle of the same name; Lemnos is placed among the Cyclades; the battles of Mycale and the Eurymedon are confused; the narrative of Hannibal's crossing of the Alps was a travesty – and Nepos was a native of Pavia! Nor will it do to palliate the deficiencies of Nepos' style by arguing that the Latin language was as yet undeveloped: the 'Lives' postdate the whole corpus of Cicero's work. His periods are not sustained, his excessive alliteration and strivings for antithesis annoy, his archaisms and colloquialisms are used without apparent purpose.

Nepos' scheme was ambitious and influential (for Plutarch, evidently), yet the execution often fell regrettably short.

[1] 16.3.1.   [2] 25.17.4.

3. THE LITERARY MIME

About 90 B.C. Pomponius and Novius gave some semblance of literary form to the *Atellana fabula*, a type of *commedia dell'arte* imported from Campania; a generation later Decimus Laberius and Publilius Syrus took the lead in effecting a similar development in the mime, which seems originally to have reached Rome from Sicily during the third century B.C., and the mime now took over from the *Atellana* as the *exodium* (epilogue) to comedies proper. The changes brought about cannot be defined with confidence, beyond saying that the role of improvisation in the mime was reduced, though not eliminated, and the place of verse, usually iambic, sometimes trochaic, was consequently increased. Improvised mime had made for notoriously slight and trivial plots (reversals of fortune, the marital triangle), with abrupt endings when inspiration failed; some consequence and credibility were now injected and the range of plots grew wider, while the role of slapstick was modified under the influence of comedy, both Greek-based and Roman-based. We even find the assumptions of Hellenistic popular philosophy both exploited and criticized. But the mime's appeal never rested upon sophistication. Its aim was laughter and nothing was done to refine it; moralists' condemnations continue ineffective and unabated into the Byzantine period. Parody of religion and myth, ripe obscenity and double meanings are all attested. Cicero acknowledges with embarrassment his pleasure in the mime's humour.[1]

There were other attractions: songs, striptease,[2] live sex and live animals on stage, imitations of beasts and humans, both by voice and by movement, and topical, personal and satiric allusions; Cicero recognized performance and audience reaction as valuable barometers of public opinion.[3] No masks or shoes were worn, staging and costume were simple and performers normally few. Yet the mime bred a certain wit and grace: Sulla was the first of Rome's rulers to relish the company of mimic actors: female roles were played by real women, and actresses – Tertia, Arbuscula, Cytheris – feature prominently in the scandal of the late Republic. The orator Cassius Severus and the philosopher Seneca were understandably surprised at finding in Publilius finely expressed moral maxims and it is ironic that we owe our fragments of a great popular entertainer to his moments of sententious virtue.

Laberius and Publilius must be differentiated sharply: Laberius revelled in neologisms and vulgarisms; Publilius wrote pointedly but plainly. Laberius, as a Roman knight, might not himself act, while Publilius, a Levantine and the freedman of a freedman, regularly performed in his own plays and rapidly

---

[1] *De or.* 2.173.

[2] Val. Max. 2.10.8: the younger Cato once left the theatre on hearing that his presence was inhibiting the crowd from telling the girls to strip.

[3] Cic. *Att.* 14.2.1, 3.2.

earned great popularity throughout Italy. Towards Caesar, Laberius was notoriously disrespectful; his gibes clearly reached a wider audience than Catullus' and the Dictator reacted less graciously. Events at the *Ludi Victoriae Caesaris* in July 46 (?) are confusingly recorded: Caesar induced Laberius to act in person and he lamented his loss of civil status – automatic for a mimic actor – in a moving and dignified prologue: well-received iambics on tyranny followed. Publilius probably performed on the same occasion – competitions are attested elsewhere – and was declared victorious; Laberius was restored to equestrian rank at once, but the humiliation was itself a tribute to the mime's importance.

APPENDIX OF
AUTHORS AND WORKS

VALERIUS AEDITUUS, PORCIUS LICINUS,
QUINTUS LUTATIUS CATULUS

LIVES

Listed in this order by Gellius (19.9.10) and Apuleius (*Apol.* 9). Aedituus called 'old' (*ueteris poetae*) by Gellius; Licinus wrote after the death of Terence (*c.* 159 B.C.; *FPL* 45); Catulus was consul 102 B.C. and wrote on Roscius (b. 134 B.C.). On dating see Ross (below) 141.

WORKS

Four short erotic elegiac epigrams preserved by Gellius: two by Aedituus, one each by Licinus and Catulus; one epigram by Catulus preserved by Cicero (*Nat. D.* 1.79). Licinus also wrote in trochaics on the early history of Rome.

BIBLIOGRAPHY

TEXT: *FPL* 42–6.

STUDIES: R. Büttner, *Porcius Licinus und der litterarische Kreis des Q. Lutatius Catulus* (Leipzig 1893); Bardon I 123–32; D. O. Ross, *Style and tradition in Catullus* (Cambridge, Mass. 1969) 139–47.

LAEVIUS, ?MELISSUS

LIFE

Conventionally dated to early 1st c. B.C., but the ancient sources offer little firm evidence. See Leo (below) 180 n.1 = 268 n.1.

WORKS

Erotopaegnia (Love-plays) on erotic and mythological themes in (at least) six books: Charisius 2, p. 265. 12 B (*GLK* I 204.16). Other titles are probably those of works in the collection: cf. Charisius 4, p. 376. 1–2 B (*GLK* I 288.6). Nearly thirty fragments survive in a variety of metres.

BIBLIOGRAPHY

TEXT: *FPL* 55–63.

STUDIES: F. Leo, *Hermes* 49 (1914) 180–8 = *Ausgew. kl. Schriften*, ed. E. Fraenkel (Rome 1960) I 268–75; D. O. Ross, *Style and tradition in Catullus* (Cambridge, Mass. 1969) 155–60; J. Granarolo, *D'Ennius à Catulle. Recherches sur les antécédents romains de la 'poésie nouvelle'* (Paris 1971).

CATULLUS, GAIUS VALERIUS

LIFE

Dates probably 84–54 B.C.; b. in Verona. Jerome (*Chron.*) gives dates as 87–57, but C. was certainly alive in 55 (Pompey's consulship, 113.2; *porticus Pompeii*, 55.6; invasions of Britain, 11.12, 29.4, cf. 45.22). At Rome had affair with a Clodia (called Lesbia in his poems), possibly the elder sister of P. Clodius and wife of Q. Metellus Celer. Visited Asia Minor 57/56 as member of entourage of C. Memmius, governor of Bithynia. Sources: own poems; Apul. *Apol.* 10 (Lesbia's real name); Suet. *Iul.* 73 (Caesar entertained by C.'s father). On identity of Clodia see T. P. Wiseman, *Catullan Questions* (Leicester 1969) 50ff.

WORKS

Collection of 116 poems, in various lyric metres (1–61, 63; mainly phalaecian hendecasyllables), hexameters (62, 64), and elegiac couplets (65–116). On arrangement and publication see pp. 20–3.

BIBLIOGRAPHY

(for 1934–59 see H. J. Leon, *C.W.* 65 (1959–60) 104–13, 141–8, 174–80, 281–2; for 1960–9, D. F. Thomson, *C.W.* 65 (1971–2) 116–26; also (1929–57) J. Kroymann in Kroll, under *Texts* below)

TEXTS AND COMMENTARIES: TEXTS: L. Schwabe (Berlin 1886); R. A. B. Mynors (OCT, 1958); D. F. Thomson (Chapel Hill 1978). COMMENTARIES: R. Ellis, 2nd ed. (Oxford 1889); W. Kroll, 3rd ed. (Stuttgart 1959); C. J. Fordyce (Oxford

1961; corrected ed. 1973), reviewed by E. Fraenkel, *Gnomon* 34 (1962) 253–63; K. Quinn, 2nd ed. (London 1973).

TRANSLATIONS: E. S. Duckett, *Catullus in English poetry* (Northampton, Mass. 1925); F. W. Cornish (Loeb, 1913).

STUDIES: (1) HELLENISTIC AND NEW POETRY: F. Leo, 'Die römische Poesie in der sullanischen Zeit', *Hermes* 49 (1914) 161–95; S. Gaselee, *The love romances of Parthenius* (Loeb, 1916); R. Pfeiffer, 'A fragment of Parthenios' Arete', *C.Q.* 37 (1943) 23–32; W. Clausen, 'Callimachus and Latin poetry', *G.R.B.S.* 5 (1964) 181–96; G. W. Bowersock, *Augustus and the Greek world* (Oxford 1965) 122–39 (Greek teachers in Rome); H. Tränkle, 'Neoterische Kleinigkeiten', *M.H.* 24 (1967) 87–103; D. O. Ross, 'Nine epigrams from Pompeii (*CIL* 4.4966–73)', *Y.Cl.S.* 21 (1969) 127–42; N. B. Crowther, 'οἱ νεώτεροι, Poetae Novi and Cantores Euphorionis', *C.Q.* n.s.20 (1970) 322–7; idem, 'Valerius Cato, Furius Bibaculus, and Ticidas', *C.Ph.* 66 (1971) 108–9; idem, 'Parthenius and Roman poetry', *Mnemosyne* 29 (1976) 65–71; J. Soubiran, *Cicéron: Aratea, fragments poétiques* (Budé, 1972); T. P. Wiseman, *Cinna the poet* (Leicester 1974); R. O. A. M. Lyne, 'The neoteric poets', *C.Q.* n.s.28 (1978) 167–87.

(2) CATULLUS – GENERAL: R. Reitzenstein, 'Zur Sprache der lateinischen Erotik', *S.H.A.W.* 12 (1912) 9–36; A. L. Wheeler, *Catullus and the traditions of ancient poetry* (Berkeley 1934); E. A. Havelock, *The lyric genius of Catullus* (Oxford 1939; 2nd ed. New York 1967); J. P. Elder, 'Notes on some conscious and subconscious elements in Catullus' poetry', *H.S.Ph.* 60 (1951) 101–36; K. Quinn, *The Catullan revolution* (Melbourne 1959); D. O. Ross, *Style and tradition in Catullus* (Cambridge, Mass. 1969); T. P. Wiseman, *Catullan questions* (Leicester 1969); J. W. Loomis, *Studies in Catullan verse, Mnemosyne* suppl. 24 (1972).

(3) INDIVIDUAL POEMS: 1: J. P. Elder, *H.S.Ph.* 71 (1966) 143–9; P. Levine, *C.S.C.A.* 2 (1969) 209–16; F. Cairns, *Mnemosyne* 22 (1969) 153–8. 4: E. Fraenkel, *Iktus und Akzent im lateinischen Sprechvers* (Berlin 1928) 322–6 (rhythms of ordinary speech in 4, 8, 25); J. Svennung, *Opuscula Romana* 1 (Lund 1954) 109–24; M. C. J. Putnam, *C.Ph.* 57 (1962) 10–19 (also 31, 46, 101). 5: F. Cairns, *Mnemosyne* 26 (1973) 11–21; E. A. Fredericksmeyer, *A.J.Ph.* 91 (1970) 431–45. 8: E. Fraenkel, *J.R.S.* 51 (1961) 46–53 (also 42). 27: F. Cairns, *Mnemosyne* 28 (1975) 24–9. 31: F. Cairns, in (edd.) A. J. Woodman and D. West, *Quality and pleasure in Latin poetry* (Cambridge 1975) 1–17. 36: V. Buchheit, *Hermes* 87 (1959) 309–27; D. O. Ross, *Mnemosyne* 26 (1973) 60–2. 44: C. P. Jones, *Hermes* 96 (1968) 379–83. 45: D. O. Ross, *C.Ph.* 60 (1965) 256–9. 51: W. Ferrari, *A.S.N.P.* 7 (1938) 59–72; R. Lattimore, *C.Ph.* 39 (1944) 184–7; E. Fraenkel, *Horace* (Oxford 1957) 211–14 (vv. 13–16). 56.5–7: A. E. Housman, *Hermes* 66 (1931) 402. 58.5: R. J. Penella, *Hermes* 104 (1976) 118–20. 61: P. Fedeli, *Seges* 16 (Freiburg 1972; repr. in *London Studies in Classical Philology*, vol. VI, 1980). 62: U. von Wilamowitz-Moellendorff, *Hellenistische Dichtung* II (1924) 277–310 (also 61, 34, 4, 64–5); E. Fraenkel, *J.R.S.* 45 (1955) 1–8. 64: R. Reitzenstein, *Hermes* 35 (1900)

73–105; F. Klingner, *S.B.A.W.* 6 (1956); M. C. J. Putnam, *H.S.C.Ph.* 65 (1961) 165–201; L. C. Curran, *Y.Cl.S.* 21 (1969) 171–92; J. C. Bramble, *P.C.Ph.S.* 16 (1970) 22–41; W. Clausen, *I.C.S.* 2 (1976) 219–23 (vv. 116–20). 66: R. Pfeiffer, *Philologus* 87 (1932) 179–228; B. Axelson, *Studi in onore di Luigi Castiglioni* 1 (Florence 1960) 15–21; M. C. J. Putnam, *C.Ph.* 55 (1960) 223–8 (vv. 75–88); W. Clausen, *H.S.C.Ph.* 74 (1968) 85–94 (65 and 66). 68: H. W. Prescott, *T.A.Ph.A.* 71 (1940) 473–500; G. Luck, *The Latin love elegy*, 2nd ed. (London 1969) 58–69; T. P. Wiseman, *Cinna the poet* (Leicester 1974) 77–103. 96: E. Fraenkel, *W.S.* 69 (1956) 279–88 (also 53, 14, 50). 106, 112, 93, 94, 105, 85: O. Weinreich, *Die Distichen des Catull* (Tübingen 1926).

INDEX: M. N. Wetmore (New Haven 1912; repr. Hildesheim 1961).

LUCRETIUS CARUS, TITUS

LIFE

Dates *c.* 98–55 B.C., but certainty impossible. Jerome (*Chron.*) gives year of birth as 94 or 93, the *Codex Monacensis* (ed. H. Usener, *Rh.M.* 22 (1867) 442) as 97. According to Jerome L. died 'in his forty-fourth year'; Donatus (*Vit. Verg.* 6) makes his death coincide with Virgil's assumption of the *toga virilis* and improbably dates this event to the consulship of Pompey and Crassus (55). Cicero's letter (*Q.Fr.* 2.9.3) suggests, but does not prove, that L. was dead by Feb. 54. Tradition of his madness and suicide is attested only by Jerome and the 'Borgia life' (printed by J. Masson, *J.Ph.* 23 (1895) 220–37; probably a Renaissance forgery); for criticism of the story see K. Ziegler, *Hermes* 71 (1936) 420–40. Refs. to L. in contemporary and Augustan writers: Cic. (cited above); Nepos, *Att.* 12.4; Vitr. 9 *praef.* 17; Ovid, *Am.* 1.15.23 and *Trist.* 2.425; cf. Virg. *Geo.* 2.490–2.

WORKS

De rerum natura (6 bks): L.'s only known work, unfinished at his death (unfulfilled promise at 5.155 to write about abodes of the gods). Internal evidence for date of composition is thin: the dedicatee Memmius is probably the praetor of 58; 2.40–1 cannot refer to troop movements in 58, as is often supposed (see T. P. Wiseman, *Cinna the poet* (Leicester 1974) 11–12); 4.75–86 need not have been written after the opening of Rome's first permanent theatre in 55 (but see L. R. Taylor, in (ed.) M. E. White, *Studies in honour of Gilbert Norwood* (Toronto 1952) 149–50).

BIBLIOGRAPHY

(see A. Dalzell, *C.W.* 66 (1972–3) 389–427, and 67 (1973–4) 65–112; Boyancé (1963) under *Studies* below; E. J. Kenney, *G. & R. New surveys in the classics* 11 (1977))

TEXTS AND COMMENTARIES: TEXTS: A. Ernout, 10th ed. (Budé, 1966); J. Martin, 6th ed. (BT, 1969); C. Müller (Zurich 1975); W. H. D. Rouse, rev. M. F. Smith (Loeb, 1975). COMMENTARIES: C. Lachmann (Berlin 1850); H. A. J. Munro, 4th ed. (Cambridge 1886); C. Guissani, 4 vols. (Turin 1896–8); A. Ernout and L. Robin, 3 vols. (Paris 1925–8); W. E. Leonard and S. B. Smith (Madison 1942); C. Bailey, 3 vols. (Oxford 1947; repr. with corrections 1950: with prolegomena and tr.). Bk 3: R. Heinze (Leipzig 1897); E. J. Kenney (Cambridge 1971). Bk 6: A. Barigazzi (Turin 1946).

TRANSLATIONS: Prose: H. A. J. Munro (Cambridge 1864); R. E. Latham (Penguin, 1951); M. F. Smith (London 1969). Verse: R. Humphries (Bloomington 1968.)

STUDIES: C. Martha, *Le poème de Lucrèce* (Paris 1867); W. Y. Sellar, *The Roman poets of the republic*, 3rd ed. (Oxford 1889) chs. 10–14; J. Masson, *Lucretius: Epicurean and poet* (London 1907–9); G. Santayana, *Three philosophical poets: Lucretius, Dante and Goethe* (Cambridge, Mass. 1910); O. Regenbogen, *Lukreʒ, seine Gestalt in seinem Gedicht, Neue Wege ʒur Antike* 2.1 (Leipzig 1932) = *Kl. Schr.* (Munich 1961) 296–386; E. E. Sikes, *Lucretius: poet and philosopher* (Cambridge 1936); M. Roselaar, *Lukreʒ: Versuch einer Deutung* (Amsterdam 1943); E. Bignone, *Storia della letteratura latina* II (Florence 1945) chs. 6–8; J. B. Logre, *L'anxiété de Lucrèce* (Paris 1946); A. Ernout, *Lucrèce* (Brussels 1947); A. Traglia, *Sulla formaʒione spirituale di Lucreʒio* (Rome 1948); F. Klingner, 'Philosophie und Dichtkunst am Ende des zweiten Buches des Lukrez', *Hermes* 80 (1952) 3–31; J.-H. Waszink, 'Lucretius and poetry', *Mededelingen Nederl. Akad. van Wetensch., Afd. Letterkunde* 17 (1954) no. 8, 243–57; F. Giancotti, *Il preludio di Lucreʒio* (Messina 1959); U. Pizzani, *Il problema del testo e della composiʒione del De rerum natura di Lucreʒio* (Rome 1959); P. Boyance, *Lucrèce et l'Épicurisme* (Paris 1963); (ed.) D. R. Dudley, *Lucretius* (London 1965); C. J. Classen, 'Poetry and rhetoric in Lucretius', *T.A.Ph.A.* 99 (1968) 77–118; A. Amory, 'Obscura de re lucida carmina: science and poetry in *De rerum natura*', *Y.Cl.S.* 21 (1969) 145–68; D. West, *The imagery and poetry of Lucretius* (Edinburgh 1969); E. J. Kenney, 'Doctus Lucretius', *Mnemosyne* 23 (1970) 366–92; P. H. Schrijvers, *Horror ac divina voluptas: études sur la poétique et la poésie de Lucrèce* (Amsterdam 1970). *Concordance.* L. Roberts, ΑΓωΝ suppl. (1968).

CICERO:
THE RELATIONSHIP OF ORATORY TO LITERATURE
GENERAL WORKS

(1) Background

Boissier, G., *Cicéron et ses amis* (Paris 1865), tr. Jones, A. D., *Cicero and his friends* (London 1897).

Heinemann, I., 'Humanitas' in *RE* suppl. V (1931) 282–310.

Kroll, W., *Die Kultur der ciceronischen Zeit*, 2 vols. (Leipzig 1933).

Warde Fowler, W., *Social life at Rome in the age of Cicero* (London 1908; repr. 1963).

(2) Rhetoric and dialogue

Clarke, M. L., *Rhetoric at Rome: a historical survey* (London 1953).

Hirzel, R., *Der Dialog* (Leipzig 1895).

Kennedy, G., *The art of rhetoric in the Roman world* (Princeton 1972).

Kroll, W., 'Rhetorik', in *RE* suppl. VII (1940) 1039–1138.

Lansberg, H., *Handbuch der lateinischen Rhetorik* (Munich 1940: elucidation of technical terms).

Leeman, A. D., *Orationis ratio*, 2 vols. (Amsterdam 1963).

Norden, E., *Die antike Kunstprosa*, 2 vols. (Leipzig 1898; repr. Stuttgart 1973).

CICERO, MARCUS TULLIUS

LIFE

b. 106 B.C. Arpinum; equestrian family. Educ. at Rome with younger brother Quintus; mentors L. Crassus and two Scaevolas. Friendship with Atticus begun. 89: served in Social War under Pompeius Strabo; got to know his famous son. 81: debut as advocate. 79–77: peregrination; Athens (joined Academy), Asia Minor, Rhodes. On return married Terentia (d. Tullia b. 76, s. Marcus b. 65). 75: quaestor, W. Sicily. 70: triumphantly prosecuted Verres, governor, for Sicilians; recognized as leader of Bar. 69: curule aedile. 66: praetor, supported Pompey. 60: pubd *Catilinarians*; refused invitation to join First Triumvirate (Caesar, Pompey, Crassus). 58: exiled, nominally for having put Catilinarians to death without trial; his house wrecked. 57: triumphant recall. 56–51: having attempted independence, was brought to heel and used by Triumvirs; active as advocate and as writer (*De oratore; De republica*; began *De legibus*). 51–50: unwilling but upright governor of Cilicia. 49: on outbreak of civil war attempted neutrality, but eventually joined Pompeians as the more republican side. Crossed to Epirus, but not present at Pharsalus. Returned after the defeat and submitted to Caesar's clemency. 46: resumed writing (*Brutus* and *Orator*). Divorced Terentia; briefly married to his young ward Publilia. 45: Tullia died; series of philosophical works begun, lasting sixteen months. 44: after Caesar's murder, resumed political activity in September, to combat Antony (*Philippics*). Coordinated activity of senatorial majority till 43, when his young protégé Octavian discarded him, seized Rome and the consulship, and joined the Second Triumvirate, which outlawed him. Killed in consequence, 7 December 43 B.C. Main sources his own works, esp. correspondence, *Brutus*, prologues in dialogues and treatises, some speeches. Also Plutarch's Life.

WORKS (dates B.C. in brackets)

TEXTS AND COMMENTARIES: (1) IN SERIES: Mondadori (for *Collegium Ciceronianis Studiis Provehendis*; in progress); BT (under revision); OCT (except philosophical works and fragments); Budé; Loeb.

(2) SPEECHES (some with comm.): All: G. Long, 4 vols. (London 1851–8); C. Halm, rev. Laubmann–Sternkopf (1886–93); M. Fuhrmann, 7 vols. (Zurich–Stuttgart 1970–: with German tr.). *Pro Quinctio* (81): T. E. Kinsey (Sydney 1971). *Pro Roscio Amerino* (80): G. Landgraf, 2nd ed. (Leipzig 1914). *Pro Roscio comoedo* (?77). *Divinatio in Caecilium* and *Verrines* (70): E. Thomas (Paris 1894); *Verr.*, W. Peterson (London 1907). *Pro Tullio* (69). *Pro Fonteio* (69). *Pro Caecina* (69). *Pro Cluentio* (66): W. Y. Fausset (London 1887); W. Peterson (London 1899). *De imperio Cn. Pompeii = Pro lege Manilia* (66): F. P. Donnelly (New York 1939); C. Macdonald (London–Harvard 1966). *Contra Rullum* I-III (63). *Pro Rabirio perduellionis reo* (63): W. E. Heitland (Cambridge 1882). *Pro Murena* (63): W. E. Heitland (Cambridge 1874). *In Catilinam* I–IV (63): A. Haury (Paris 1969). *Pro Sulla* (62): J. S. Reid (Cambridge 1902). *Pro Archia* (62): J. S. Reid (Cambridge 1877; repr. 1938). *Pro Flacco* (59): T. B. L. Webster (Oxford 1931). *Post reditum in senatu* (57). *De domo sua* (57): R. G. Nisbet (Oxford 1939). *De haruspicum responso* (56). *Pro Sestio* (56): H. A. Holden, 9th ed. (1933). *In Vatinium* (56): L. Pocock (London 1926: comm. only). *Pro Caelio* (56): R. G. Austin, 3rd ed. (Oxford 1960). *De provinciis consularibus* (56): H. E. Butler and M. Cary (Oxford 1924). *Pro Balbo* (56): J. S. Reid (Cambridge 1878). *In Pisonem* (55): R. G. M. Nisbet (Oxford 1961). *Pro Plancio* (54): H. A. Holden, 3rd ed. (Cambridge 1891). *Pro Scauro* (54). *Pro Rabirio Postumo* (54). *Pro Milone* (52): A. G. Poynton, 3rd ed. (Oxford 1902); J. Quémener (Paris 1972). *Pro Marcello* (46): M. Ruch (Paris 1965). *Pro Ligario* (46). *Pro rege Deiotaro* (45). *Philippics* (44–3): J. R King, 2nd ed. (Oxford 1878); I and II, J. D. Denniston (Oxford 1926).

(3) RHETORICA: *De inventione* (c. 84). *De oratore* (55–4): K. W. Piderit and O. Harnecker, 6th ed. (Leipzig 1886–90; repr. Amsterdam 1962). *Partitiones oratoriae* (c. 54). *De optimo genere oratorum* (52). *Brutus* (46): O. Jahn and W. Kroll, 7th ed. rev. B. Kytzler (Berlin 1964); A. E. Douglas (Oxford 1966). *Orator* (46): J. E. Sandys (Cambridge 1885); O. Jahn and W. Kroll, 8th ed. (Berlin 1913; repr. 1961); O. Seel (Heidelberg 1962). *Topica* (44): A. S. Wilkins (Oxford 1901).

(4) POLITICA: *De republica* (54–1): G. H. Sabine and S. B. Smith, *Cicero on the commonwealth* (Columbus, Ohio 1929: intr. and tr.); K. Ziegler, 5th ed. (Leipzig 1960). *De legibus* (51–?): W. D. Pearman (Cambridge 1881); K. Ziegler (Heidelberg 1950; 2nd ed. 1963).

(5) PHILOSOPHICA: *Paradoxa Stoicorum* (46): A. G. Lee (London 1953). *Academica* (45): J. S. Reid (Cambridge 1885). *De finibus* (45): W. M. L. Hutchinson (London 1909); I and II, J. S. Reid (Cambridge 1925). *Tusculans* (45): J. W. Dougan (vol. I Cambridge 1905; vol. II ed. R. M. Henry 1934); M. Pohlenz and O. Heine, 4th ed. (Leipzig 1929; repr. 1957); O. Gigon, 2nd ed. (Munich 1970). *De natura deorum* (45):

A. S. Pease, 2 vols. (Cambridge, Mass. 1955–8). *De fato* (44): A. Yon, 3rd ed. (Paris 1950). *Cato maior de senectute* (44): L. Huxley (Oxford 1887; repr. 1951); F. G. Moore (New York 1903); M. Ruch (Paris 1972). *Laelius de amicitia* (44): J. S. Reid (Cambridge 1887; 2nd ed. 1893). *De officiis* (44): H. A. Holden, 3rd ed. (Cambridge 1899; repr. Amsterdam 1966); J. Higginbotham (London 1967; intr., tr. and notes).

(6) CORRESPONDENCE: *Ad familiares* (16 bks), *Ad Atticum* (16 bks), and *Ad Quintum fratrem* (27 letters). Complete: R. Y. Tyrrell and L. C. Purser, 2nd ed. (Dublin 1885–1933); D. R. Shackleton Bailey, 10 vols. (Cambridge 1965–81). (Translation by D. R. Shackleton Bailey, Penguin 1978 (*Ad Att.*), 1979 (remainder).)

(7) TRANSLATIONS: Plato's *Timaeus*. See R. Poncelet, *Cicéron traducteur de Platon* (Paris 1957).

(8) VERSE (fragments): *Juvenilia*: *Aratea* (tr.); *De consulatu suo*; *De temporibus suis*; *Marius*; *Limon* (a miscellany). W. W. Ewbank, *The poems of Cicero* (London 1933); A. Traglia, *Ciceronis poetica fragmenta* (Rome 1952); J. Soubiran, *Cicéron: Aratea, fragments poétiques* (Budé, 1972). *Studies*. E. Malcovati, *Cicerone e la poesia* (Pavia 1943); A. Traglia, *La lingua di Cicerone poeta* (Bari 1950).

(9) LOST PROSE WORKS: *Consolatio* (45). *Hortensius* (45): M. Ruch (Paris 1958). *Laus Catonis* (45). *De gloria* (44). *De consiliis suis* (? = *Anecdota*). *Geographica* (? = *Admiranda*). Translations: Plato's *Protagoras*; Xenophon's *Oeconomica*.

(10) SCHOLIA: T. Stengl (Vienna–Leipzig 1912). Asconius on five speeches: A. C. Clark (Oxford 1907).

STUDIES: (1) CRITICAL SURVEYS OF LITERATURE: W. Allen, *C.W.* 47 (1954) 129–39 (for 1935–53); R. J. Rowland, *C.W.* 60 (1966) 51–65, 101–15 (for 1953–65); P. Boyancé, in *Actes Congr. Budé* (1960) 254–91 (for 1933–58), repr. in *Études sur l'humanisme Cicéronien*, *Coll. Latomus* 121 (Brussels 1970); A. E. Douglas, *G.&R.*, *New surveys in the classics* 2 (1968). *Rhetorica*: *FYAT* 416–64; A. E. Douglas, *ANRW* 1.3 (1973) 95–138. *Philosophica*: S. E. Smethurst, *C.W.* 51 (1957) 1–4, 32–41; *C.W.* 58 (1964–5) 36–44; *C.W.* 61 (1967) 125–33.

(2) GENERAL ACCOUNTS OF CICERO: J. W. Duff, *A literary history of Rome from the origins to the close of the golden age* (London 1909; rev. A. M. Duff 1953); T. Petersson, *Cicero: a biography* (Berkeley 1920); O. Plasberg, in (ed.) W. Ax, *Cicero in seinen Werken und Briefen* (1926; repr. Darmstadt 1962); M. Gelzer et al., *RE* VIIA.1 (1939) 827–1274, separately printed for 'Studierende' only (Stuttgart 1961); E. Bignone, *Storia della letteratura latina* (Florence 1950) III 442–685; F. Klingner, *Römische Geisteswelt*, 4th ed. (Munich 1961) 110–59; Schanz–Hosius I 400–550, in I. von Müller's *Handbuch der Altertumsw.*, 4th ed. (Munich 1966).

(3) STUDIES OF CICERONIAN TOPICS: E. Becker, *Technik und Szenerie des ciceronischen Dialogs* (Osnabrück 1938); M. Rambaud, *Cicéron et l'histoire romaine* (Paris 1953); A. Haury, *Ironie et humour chez Cicéron* (Leiden 1955); M. Ruch, *Le prooemium philosophique chez Cicéron* (Paris 1958); A. Michel, *Rhétorique et philosophie chez Cicéron* (Paris 1960); (ed.) E. Paratore, *Collana di studi ciceroniani*, 2 vols. (Rome 1961–2);

K. Büchner, *Cicero: Studien zur römischen Literatur* II (Wiesbaden 1962); (ed.) T. A. Dorey, *Cicero* (London 1965); (ed.) G. Radke, *Cicero, ein Mensch seiner Zeit* (Berlin 1968); P. Boyancé, *Études sur l'humanisme cicéronien* (Paris 1970); K. Büchner, *Das neue Cicerobild*, *Wege der Forschung* 27 (Darmstadt 1971).

(4) SPEECHES: T. Zieliński, 'Das Clauselgesetz in Ciceros Reden: Grundzüge einer oratorischen Rhythmik', *Philologus* suppl. 9 (1904) 589–875; L. Laurand, *Études sur le style des discours de Cicéron*, 3 vols. (Paris 1907; 4th ed. 1936–8); J. Humbert, *Les plaidoyers écrits et les plaidoiries réelles de Cicéron* (Paris 1925); F. Klingner, 'Ciceros Rede für den Schauspieler Roscius: eine Episode in der Entwicklung seiner Kunstprosa' *S.B.A.W.* 1953, 4; C. Neumeister, *Grundsätze der forensischen Rhetorik gezeigt in Gerichtsreden Ciceros* (Munich 1964); R.G.M. Nisbet, in (ed.) T. A. Dorey, *Cicero* (London 1965) 48–80.

(5) RHETORICA (see also under *General works* (2) above): H. C. Hubbell, *The influence of Isocrates on Cicero, Dionysius and Aristides* (New Haven 1913); H. K. Schulte, *Orator: Untersuchungen über das ciceronische Bildungsideal* (Frankfurt 1935); K. Barwick, 'Das Rednerische Bildungsideal Ciceros', *Abh. der Sächs. Akad. der Wiss. in Leipzig* 54 (1963) 3; A. Weische, *Ciceros Nachahmung der attischen Redner* (Heidelberg 1972).

(6) POLITICA: R. Harder, 'Über Ciceros "Somnium Scipionis"', *Abh. Königsb., Geistesw. Kl.* 1929, *Heft* 3, 115–50 = *Kleine Schriften*, ed. W. Marg (Munich 1960) 354–95; V. Pöschl, *Römischer Staat und griechisches Staatsdenken bei Cicero* (Berlin 1936); K. Büchner, 'Die beste Verfassung', *S.I.F.C.* 26 (1952) 37–140 = *Cicero: Studien zur römischen Literatur* II (Wiesbaden 1962) 25–115.

(7) PHILOSOPHICA: M. Pohlenz, *Antikes Führertum: Cicero 'De officiis' und das Lebensideal des Panaitios* (Leipzig 1934); L. Labowsky, *Der Begriff des 'prepon' in der Ethik des Panaitios* (Leipzig 1934); M. van den Bruwaene, *La théologie de Cicéron* (Louvain 1937); M. O. Lişcu, *L'expression des idées philosophiques chez Cicéron* (Paris 1937); H. A. K. Hunt, *The humanism of Cicero* (Melbourne 1954); W. Süss, 'Cicero: eine Einführung in seine philosophische Schriften', *A.A.W.M.* 1965, 5, 210–385.

(8) INFLUENCE: T. Zieliński, *Cicero im Wandel der Jahrhunderte*, 4th ed. (Leipzig 1929); C. Becker, s.v. 'Cicero' in *RAC* III 86–127; M. L. Clarke and A. E. Douglas, in (ed.) T. A. Dorey, *Cicero* (London 1965) 81–103, 135–70.

(9) LEXICA: Speeches: H. Merguet, 4 vols. (Jena 1873–84). *Philosophica*: H. Merguet, 3 vols. (Jena 1887–94). Letters: W. A. Oldfather et al. (Urbana 1938). Verse: M. J. W. Speath (Urbana 1955). *Rhetorica*: K. M. Abbott et al. (Urbana 1964).

SALLUSTIUS CRISPUS, GAIUS

LIFE

b. *c.* 86 B.C. at Amiternum. Tribune of the plebs 52; opposed T. Annius Milo. Expelled from senate 50, but reinstated as quaestor a year or two later. Served under Caesar during civil war 49–45. Elected praetor 46 and appointed first governor of *Africa Nova* Retired to write after Caesar's death and d. in Rome 35 or 34 B.C. Main sources: Jerome, *Chron.* (birth); Ascon. *ad Cic. Milo* p. 34 Stangl (tribunate); *Invect. in Sall. passim* (esp. 15 for evidence of a previous quaestorship); Dio 40.63.2ff. (expulsion from Senate); idem 42.52.1ff., 43.9.2; *Bell. Afr.* 8.3, 34.1–3, 97.1; App. 2.92, 100 (praetorship and African career); Sall. *Cat.* 3.3–4.2 (retirement); Gell. 17.18; ps.-Acron *ad Hor. Sat.* 1.2.41, 49. See Syme (1964, under *Studies* below) 1–59; G. Perl, 'Sallusts Todesjahr', *Klio* 48 (1967) 97–105. Further testimonia in preface to Kurfess's ed.

WORKS

(1) *Bellum Catilinae*, pubd *c.* 42, and *Bellum Iugurthinum*, pubd *c.* 40: historical monographs, each in a single book. *Historiae*: preserved by over 500 fragments covering the years 78–67, including four complete speeches and two complete letters; begun *c.* 39 and left incomplete in bk 5 at S.'s death.

(2) Spurious. Two *Epistulae ad Caesarem senem de re publica*, and *In M. Tullium Ciceronem invectiva*: probably emanate from the rhetorical schools.

BIBLIOGRAPHY

(for 1879–1964, see A. D. Leeman (Leiden 1965))

TEXTS AND COMMENTARIES: TEXTS: *Cat.* and *Iug.*: H. Jordan (Berlin 1866); A. W. Ahlberg (BT, 1919); A. Kurfess (BT, 1951); A. Ernout (Budé, 1946). *Invect.* and *Epist.*: A. Kurfess (BT, 1914); A. Ernout (Budé, 1962). COMMENTARIES: *Cat.* and *Iug.*: R. Dietsch (Leipzig 1846); F. Kritz (Leipzig 1853). *Cat.*: R. Jacobs, H. Wirz, A. Kurfess (Berlin 1922); J. Hellegouarc'h (Paris 1972); K. Vretska (Heidelberg 1976); P. McGushin (Leiden 1977). *Iug.*: R. Jacobs and H. Wirz (Berlin 1922); E. Koestermann (Heidelberg 1971). *Hist.*: B. Maurenbrecher (Leipzig 1891–3). *Invect.* and *Epist.*: K. Vretska (Heidelberg 1961).

STUDIES: H. Schnorr von Carolsfeld, *Über die Reden und Briefe bei Sallust* (Leipzig 1888); A. Kunze, *Sallustiana* (Leipzig 1892–8); E. Schwartz, 'Die Berichte über die catilinarische Verschwörung', *Hermes* 32 (1897) 554–608 = *Gesamm. Schr.* (Berlin 1956) II 275–336; G. Boissier, 'Les prologues de Salluste', *J.S.* n.s.1 (1903) 59–66; idem, *La conjuration de Catilina* (Paris 1905); A. W. Ahlberg, *Prolegomena in Sallustium* (Göteborg 1911); R. Ullmann, 'Essai sur le Catilina de Salluste', *R.Ph.* 42 (1918) 5–27; G. Funaioli, in *RE* IA (1920) 1913–55; W. Kroll, 'Die Sprache des Sallust', *Glotta* 15 (1927) 280–305; R. Ullmann, *La technique des discours dans Salluste, Tite-Live et Tacite* (Oslo 1927); F. Klingner, 'Über die Einleitung der Historien Sallusts', *Hermes* 63 (1928) 165–92 = *Studien* (Zurich 1964) 571–93; O. Seel, *Sallust von den Briefen ad Caesarem zur Coniuratio Catilinae* (Leipzig 1930); F. Egermann, *Die*

Prooemien zu den Werken des Sallust, S.B.A.W. 214.3 (1932); E. Skard, *Ennius und Sallustius* (Oslo 1933); W. Schur, *Sallust als Historiker* (Stuttgart 1934); K. Bauhofer, *Die Komposition der Historien Sallusts* (diss. Munich 1935); K. Latte, *Sallust, Neue Wege zur Antike* 2.4 (1935); S. Pantzerhielm-Thomas, 'The prologues of Sallust', S.O. 15–16 (1936) 140–62; K. Vretska, 'Der Aufbau des Bellum Catilinae', *Hermes* 72 (1937) 202–22; V. Pöschl, *Grundwerte römischer Staatsgesinnung in den Geschichtswerken des Sallust* (Berlin 1940); P. Zancan, 'Prolegomeni alla Giugurtina I', A.I.V. 102 (1942–3) 637–65; K. von Fritz, 'Sallust and the attitude of the Roman nobility at the time of the wars against Jugurtha', T.A.Ph.A. 74 (1943) 134–68; E. Skard, 'Die Bildersprache des Sallust', S.O. suppl. 11 (1943) 141–64; H. Last, 'Sallust and Caesar in the Bellum Catilinae', *Mélanges Marouzeau* (Paris 1948) 355–69; P. Perrochat, *Les modèles grecs de Salluste* (Paris 1949); K. Büchner, *Der Aufbau von Sallusts Bellum Iugurthinum, Hermes Einzelschriften* 9 (1953); A. D. Leeman, 'Sallusts Prologe und seine Auffassung von der Historiographie', *Mnemosyne* 7 (1954) 323–39, and 8 (1955) 38–48; K. Vretska, *Studien zu Sallusts Bellum Iugurthinum*, S.B.A.W. 229.4 (1955); E. Skard, *Sallust und seine Vorgänger* (Oslo 1956); W. Avenarius, 'Die griechischen Vorbilder des Sallust', S.O. 33 (1957) 48–86; A. D. Leeman, *Aufbau und Absicht von Sallusts Bellum Iugurthinum* (Amsterdam 1957); W. Steidle, *Sallusts historisch Monographien, Historia Einzelschriften* 3 (1958); K. Büchner, *Sallust* (Heidelberg 1960); D. C. Earl, *The political thought of Sallust* (Cambridge 1961); R. Syme, *Sallust* (California 1964); A. la Penna, *Sallustio e la 'rivoluzione' romana* (Milan 1968); H. Gugel, 'Bemerkungen zur Darstellung von Catilinas Ende bei Sallust', *Festschrift Vretska* (Heidelberg 1970) 361–81; V. Pöschl, 'Die Reden Caesars und Catos in Sallusts Catilina', in *Sallust, Wege der Forschung* 94 (Darmstadt 1970) 368–97; A. la Penna, 'Congetture sulla fortuna di Sallustio nell'antichità', *Studia Florentina A. Ronconi oblata* (Rome 1971) 195–206; K. Bringmann, 'Sallusts Umgang mit der historischen Wahrheit in seiner Darstellung der catilinarischen Verschwörung', *Philologus* 116 (1972) 98–113; L. Canfora, 'Il programma di Sallustio', *Belfagor* 27 (1972) 137–48; D. Flach, 'Die Vorrede zu Sallusts Historien in neuer Rekonstruktion', *Philologus* 117 (1973) 76–86; C. Questa, 'Sallustio, Tacito e l'imperialismo Romano', *Atti e memorie dell' Arcadia* 3.6 (1975–6) 1–43.

INDEXES: O. Eichert, 4th ed. (Hannover 1890); A. D. Bennett (Hildesheim 1970).

APPENDIX (mainly concerning the spurious pieces). H. Last, 'On the Sallustian Suasoriae', C.Q. 17 (1923) 87–100, 151–62; W. Kroll, 'Sallusts Staatsschriften', *Hermes* 62 (1927) 373–92; B. Edmar, *Studien zu den Epistulae ad Caesarem senem de re publica* (Lund 1931); E. Skard, 'Studien zur Sprache der Epistulae ad Caesarem', S.O. 10 (1931) 61–98; G. Carlsson, *Eine Denkschrift an Cäsar über den Staat, historisch-philologisch untersucht* (Lund 1936); O. Seel, *Die Invektive gegen Cicero, Klio Beiheft* 47 (1943); M. Chouet, *Les lettres de Salluste à César* (Paris 1950), reviewed by E. Fraenkel, J.R.S. 41 (1951) 192–4; A. Dihle, 'Zu den Epistolae ad Caesarem senem',

APPENDIX OF AUTHORS AND WORKS

M.H. 11 (1954) 126–30; R. G. M. Nisbet, 'The *Invectiva in Ciceronem* and *Epistula Secunda* of Pseudo-Sallust', *J.R.S.* 48 (1958) 30–2; O. Seel, *Sallusts Briefe und die pseudo-sallustische Invektive, Erlanger Beiträge* 25 (Nuremberg 1967); E. Pasoli, *Problemi delle Epistulae ad Caesarem sallustiane* (Bologna 1970).

CAESAR, GAIUS IULIUS

LIFE

b. 13 July 100 B.C. Consul 59, proconsul of Cisalpine and Transalpine Gaul 58–50, dictator 49, campaigns against Pompey and his sons 48–45. Assassinated 15 March 44 B.C. Main sources: his own writings and the spurious works mentioned below; Suetonius, *Divus Iulius*; Cicero's speeches and letters; Plutarch, *Caesar* and other lives; Appian, *Bellum civile*; Dio Cassius 36–44. Evidence fully treated by M. Gelzer, *Caesar: politician and statesman*, tr. P. Needham (Oxford 1968).

WORKS

(1) EXTANT: *Commentarii de bello Gallico* (7 bks; bk 8 composed by his subordinate A. Hirtius to complete account of campaign), and *Commentarii de bello civili* (3 bks); verse epigram to Terence (*FPL* 91). (2) LOST (Suet. *Iul.* 56.5–7): Speeches (several collected and pubd; out of fashion by end of 1st c. A.D., Tac. *Dial.* 21); two books on style, *De analogia*, written early summer 54; poem *Iter* on his journey to Spain 45; pamphlet in two books attacking memory of Cato (Plut. *Cato min.* 36.4–5, 52.5–7). (3) SPURIOUS: *Bellum Alexandrinum, Bellum Africum, Bellum Hispaniense*, dealing with later episodes of the civil wars; subsequently attached to C.'s name but written by unknown officers.

BIBLIOGRAPHY

(see H. Gesche, *Caesar, Erträge der Forschung* (Darmstadt 1976))

TEXTS AND COMMENTARIES: TEXTS: A. Klotz and W. Trillitzsch (BT, 1927–64). COMMENTARIES: *Bell. Gall.*: F. Kraner, W. Dittenberger, H. Meusel, H. Oppermann (Zurich–Berlin 1964–6). *Bell. Civ.*: F. Kraner, F. Hofmann, H. Meusel, H. Oppermann (Berlin 1959). TEXTUAL PROBLEMS: F. Beckmann, *Geographie und Ethnographie in Caesars Bellum Gallicum* (Dortmund 1930); G. Jachmann, 'Caesartext und Caesarinterpolation', *Rh.M.* 89 (1940) 161–88; K. Barwick, 'Ist der Caesartext heillos interpoliert?', *Rh.M.* 91 (1942) 28–51.

STUDIES: H. Drexler, 'Zum Begriff Commentarii', *Hermes* 70 (1935) 227–34; K. Barwick, *Caesars Bellum Civile: Tendenz, Abfassungszeit und Stil* (Leipzig 1951); U. Knoche, 'Caesars Commentarii, ihr Gegenstand und ihre Absicht', *Gymnasium* 58

(1951) 139–60; F. Bömer, 'Der Commentarius', *Hermes* 81 (1953) 210–50; M. Rambaud, *L'art de la déformation historique dans les Commentaires de César*, 2nd ed. (Paris 1966); J. P. V. D. Balsdon, *J.R.S.* 45 (1955) 161–4 (review of Barwick and Rambaud); G. Walser, 'Caesar und die Germanen', *Historia Einzelschriften* 1 (1956); F. E. Adcock, *Caesar as man of letters* (Cambridge 1956); D. Rasmussen, *Caesars Commentarii: Stil und Stilwandel* (Göttingen 1963); S. Weinstock, *Divus Julius* (Oxford 1971); J. H. Collins, 'Caesar as political propagandist', *ANRW* 1.1 (1972) 922–66; F.-M. Mutschler, *Erzählstil und Propaganda in Caesars Kommentarien* (Heidelberg 1975); H. A. Gärtner, *Beobachtungen zu Bauelementen in der antiken Historiographie, Historia Einzelschriften* 25 (1975).

LEXICON: H. Merguet (Jena 1886; repr. Hildesheim 1963).

VARRO, MARCUS TERENTIUS

LIFE

b. 116 B.C., possibly at Reate (mod. Rieti). Pupil of antiquarian L. Aelius Stilo and philosopher Antiochus of Ascalon. *IIIvir capitalis* in 90s, quaestor 85 (?), tribune of the plebs and praetor at uncertain dates. Served in Dalmatian campaign 78–7; proquaestor under Pompey against Sertorius 76–1 and legate in pirate war 67–? (awarded *corona rostrata*). *XXvir agris dandis assignandis* 59. Legate under Pompey in Spain ?–49. Joined Pompeians at Dyrrhachium; returned to Italy after Pharsalus and regained his property which was then threatened by Antony and rescued by Caesar. Commissioned by Caesar to collect a great library 46; lost some property 44; proscribed 43 to his own library's detriment, but saved by Fufius Calenus. d. pen in hand 27 B.C. Sources: Jerome, *Chron. ann. Abr.* 1901 and 1989, Symm. *Epist.* 1.2, Val. Max. 7.3 (birth, death); Varro, *Ling. Lat.* 7.2, Cic. *Brut.* 205 and *Acad. post.* 1.7.12 (teachers); Gell. 13.12.6 (*IIIvir*, tribune); Varro, *Sat. Men.* 478 (quaestor); App. 4.47 (praetor); Varro, *Res Rust.* 2.10.8, 3.12.7, 2. *proem.* 6 (Dalmatia, proquaestor, pirate war); Pliny, *N.H.* 7.115 and 176 (*corona, XXvir*); Caes. *Bell. Civ.* 2.17 (in Spain); Cic. *Fam.* 9.6.3 (Dyrrhachium); Suet. *Iul.* 44.2 (library); Cic. *Phil.* 2.103, App. 4.47, Gell. 3.10.17 (property threatened, proscription etc.).

WORKS

Had written 490 books (as distinct from whole works) by age of 77 (Gell. 3.10.17) and over 600 by time of his death (Auson. *Prof. Burd.* 20.10; 620 according to F. Ritschl, *Opuscula philologica* III (Leipzig 1877) 488). Jerome's incomplete catalogue, of uncertain origin, has been accidentally preserved (see G. L. Hendrickson, *C.Ph.* 6 (1911) 334–43); numerous titles attested elsewhere (Ritschl 472–4). A representative selection follows.

(1) EXTANT: *De lingua Latina*: six mutilated books survive out of twenty-five. Completed after July 45 and before Cicero's death (Cic. *Att.* 13.12.3). Bks 2–4 ·dedicated to his quaestor P. Septimius, 5–7 (and possibly rest of work) to Cicero (*Ling. Lat.* 7.109). *De re rustica*: completed 37 B.C. (1.1.1), but perhaps written in sections over previous twenty years (see Martin and White, under *Studies* (4) below). Bk 1 dedicated to his wife Fundania, who has just bought a farm, 2 to his landowner friend Turranius Niger, 3 to his neighbour Pinnius.

(2) LOST OR FRAGMENTARY (no. of bks in Roman numerals): Verse. *Saturarum Menippearum* CL: about ninety titles and 600 fragments preserved; of early date (Cic. *Acad. post.* 1.8). Also ten books of 'poems', four of satires, six of tragedies. Prose. (*a*) History, geography, antiquities. *Antiquitates: Rerum humanarum* XXV written first; *Rerum divinarum* XVI probably completed and dedicated to Caesar as pontifex maximus 46. *De vita populi Romani* IV (dedicated to Atticus); *De gente populi Romani* IV, 43–2; *De familiis Troianis* (cf. Virg. *Aen.* 5.117ff., etc.); *De vita sua* III and *Legationum* III (both autobiographical); *Annales* (see p. 291); Εἰσαγωγικὸς *ad Pompeium* (70: instructions to P. on how to behave in the senate; Gell. 14.7); *Ephemeris navalis ad Pompeium* (probably 77: cf. *De ora maritima*, *De litoralibus*, *De aestuariis*). (*b*) Language and literary history. *De antiquitate litterarum ad L. Accium*; *De origine linguae Latinae*; *De similitudine verborum*; *De sermone Latino* V (after 46); *Quaestionum Plautinarum* V; *De scaenicis originibus* III; *De actionibus scaenicis* III; *De poematis* III (cf. Aristotle's *Poetics*, Neoptolemus of Parium, Philodemus); *De poetis* (fundamental literary chronology); *Hebdomades vel De imaginibus* XV (probably completed 39: see p. 291). (*c*) Rhetoric and law. *Orationum* XII; *Laudationes* (Cic. *Acad. post.* 1.8, *Att.* 13.48.2); *De iure civili* XV. (*d*) Philosophy and science. *De philosophia*; *De forma philosophiae*; *Logistoricon* LXXVI, dialogues on philosophical and historical themes whose double titles (eleven extant plus eight fragmentary titles) signify the chief participant in the dialogue and the subject matter on which he is an expert; of late date; *Disciplinarum* IX (written 34–3?).

BIBLIOGRAPHY

(see B. Cardauns in *Entretiens IX: Varron* (Fondation Hardt, Geneva 1963) 209–12 (for 1950–62); H. Dahlmann, *ANRW* 1.3 (1973) 3–18; J. Collart, *Lustrum* 9 (1964) 213–41 (grammatical works); K. D. White, *ANRW* 1.4 (1973) 495–7 (*Res Rust.*))

TEXTS AND COMMENTARIES: (1) EXTANT: TEXTS: Complete: F. Semi (Venice 1965–Padua 1966: reprints many earlier texts). *Ling. Lat.*, *Res Rust.* and grammatical fragments: A. Traglia (Turin 1974). *Ling. Lat.*: G. Goetz and F. Schoell (Leipzig 1910: with gramm. fragments); R. G. Kent, rev. ed. (Loeb, 1951). *Res Rust.*: G. Goetz, 2nd ed. (BT, 1929); W. D. Hooper and H. B. Ash, rev. ed. (Loeb, 1935: with Cato); J. Heurgon (Budé, 1978: bk 1 only, with brief notes). COMMENTARIES: *Ling. Lat.* Bk 5: J. Collart (Paris 1954: with French tr.). Bk 8: H. Dahlmann, *Hermes*

Einzelschriften 7 (1940: with German tr.). Bk 10: A. Traglia (Bari 1956). *Res. Rust.* J. G. Schneider, *Scriptorum rei rusticae*, vol. 1 (Leipzig 1794: only full comm. on agricultural matters); H. Keil, 3 vols. (Leipzig 1891–1902: with Cato).

(2) FRAGMENTS: Verse. *Sat. Men.*: A. Riese (Leipzig 1865); F. Buecheler and W. Heraeus, *Petronii Saturae* (Berlin 1922) 177–250; E. Bolisani (Padua 1936); J.-P. Cèbe, 3 vols. so far (Rome 1972–5). Prose. (*a*) Historical etc. *Antiquitates*: P. Mirsch, *Leipzig Studien* 5 (1882). *Res divinae*: R. Merkel, *Ovidi Fasti* (Berlin 1841) 106–247; R. Agahd, *N.J.Kl.P.* suppl. 24 (1895: bks 1, 14–16); B. Cardauns, *Abh. Akad. Mainz* 1976. *De vita pop. Rom.*: B. Riposati (Padua 1907). *De gente pop. Rom.*: P. Fraccaro (Milan 1939); see also *HRR* II 9–25. (*b*) Language etc. G. Funaioli, *Grammaticae Romanae fragmenta* (BT, 1907). (*c*) Law. F. P. Bremer, *Iurisprudentiae antehadrianae quae supersunt* (BT, 1896) I 122–7. (*d*) Philosophy etc. *De philosophia*: G. Langenberg (diss. Köln 1959). *Logistorici*: Riese, with *Sat. Men.* above; C. Chappuis (Paris 1868: with *De forma philosophiae* and *Imagines*); E. Bolisani (Padua 1937). *Catus de liberis educandis*: R. Müller (diss. Bonn 1938). *Curio de cultu*: B. Cardauns (diss. Köln 1960). *Tubero de origine humana*: R. Heisterhagen, *Abh. Akad. Mainz* 4, 1957, 20–37. *Disciplinae*: see F. Ritschl, *Opuscula philologica* III (Leipzig 1877) 352–402, and M. Simon, *Philologus* 110 (1966) 88–101. (*e*) Others. *Epistulae*: Riese, with *Sat. Men.* above; D. Wolff (diss. Marburg 1960); see too *R.C.C.M.* 9 (1967) 78–85. *Sententiae*: C. Chappuis (Paris 1856); P. Germann (Paderborn 1910).

TRANSLATIONS: *Res Rust.*: L. Storr-Best (London 1912); B. Tilly, *Varro the farmer* (London 1973: selections).

STUDIES: (1) GENERAL: G. Boissier, *Étude sur la vie et les ouvrages de Varron* (Paris 1861); Ritschl, under (*d*) above, III 419–505 and *passim*; H. Dahlmann, *RE* suppl. VI (1935) 1172ff.; *Entretiens IX: Varron* (Fondation Hardt, Geneva 1963). (2) BIOGRAPHICAL: C. Cichorius, *Römische Studien* (Leipzig 1922) 189–241; K. Kumianecki *Athenaeum* 40 (1962) 221–43; R. Astbury, *C.Q.* n.s.17 (1967) 403–7; N. M. Horsfall, *B.I.C.S.* 19 (1972) 120–8. (3) 'LING. LAT.' etc.: H. Dahlmann, *Varro und die hellenistische Sprachtheorie* (Berlin 1935); F. della Corte, *La filologia latina delle origini a Varrone* (Turin 1937) 101–46, 149–60; H. Dahlmann, 'Varros schrift "De poematis"' *Abh. Akad. Mainz* 3, 1953; idem, 'Studien zu Varros "De poetis,"' *Abh. Akad. Mainz* 10, 1962; J. Collart, *Varron, grammarien latin* (Paris 1954); D. J. Taylor, *Declinatio* (Amsterdam 1973). (4) 'RES RUST.': J. Heurgon, 'L'effort de style de Varron dans les Res rusticae', *R.Ph.* 76 (1950) 57–71; H. Dohr, *Die italischen Gutshöfe* (diss. Köln 1965); J. E. Skydsgaard, *Varro the scholar* (Copenhagen 1967); R. Martin, *Recherches sur les agronomes latins* (Paris 1971) 213–35, 257–86; K. D. White, *ANRW* I.3 (1973) 463–94. (5) 'SAT. MEN.': F. della Corte, *La poesia di Varrone reatino ricostituita*, *Mem. Acad. Torino* n.s.69.2 (1937–8); E. Norden, *Kleine Schriften* (Berlin 1966) 1–87; E. Woytek, *Sprachliche Studien zur Satura Menippea Varros*, *W.S.* suppl. 2 (1970) (6) HISTORY etc.: P. Boyancé, 'Sur la théologie de Varron', *R.E.A.* 52 (1955) 57–84; H.

Hagendahl, *Augustine and the Latin classics* (Göteborg 1967) 589–630; K. G. Sallmann, *Die Geographie des älteren Plinius in ihrem Verhältnis ʒu Varro* (Berlin 1971); G. Lieberg, 'Die Theologia tripartita', *ANRW* 1.4 (1973) 63–115. (7) 'LOGISTORICI': H. Dahlmann, 'Varronische Studien' I (with R. Heisterhagen), *Abh. Akad. Mainʒ* 4, 1957, and II, ibid. 11, 1959, 5–25. (8) 'IMAGINES': E. Bethe, *Buch und Bild im Altertum* (Leipzig 1945) *passim*; A. von Salis, 'Imagines illustrium', in *Eumusia, Festgabe E. Howald* (Zurich 1947) 11–29. (9) OTHERS. E. Laughton, 'Observations on the style of Varro', *C.Q.* n.s.10 (1960) 1–28.

NEPOS, CORNELIUS

LIFE

b. in Po valley possibly *c.* 109 B.C.; probably a native of Ticinum. Associated with Catullus (Cat. 1), Atticus and Cicero. d. after 27 B.C. Praenomen unknown. Sources: Nepos 25.19.1 (birth); 25.13.7 (Atticus); Pliny, *N.H.* 3.127, 10.60; Pliny, *Epist.* 3.28.1 (birthplace and death); Macr. *Sat.* 2.1.14 (Cic.'s letters to him); Fronto p. 20N (N.'s role as editor of Cic.).

WORKS

(1) *De viris illustribus* (at least sixteen books, *GLK* I 141.13). Extant: *De excellentibus ducibus exterarum gentium* (title not quite certain); *Cato* and *Atticus* from *De historicis Latinis*. Books *De Romanorum imperatoribus* (23.13.2), *De historicis Graecis* (10.3.2), and *De regibus* (21.1.1) are certain; categories *De poetis*, *De oratoribus* and *De grammaticis* are likely. First pubd probably 35/34 B.C. (25.12.1f., 19.2); 2nd ed. before 27. Was there a 2nd ed. of the whole work? See H. Rahn, *Hermes* 85 (1957) 205–15. (2) Lost. Separate lives of Cato (24.3.5) and Cicero (Gell. 15.28.1); *Chronica*, 3 bks (Cat. 1.6; cf. Gell. 17.21.3); *Exempla*, at least 5 bks (Gell. 6.18.11); a geographical work (?), see K. G. Sallmann, *Die Geographie des älteren Plinius in ihrem Verhältnis ʒu Varro* (Berlin 1971) 119ff.; *versiculi severi parum* (Pliny, *Epist.* 5.3.6); letters to Cicero (Lact. *Inst.* 3.15.10).

BIBLIOGRAPHY

TEXTS AND COMMENTARIES: TEXTS: E. O. Winstedt (OCT, 1904); J. C. Rolfe (Loeb, 1929: with Florus); E. Malcovati (Paravia, 1945); P. K. Marshall (BT, 1977: bibliography xiii-xvi). COMMENTARIES: K. Nipperdey and K. Witte, 12th ed. (Berlin 1962). *Hannibal, Cato, Atticus*: M. Ruch (Paris 1968).

STUDIES: E. Jenkinson, 'Nepos. An introduction to Latin biography', in (ed.) T. A. Dorey, *Latin biography* (London 1967) 1–15; idem, 'Cornelius Nepos and biography at Rome', *ANRW* 1.3 (1973) 703–19 (718–19 provide bibliography for 1939–72); A. D. Momigliano, *The development of Greek biography* (Harvard 1971) 96–9.

THE LITERARY MIME

LIVES

DECIMUS LABERIUS: b. *c.* 106 B.C. (Macr. *Sat.* 2.7.5(12) = Laber. *Mim.* 109). Acted in own mime at celebrations following Caesar's triumphs 46. d. 43 B.C. (Jerome, *Chron. ann. Abr.* 1974). PUBLILIUS SYRUS: probably an Antiochene (Pliny, *N.H.* 35.199.) Brought to Rome as a slave and manumitted. Surpassed Laberius in competition commissioned by Caesar (Macr. *Sat.* 2.7.6f.). *fl.* 43 B.C. (Jerome, loc. cit.).

WORKS

Laberius: titles of forty-three mimes and 183 lines survive in part or complete, including twenty-seven lines (Macr. *Sat.* 2.7.3) of his prologue before Caesar; perhaps this was the only part of the mime regularly committed to writing in advance. Publilius: titles of two mimes only (one hopelessly corrupt) and less than five lines survive, outside the *Sententiae* (700 lines), an incomplete reproduction made under Nero or earlier (Sen. *Epist.* 8.9, 94.43, 108.8ff. etc., O. Skutsch, *RE* XXIII.2 (1959) 1924) and used in Roman schools (Jerome, *Epist.* 104.8; cf. Sen. *Epist.* 33.6); not all the *Sententiae* (like those attributed to Epicharmus, Menander, Cato, Varro and Seneca) need be authentic: see Gratwick and Jory under *Studies* below.

BIBLIOGRAPHY

(see P. Hamblenne, *ANRW* I.3 (1973) 698–70)

TEXTS AND COMMENTARIES: *CRF* 337–85; M. Bonaria, *Mimorum Romanorum fragmenta* (Genoa 1956); idem, *I mimi romani* (Rome 1965). *Sententiae*: J. W. and A. M. Duff, *Minor Latin poets* (Loeb, 1934) 1–111; O. Friedrich (1880: repr. Hildesheim 1964: with comm.); H. Beckby (Munich 1969).

STUDIES: G. Boissier, in Daremberg–Saglio, s.v. 'Mimus'; J.-P. Cèbe, *La caricature et la parodie* (Paris 1966) *passim*; F. Giancotti, *Mimo e gnome* (Messina 1967), reviewed by A. S. Gratwick, *C.R.* n.s.19 (1969) 185–7 and E. J. Jory, *Gnomon* 42 (1970) 125–9; W. Beare, *The Roman stage* 3rd ed. (London 1964) 149–58.

METRICAL APPENDIX

(1) BASIC PRINCIPLES

(A) STRESSED AND QUANTITATIVE VERSE

In metres familiar to speakers of English, rhythm is measured by the predictable alternation of one or more stressed syllables with one or more unstressed syllables (distinguished by the notation – and ᴗ, or ′ and ˣ). Consequently, it is word-accent that determines whether or not a word or sequence of words may stand in a certain part of the verse. Thus the word *classical* may occupy the metrical unit represented by the notation –ᴗᴗ by virtue of the stress imparted to its first syllable in everyday pronunciation. In contrast, the rhythms of classical Latin metres are measured by the predictable alternation of one or more 'heavy' syllables with one or more 'light' syllables (defined below, and distinguished by the notation – and ᴗ), so that in the construction of Latin verse the factor of primary importance is not word-accent but syllabic 'weight'. Thus the word *facerent*, although accented in normal speech on the first syllable, consists for metrical purposes of two light syllables followed by one heavy syllable, and for this reason can only occupy the metrical unit ᴗᴗ–. Verse constructed upon this principle is conventionally designated *quantitative*: it should be emphasized that this term refers to the quantity (or 'weight') of syllables, and that throughout this account such quantity is described by the terms 'heavy' and 'light' to distinguish it from the intrinsic length of vowels; unfortunately, both syllabic weight and vowel-length are still generally denoted by the same symbols, – and ᴗ.

(B) SYLLABIFICATION

A syllable containing a long vowel or diphthong is heavy (e.g. the first syllables of *pacem* and *laudo*).

A syllable containing a short vowel is light if it ends with that vowel (e.g. the first syllable of *pecus*), but heavy if it ends with a consonant (e.g. the first syllable of *pectus*).

To decide whether or not a short-vowelled syllable ends with a consonant (and thus to establish its quantity), the following rules should be observed:[1] (i) word-division

---

[1] The resulting division is practical only; for the difficulties involved in an absolute definition of the syllabic unit see Allen (1973) under (4) below, esp. 27–40.

should be disregarded; (ii) a single consonant between two vowels or diphthongs belongs to the succeeding syllable (thus *pecus* →*pe–cus*; *genus omne* →*ge–nu–som–ne*); (iii) of two or more successive consonants, at least one belongs to the preceding syllable (thus *pectus* →*pec–tus*; also *nulla spes* →*nul–las–pes*, though short final vowels are normally avoided in this position), except as allowed for below.

Note: for this purpose *h* is disregarded; *x* and *z* count as double consonants, 'semi-consonantal' *i* and *u* as consonants (except in the combination *qu*, regarded as a single consonant).

To (iii) there is an important exception. In the case of the combination of a plosive and liquid consonant (*p*, *t*, *c*, *b*, *d*, *g* followed by *r* or *l*), the syllabic division may be made either between the consonants (e.g. *pat–ris*) or before them (e.g. *pa–tris*), resulting in *either* a heavy *or* a light preceding syllable. However, when two such consonants belong to different parts of a compound or to two different words, the division is always made between them, giving a heavy preceding syllable (e.g. *ablego* → *ab–lego*, not *a–blego*; *at rabidae* →*at–rabidae*, not *a–trabidae*). Lastly, when, after a short final vowel, these consonants begin the next word, the division is nearly always made before them, giving a light preceding syllable (e.g. *plumbea glans* →*plum–be–a–glans*).

(C) ACCENT

The nature of the Latin word-accent (whether one of pitch or stress) and its importance in the construction of verse are both matters of controversy: for a clear discussion of the basic problems see Wilkinson under (4) below, 89–96, 221–36. By way of practical guidance in reading Latin verse, all that may be said is that for the present-day English speaker, accustomed to a naturalistic manner of reading poetry, it will sound as strange (and monotonous) to emphasize the heavy syllables of a metrical structure ('Quális Théseá iacuít cedénte carína') as it does to read Shakespearian verse with attention only to its iambic structure ('Now ís the wínter óf our discontént'); furthermore that, even in giving stress to the word-accent in Latin verse, heavy syllables will generally coincide with accented syllables with sufficient frequency to ensure that the metre is not forgotten – particularly at the beginning and end of many metres, as in the hexameter quoted above. It should be remembered, however, that what sounds natural is not thereby authentic, and that poetic delivery is highly susceptible to whims of fashion, idiosyncrasy and affectation. Even now it is not uncommon criticism of a Shakespearian actor that he 'mutilates' the shape of the verse by reading it as prose, while recordings of Tennyson and Eliot reading their poetry already sound bizarre (in different ways) to the modern ear.

(2) TECHNICAL TERMS

Anceps ('unfixed'): term used to describe a metrical element which may be represented by either a heavy or a light syllable. The final element of many Latin metres is regularly of this nature, but not in certain lyric metres in which there is metrical continuity (*synaphea*) between as well as within lines.

Brevis brevians, or *the law of iambic shortening*: in comedy and other early Latin verse a heavy syllable may be lightened if it directly follows a light syllable and is adjacent to an accented syllable.

Caesura ('cutting') and *diaeresis*: division between words within a verse is termed *caesura* when occurring inside a metrical foot, or *diaeresis* when occurring at the end of a foot. The varied distribution of these plays an important part in avoiding monotony in the structure of verse; in particular, the caesura prevents a succession of words co-extensive with the feet of a metre (as found in Ennius' hexameter, 'sparsis hastis longis campus splendet et horret').

Elision and *hiatus*: a vowel (or vowel $+m$) ending a word is generally suppressed or *elided* when immediately preceding another vowel or *h*. When it is not elided in these circumstances (a phenomenon most frequently found in comedy), it is said to be in *hiatus*; by the rare process of *correption* a long vowel or diphthong in hiatus may be scanned short to make a light syllable. *Prodelision* (or *aphaeresis*) signifies the suppression of *e* in *est* after a final vowel or *m*, *hypermetric elision* the suppression of a vowel between lines (nearly always that of *–que*).

Resolution: the substitution of two light syllables for a heavy one.

(3) COMMON METRES

For the sake of simplicity only the most basic characteristics of each metre are given here. For the numerous divergencies regarding anceps, resolution, position of caesura etc., see Raven under (4) below.

(a) Stichic verse (constructed by repetition of the same metrical line)
Iambic senarius (or trimeter):

$$\times-\cup-\ |\ \times-\cup-\ |\ \times-\cup\times$$

(commonest dialogue metre in early Roman drama; also used in Seneca's tragedies, Phaedrus' *Fables*, and, in alternation with an iambic dimeter ($=\times-\cup-\ |\ \times-\cup-$), Horace's *Epodes* 1–10)
Iambic septenarius (or tetrameter catalectic):

$$\times-\cup-\ |\ \times-\cup-\ |\ \times-\cup-\ |\ \cup-\times$$

(common dialogue metre of comedy)

Trochaic septenarius (or tetrameter catalectic):

$$-\cup-\underline{\cup}\,|\,-\cup-\underline{\cup}\,|\,-\cup-\underline{\cup}\,|\,-\cup\cup$$

(very common dialogue metre in early Roman drama)

Hexameter:

$$-\cup\cup\,|\,-\cup\cup\,|\,-\cup\cup\,|\,-\cup\cup\,|\,-\cup\cup\,|\,-\underline{\cup}$$

(regular metre for epic, satiric, pastoral and didactic poetry)

Pentameter:

$$-\cup\cup-\cup\cup-\,|\,-\cup\cup-\cup\cup\underline{\cup}$$

(following the hexameter this forms the elegiac couplet, which is regarded as an entity and hence as stichic; regular metre for love-poetry and epigram)

Phalaecean hendecasyllables:

$$\underline{\cup\cup}\,|\,-\cup\cup-\,|\,\cup-\cup-\underline{\cup}$$

(i.e. first foot may be a spondee, iamb or trochee; used by Catullus, Martial and Statius)

(b) Non-stichic verse (constructed by combination of different metrical lines)

Alcaic stanza:	$--\cup--\,|\,-\cup\cup-\,|\,\cup\underline{\cup}$	(twice)
	$--\cup---\cup\underline{\cup}$	
	$-\cup\cup-\cup\cup-\,|\,\cup-\underline{\cup}$	
Sapphic stanza:	$-\cup--\,|\,-\cup\cup-\,|\,\cup-\underline{\cup}$	(three times)
	$-\cup\cup-\,|\,\underline{\cup}$	(adonean)
Third asclepiad:	$--\,|\,-\cup\cup-\,|\,\cup\underline{\cup}$	(glyconic)
	$--\,|\,-\cup\cup--\cup\cup-\,|\,\cup\underline{\cup}$	(lesser asclepiad)
Fourth asclepiad:	$--\,|\,-\cup\cup--\cup\cup-\,|\,\cup\underline{\cup}$	(lesser asclepiad, three times)
	$--\,|\,-\cup\cup-\,|\,\cup\underline{\cup}$	(glyconic)
Fifth asclepiad	$--\,|\,-\cup\cup--\cup\cup-\,|\,\cup\underline{\cup}$	(lesser asclepiad, twice)
	$--\,|\,-\cup\cup-\,|\,\underline{\cup}$	(pherecratean)
	$--\,|\,-\cup\cup-\,|\,\cup\underline{\cup}$	(glyconic)

(the First and Second asclepiad consist, respectively, of the lesser and greater asclepiad only; the latter $=--\,|\,-\cup\cup--\cup\cup--\cup\cup-\,|\,\cup\underline{\cup}$)

All the above found in Horace's *Odes*; some in Catullus and Statius.

(4) BIBLIOGRAPHY

Allen, W. S., *Vox Latina*, 2nd ed. (Cambridge 1978).

idem, *Accent and rhythm* (Cambridge 1973).

Raven, D. S., *Latin metre* (London 1965).

Wilkinson, L. P., *Golden Latin artistry* (Cambridge 1963) 89–134 and *passim*

ABBREVIATIONS

Anth. Lat.	A. Riese–F. Bücheler–E. Lommatzsch, *Anthologia Latina* (Leipzig, 1894–1926). (Cf. *CLE*)
ANRW	H. Temporini, *Aufstieg und Niedergang der römischen Welt* (Berlin, 1972–)
Bardon	H. Bardon, *La littérature latine inconnue* (Paris 1951–6)
BT	Bibliotheca Scriptorum Graecorum et Romanorum Teubneriana (Leipzig & Stuttgart)
Budé	Collection des Universités de France, publiée sous le patronage de l'Association Guillaume Budé (Paris)
Bursian	Bursian's *Jahresbericht über die Fortschritte der klassischen Altertumswissenschaft* (Berlin, 1873–1945)
CAF	T. Kock, *Comicorum Atticorum Fragmenta* (Leipzig, 1880–8)
CAH	*The Cambridge Ancient History* (Cambridge, 1923–39)
CAH[2]	2nd ed. (Cambridge, 1961–)
CC	*Corpus Christianorum.* Series Latina (Turnholt, 1953–)
CGF	G. Kaibel, *Comicorum Graecorum Fragmenta* (Berlin, 1899)
CGFPap.	C. F. L. Austin, *Comicorum Graecorum Fragmenta in papyris reperta* (Berlin, 1973)
CIL	*Corpus Inscriptionum Latinarum* (Berlin, 1863–)
CLE	F. Bücheler–E. Lommatzsch, *Carmina Latina Epigraphica* (Leipzig, 1897–1930). (= *Anth. Lat.* Pars II)
CRF	O. Ribbeck, *Comicorum Romanorum Fragmenta*, 3rd. ed. (Leipzig, 1897)
CSEL	*Corpus Scriptorum Ecclesiasticorum Latinorum* (Vienna, 1866–)
CVA	*Corpus Vasorum Antiquorum* (Paris & elsewhere, 1925–)
Christ–Schmid– Stählin	W. von Christ, *Geschichte der griechischen Literatur*, rev. W. Schmid and O. Stählin (Munich, 1920–1924) 6th ed. (Cf. Schmid–Stählin)
DTC	A. W. Pickard-Cambridge, *Dithyramb, tragedy and comedy.* 2nd ed., rev. T. B. L. Webster (Oxford, 1962)
DFA	A. W. Pickard-Cambridge, *The dramatic festivals of Athens.* 2nd ed., rev. J. Gould–D. M. Lewis (Oxford, 1968)

ABBREVIATIONS

DK	H. Diels–W. Kranz, *Die Fragmente der Vorsokratiker*. 6th ed. (Berlin, 1951)
EGF	G. Kinkel, *Epicorum Graecorum Fragmenta* (Leipzig, 1877)
FGrH	F. Jacoby, *Fragmente der griechischen Historiker* (Berlin, 1923–)
FHG	C. Müller, *Fragmenta Historicorum Graecorum* (Berlin, 1841–70)
FPL	W. Morel, *Fragmenta Poetarum Latinorum* (Leipzig, 1927)
FPR	E. Baehrens, *Fragmenta Poetarum Romanorum* (Leipzig, 1886)
FYAT	(ed.) M. Platnauer, *Fifty years (and twelve) of classical scholarship* (Oxford, 1968)
GLK	H. Keil, *Grammatici Latini* (Leipzig, 1855–1923)
GLP	D. L. Page, *Greek Literary Papyri* (Cambridge, Mass. & London, 1942–)
Gow–Page, *Hell. Ep.*	A. S. F. Gow–D. L. Page, *The Greek Anthology: Hellenistic Epigrams* (Cambridge, 1965)
Gow–Page, *Garland*	A. S. F. Gow–D. L. Page, *The Greek Anthology: The Garland of Philip* (Cambridge, 1968)
Guthrie	W. K. C. Guthrie, *A History of Greek Philosophy* (Cambridge, 1965–81)
HRR	H. Peter, *Historicorum Romanorum reliquiae* (Leipzig, 1906–14)
HS	J. B. Hofmann, *Lateinische Syntax und Stilistik*, rev. A. Szantyr (Munich, 1965)
IEG	M. L. West, *Iambi et Elegi Graeci* (Oxford, 1971–2)
IG	*Inscriptiones Graecae* (Berlin, 1873–)
ILS	H. Dessau, *Inscriptiones Latinae Selectae* (Berlin, 1892–1916)
KG	R. Kühner–B. Gerth, *Ausführliche Grammatik der griechischen Sprache: Satzlehre*. 4th ed. (Hannover, 1955)
KS	R. Kühner–C. Stegmann, *Ausführliche Grammatik der lateinischen sprache: Satzlehre*. 3rd ed., rev. A. Thierfelder (Hannover, 1955)
Leo, *Gesch.*	F. Leo, *Geschichte der romischen Literatur*. I *Die archaische Literatur* (all pubd) (Berlin, 1913; repr. Darmstadt, 1967, w. *Die römische Poesie in der sullanischen Zeit*)
Lesky	A. Lesky, *A History of Greek Literature*, tr. J. Willis–C. de Heer (London, 1966)
Lesky, *TDH*	A. Lesky, *Die tragische Dichtung der Hellenen*, 3rd ed. (Göttingen, 1972)
LSJ	Liddell–Scott–Jones, *Greek–English Lexicon*, 9th ed. (Oxford, 1925–40)
Loeb	Loeb Classical Library (Cambridge, Mass. & London)
MGH	*Monumenta Germaniae Historica* (Berlin, 1877–91)
OCD²	*Oxford Classical Dictionary*, 2nd ed. (Oxford, 1970)

ABBREVIATIONS

OCT	Scriptorum Classicorum Bibliotheca Oxoniensis (Oxford)
Paravia	Corpus Scriptorum Latinorum Paravianum (Turin)
PIR	E. Klebs–H. Dessau, *Prosopographia Imperii Romani Saeculi I, II, III* (Berlin, 1897–8), 2nd ed. E. Groag–A. Stein (Berlin & Leipzig, 1933–)
PL	J.-P. Migne, *Patrologiae cursus completus* Series Latina (Paris, 1844–)
PLF	E. Lobel–D. Page, *Poetarum Lesbiorum Fragmenta* (Oxford, 1963)
PLM	E. Baehrens, *Poetae Latini Minores* (Leipzig, 1879–83), rev. F. Vollmer (incomplete) (1911–35)
PLRE	A. H. M. Jones–J. R. Martindale–J. Morris, *The prosopography of the later Roman Empire* (Cambridge, 1971–)
PMG	D. L. Page, *Poetae Melici Graeci* (Oxford, 1962)
PPF	H. Diels, *Poetarum Philosophorum Graecorum Fragmenta* (Berlin, 1901)
Pfeiffer	R. Pfeiffer, *A history of classical scholarship* (Oxford, 1968)
Powell	J. U. Powell, *Collectanea Alexandrina* (Oxford, 1925)
Powell–Barber	J. U. Powell–E. A. Barber, *New chapters in the history of Greek Literature* (Oxford, 1921), 2nd ser. (1929), 3rd ser. (Powell alone) (1933)
Preller–Robert	L. Preller, *Griechische Mythologie*, 4th ed., rev. C. Robert (Berlin, 1894)
RAC	*Reallexicon für Antike und Christentum* (Stuttgart, 1941–)
RE	A. Pauly–G. Wissowa–W. Kroll, *Real-Encyclopädie der klassischen Altertumswissenschaft* (Stuttgart, 1893–)
ROL	E. H. Warmington, *Remains of old Latin* (Cambridge, Mass. & London, 1935–40)
Roscher	W. H. Roscher, *Ausführliches Lexicon der griechischen und römischen Mythologie* (Leipzig, 1884–)
SEG	*Supplementum Epigraphicum Graecum* (Leyden, 1923–71; Alphen aan den Rijn, 1979–)
SVF	H. von Arnim, *Stoicorum Veterum Fragmenta* (Leipzig, 1903–)
Snell	B. Snell, *Tragicorum Graecorum Fragmenta* (Göttingen, 1971–)
Schanz–Hosius	M. Schanz–C. Hosius, *Geschichte der römischen Literatur* (Munich, 1914–1935)
Schmid–Stählin	W. Schmid–O. Stählin, *Geschichte der griechischen Literatur* (Munich, 1929–1948)
Spengel	L. Spengel, *Rhetores Graeci* (1853–6); I ii rev. C. Hammer (Leipzig, 1894)
Teuffel	W. S. Teuffel, *Geschichte der römischen Literatur* (Leipzig & Berlin, 1913–1920)

TGF   A. Nauck, *Tragicorum Graecorum Fragmenta*, 2nd ed. (Leipzig, 1889)

TLL   *Thesaurus Linguae Latinae* (Leipzig, 1900–)

TRF   O. Ribbeck, *Tragicorum Romanorum Fragmenta*, 3rd ed. (Leipzig, 1897)

Walz   C. Walz, *Rhetores Graeci* (Stuttgart, 1832–6)

Williams, *TORP*   G. Williams, *Tradition and originality in Roman Poetry* (Oxford, 1968)

WORKS CITED IN THE TEXT

Allen, W. S. (1973). *Accent and rhythm: prosodic features of Latin and Greek*. Cambridge.

Beazley, J. D. (1951). *The development of Attic black-figure*. Berkeley.

Bignone, E. (1942–50). *Storia della letteratura latina*. 3 vols. Florence.

Birt, T. (1882). *Das antike Buchwesen in seinem Verhältniss zur Litteratur mit Beiträgen zur Textgeschichte des Theokrit, Catull, Properz und anderer Autoren*. Berlin.

Bolgar, R. (1954). *The Classical heritage and its beneficiaries*. Cambridge.

Boyancé, P. (1970). *Études sur l'humanisme cicéronien*. Collection Latomus CXXI. Brussels.

Brooks, C. and Warren, R. P. (1960). *Understanding poetry*. 3rd edn. New York, Chicago, San Francisco, Toronto.

Büchner, K. (1936). *Beobachtungen über Vers- und Gedankengang bei Lukrez*. Hermes, Einzelschrift 1. Berlin.

(1964). *Cicero: Bestand und Wandel seiner geistigen Welt*. Heidelberg.

Bühler, W. (1960). *Die Europa des Moschos*. Wiesbaden.

Clarke, M. L. (1953). *Rhetoric at Rome: a historical survey*. London.

Classen, C. J. (1968). 'Poetry and rhetoric in Lucretius', *T.A.Ph.A.* 99: 77–118.

Clausen, W. V. (1976a). 'Virgil and Parthenius', *H.S.C.Ph.* 80: 179.

(1976b). 'Ariadne's leave-taking: Catullus 64.116–20', *Ill.Cl.S.* 2: 219–23.

(1976c). 'Catulli Veronensis Liber', *C.Ph.* 71: 37–43.

D'Alton, J. F. (1931). *Roman literary theory and criticism*. London.

De Lacy, P. (1948). 'Lucretius and the history of Epicureanism', *T.A.Ph.A.* 79: 12–23.

(1957). 'Process and value: an Epicurean dilemma', *T.A.Ph.A.* 88: 114–26.

Dorey, T. A. (1965). (ed.). *Cicero*. Studies in Latin literature and its influence. London.

Douglas, A. E. (1966). *M. Tulli Ciceronis Brutus*. Oxford.

(1968). *Cicero*. Greece & Rome New Surveys in the Classics II. Oxford.

Drabkin, I. E. (1930). *The Copa*. New York.

Duckett, E. S. (1925). *Catullus in English poetry*. Smith College Class. Stud. VI. Northampton, Mass.

Duckworth, G. E. (1969). *Vergil and classical hexameter poetry: a study in metrical variety*. Ann Arbor.

Ewbank, W. W. (1933). (ed.). *The poems of Cicero*. London.

Fedeli, P. (1972). 'Sulla prima bucolica di Virgilio', *G.I.F.* 24: 273–300.

WORKS CITED IN THE TEXT

Fraenkel, E. (1937). Review of Pasquali (1936), in *J.R.S.* 27: 262ff.

(1956). 'Catulls Trostgedicht für Calvus', *W.S.* 69: 279–88.

(1964). *Kleine Beiträge zur klassischen Philologie.* 2 vols. Rome.

Fraser, P. M. (1972). *Ptolemaic Alexandria.* 3 vols. Oxford.

Friedländer, P. (1912). *Johannes von Gaza und Paulus Silentiarius.* Leipzig & Berlin.

Furley, D. J. (1966). 'Lucretius and the Stoics', *B.I.C.S.* 13: 13–33.

Gelzer, M. (1968). *Caesar,* tr. P. Needham. Cambridge, Mass.

Giancotti, F. (1959). *Il preludio di Lucrezio.* Messina, Florence.

Giussani, C. (1896). *Studi lucreziani.* Turin.

Gow, A. S. F. (1952). (ed.). *Theocritus.* 2 vols. 2nd edn. Cambridge.

Granrud, J. E. (1913). 'Was Cicero successful in the art oratorical?', *C.J.* 8: 234–43.

Grant, M. A. (1924). *Ancient rhetorical theories of the laughable.* Wisconsin Studies in Language and Literature XXI. Madison.

Harder, R. (1929). 'Über Cicero's "Somnium Scipionis"', *Königsb. Abh.,* Geistesw. Kl. Heft III, 115–50 = *Kleine Schriften,* ed. W. Marg (1960) 354–95. Munich.

Haury, A. (1955). *Ironie et humour chez Cicéron.* Leiden.

Horsfall, N. M. (1969). 'Aclys and Cateia', *Class. et. Med.* 30: 297–9.

(1976). 'The *Collegium Poetarum*', *B.I.C.S.* 23: 79–95.

Humbert, J. (1925). *Les plaidoyers écrits et les plaidoiries réelles de Cicéron.* Paris.

Hunt, H. A. K. (1954). *The humanism of Cicero.* Melbourne.

Jocelyn, H. D. (1973). 'Greek poetry in Cicero's prose writings', *Y.Cl.S.* 23: 61–111.

Kennedy, G. (1972). *The art of rhetoric in the Roman world, 300 B.C. to A.D. 300.* Princeton.

Kenney, E. J. (1970). 'Doctus Lucretius', *Mnemosyne* 4.23: 366–92.

Kenyon, F. G. (1951). *Books and readers in ancient Greece and Rome.* 2nd edn. Oxford.

Kleve, K. (1969). 'Lucrèce, l'épicurisme et l'amour', *Actes du viii Congrès G. Budé* 376–83.

Kroll, W. (1929). *C. Valerius Catullus.* Stuttgart.

Laurand, L. (1907; 4th edn. 1936–8). *Études sur le style des discours de Cicéron.* 3 vols. Paris.

Lawall, G. (1966). 'Apollonius' *Argonautica*: Jason as anti-hero', *Y.Cl.S.* 19: 116–69.

Leeman, A. D. (1963). *Orationis ratio.* Amsterdam.

Lefèvre, E. (1972). (ed.). *Senecas Tragödien.* Darmstadt.

Lejay, P. (1925). *Plaute.* Paris.

Lelièvre, F. J. (1958). 'Parody in Juvenal and T. S. Eliot', *C.Ph.* 53: 22–5.

Leo, F. (1906). 'Diogenes bei Plautus', *Hermes* 41: 441–6 (= *Ausgewählte Kleine Schriften* I, Rome 1960, 185–90).

(1913). *Geschichte der römischen Literatur* I: *Die archaische Literatur.* Berlin.

Lewis, C. S. (1942). *A preface to Paradise Lost.* London, New York & Toronto.

Lişcu, M. O. (1937). *L'expression des idées philosophiques chez Cicéron.* Paris.

Malcovati, H. (1943). *Cicerone e la poesia*. Padua.

(1955). *Oratorum Romanorum fragmenta liberae rei publicae*. 2nd edn. (1st edn. 1930). 3 vols. Turin.

Marouzeau, J. (1949). *Quelques aspects de la formation du Latin littéraire*. Paris.

Meillet, A. (1928: 4th edn. 1948). *Esquisse d'une histoire de la langue latine*. Paris.

Momigliano, A. (1941). Review of B. Farrington, *Science and politics in the ancient world*, in *J.R.S.* 31: 149–57.

Müller, R. (1969). 'Lukrez v 1101ff und die Stellung der epikureischen Philosophie zum Staat und zu den Gesetzen', in O. von Jurewicz and H. Kuch (eds.), *Die Krise der griechischen Polis*. Berlin.

Mynors, R. A. B. (1958). (ed.). *C. Valerii Catulli carmina*. Oxford.

Nettleship, H. (1980). 'Literary criticism in Latin antiquity', *Journal of Philology* 18: 225–70.

Norden, E. (1898; repr. Stuttgart 1973). *Die antike Kunstprosa*. 2 vols. Leipzig.

(1916). (ed.) *P. Vergilius Maro Aeneis Buch VI*. Berlin.

Page, D. L. (1940). (ed.). *Select papyri* III. Loeb. London & Cambridge, Mass.

(1972). 'Early Hellenistic elegy', *P.C.Ph.S.* n.s. 18: 63–4.

Pasquali, G. (1936). *Preistoria della poesia romana*. Florence.

Patin, H. J. G. (1883). *Études sur la poèsie latine*. 3rd edn. Paris.

Peter, H. (1901). *Der Brief in der römischen Literatur*. Leipzig.

Petersson, T. (1920). *Cicero: a biography*. Berkeley.

Poncelet, R. (1957). *Cicéron traducteur de Platon*. Paris.

Portalupi, F. (1955). *Bruto e i neo-atticisti*. Turin.

Putnam, M. C. J. (1960). 'Catullus 66. 75–88', *C.Ph.* 55: 223–8.

Rambaud, M. (1953). *Cicéron et l'histoire romaine*. Paris.

Rawson, E. (1973). 'The interpretation of Cicero's "De Legibus"', *ANRW* 1.4, 334–56. Berlin & New York.

Regenbogen, O. (1932). *Lukrez, seine Gestalt in seinem Gedicht*. Neue Wege zur Antike II.1. Leipzig & Berlin. (Repr. (1961) in *Kleine Schriften*. Munich.)

Reitzenstein, R. (1912). 'Zur Sprache der lateinischen Erotik', *S.H.A.W.* 12: 9–36.

Rhys Roberts, W. (1901). (ed.). *Dionysius of Halicarnassus: the three Literary Letters*. Cambridge.

Robinson, R. P. (1923). 'Valerius Cato', *T.A.Ph.A.* 54: 98–116.

Rohde, E. (1914). *Der griechische Roman*. 2nd edn. Leipzig.

Ross, D. O. jr. (1969a). *Style and tradition in Catullus*. Cambridge, Mass.

(1969b). 'Nine epigrams from Pompeii (*CIL* 4.4966–73)', *Y.Cl.S.* 21: 127–42.

(1975). *Backgrounds to Augustan poetry: Gallus, elegy and Rome*. Cambridge.

Russell, D. A. (1964). *'Longinus' on the sublime*. Oxford.

Sabine, G. H. and Smith, H. B. (1929). *Cicero on the Commonwealth*. Columbus, Ohio.

Schmid, W. (1944). Review of J. Mewaldt, *Der Kampf des Dichters Lukrez gegen die Religion*, *Gnomon* 20: 97–100.

Sellar, W. Y. (1889). *The Roman poets of the Republic*. 3rd edn. Oxford.

Shackleton Bailey, D. R. (1956–70). (ed.). *Cicero's Letters to Atticus.* 7 vols. Cambridge.

Skydsgaard, J. E. (1968). *Varro the scholar.* Copenhagen.

Süss, W. (1965). 'Cicero: eine Einführung in seine philosophischen Schriften', *Abh. Mainz Geistes- und Sozialw. Kl.* 5: 210–385. Wiesbaden 1966.

Taylor, L. R. (1949). *Party politics in the age of Caesar.* Berkeley & Los Angeles.

Toynbee, J. M. C. (1971). *Death and burial in the Roman world.* London.

Tränkle, H. (1967). 'Neoterische Kleinigkeiten', *Mus.Helv.* 24: 87–103.

Wilamowitz-Moellendorff, U. von (1924). *Hellenistiche Dichtung.* 2 vols. Berlin.

(1928). *Erinnerungen 1848–1914.* Leipzig.

Wilkinson, L. P. (1963). *Golden Latin artistry.* Cambridge.

Wiseman, T. P. (1969). *Catullan questions.* Leicester.

Zieliński, Th. (1904). *Das Clauselgesetz in Ciceros Reden: Grundzüge einer oratorischen Rhythmik. Philologus* Suppl.-Band IX 589–875.

INDEX

Main references are distinguished by figures in bold type. References to the Appendix (which should normally be consulted for basic details of authors' lives and works, and for bibliographies) are given in italic figures.

Academy, 36, 56, 90
Accius, 113
Aeschines, 70n.
Aeschylus, 34, 73
Aesopus (actor), 65
Alexander the Great, 73
Anaxagoras, 34
Antiochus of Ascalon, 56n., 116
Antipater (epigrammatist), 9
Antonius, M. (orator, cos. 99 B.C.), 61, 83, 85
Antonius, M. (Mark Antony), 68, 74, 76, 78
Antonius Gnipho, 109
Apocolocyntosis, 115
Apollodorus of Athens (scholar), 117
Apollonius of Rhodes: influence: on New Poetry, 5, 13; on Catullus, 6–7, 14, 15, 17, 18
Aratus of Soli: translated by Cicero, 2, 5, 72, 73; admired by Cinna, 6; model for Alexandrians, 8
Archias, 59, 72
Aristophanes (comic poet), 34
Aristotle: view of didactic, 33, 42; Lucretius and, 36, 38, 44, 51; Cicero and, 57, 58, 83 and n., 86; view of rhetoric, 60, 61, 63
Artemo, 73
Asclepiades (epigrammatist), 7
Asellio, Sempronius, 99
Atellane farce, 119
Atticus, T. Pomponius: as Cicero's friend and correspondent, 57, 59, 69, 70–1, 74n., 75, 90; in Cicero's dialogues, 68, 88; Nepos and, 20 and n., 116, 118; Varro and, 114; writings, 117
Augustine, 90, 105, 115
Augustus (Octavian), 74n., 87

Bellum Africum, 111
Bellum Alexandrinum, 111
Bellum Hispaniense, 111

Bibaculus, M. Furius, 6, 13
Brutus, M. Junius (tyrannicide); 57, 66, 68–9, 74n., 78, 87, 88, 89, 91n.

Caecilius (New Poet), 6, 26
Caecilius Statius, 58
Caelius Rufus, 58, 82
Caesar, C. Julius, **107–11**, *132–3*; view of Terrence, 67, 110; views on style, 66, 68, 109–10; lampooned, 5, 6; Cicero and, 57, 66, 68, 74, 78, 82, 88, 109; Sallust and, 94, 99, 100–1, 103; criticized by Pollio, 108, 111; Varro and, 114, 115; Laberius and, 120
   works: *Bellum civile*, 110–11; *Bellum Gallicum*, 107–8; *De analogia*, 68, 109
Caesar Strabo, C. Julius, 82–5 *passim*
Calidus, L. Julius, 20
Callimachus, 34
   influence: on Ennius, 9; on Propertius, 1, 9; on New Poets, 6–12 *passim*; on Catullus, 12, 13–15 *passim*
Calvus, C. Licinius: as orator, 5, 66; as poet, 5–6, 15; Catullus and, 6, 30–2, 66
Carbo Arvina, C. Papirius (tr.pl. 90 B.C.), 65
Carneades, 70
Cassius Severus, 119
Catiline, 78; portrayed by Sallust, 101, 103
Cato the Censor: Cicero and 58–9, 86, 90; influence on Sallust, 97, 104, 106; *Origines*, 95, 102; speeches, 60, 61; other works, 61
Cato Uticensis, 119n.; Cicero and, 57, 77, 89; in Sallust, 99, 100–1
Catullus, *122–4*; attacks on politicians, 5, 6; Lesbia and, 19, 24–6, 30; arrangement and publication of poems, **20–3**; style and vocabulary, 29, 30 and n., 31, 69n.; metre, 72
   relation to models and contemporaries, **1–13** *passim*; Ennius, 14; Meleager, 1, 20; Laevius, 2; Cicero, 3; Apollonius, 6–7, 13–18

Catullus (*cont.*)

passim; Callimachus, 6–7, 12–15 *passim*; Calvus, 6, 30–2, 66; Cinna, 10–11, 13, 27; Euphorion, 12–13; Parthenius, 12; Moschus, 17; Theocritus, 17, 27; Sappho, 24–5; Terence, 30

influence: on Virgil, 14–15; on Martial, 21, 69

poems discussed: (1), 19–21; (31), 27–9; (36), 26–7; (50), 30–2; (51), 24–5; (58), 25–6; (64), 13–19, 72; (85), 29; (109), 29–30

Catulus, Q. Lutatius, *121*; epigrams, 1, 9–10; memoirs, 107; in Cicero's *De oratore*, 83, 84

Cethegus, M. Cornelius, 50

Cicero, M. Tullius, **56–93**, *125–9*; popularity and influence, 92–3; ancient views on, 65, 68, 71, 79, 92–3; use of *clausulae*, 63 and n., 64–5, 74–5; edited Lucretius (?), 39, 58; Caesar and, 57, 66, 68, 74, 78, 82, 88, 109; Varro and, 59, 68, 114, 115; oratorical theory and practice, 59–62 (his predecessors'), 62–71 (his own); Nepos and, 75, 116, 118; wit of, 82; Sallust and, 98, 100; *De consiliis suis*, 100

views: on Ennius, 4; on New Poets, 4–5; on culture, **56–9**, 117; on historiography, 96, 99; on mime, 119

letters, 69, **73–5**, 78; Catullus' poetry and, 29, 31

philosophica, **88–92**; Lucretius' poem compared with, 34; vocabulary of, 69–70; *Academica*, 71, 89, 90; *Consolatio*, 89; *De amicitia*, 59, 90; *De divinatione*, 37–8, 89–90; *De fato*, 90, 91n.; *De finibus*, 59, 89, 91; *De gloria*, 90; *De natura deorum*, 56–7, 83, 90, 91; *De officiis*, 90, 91–2; *De senectute*, 58–9, 90; eulogy of Cato Uticensis, 90; *Hortensius*, 89, 90; *Paradoxa Stoicorum*, 91n.; *Tusculans*, 89, 91

politica: *De legibus*, 88, 90; *De republica*, 57, 58, 82, **85–8**, 98

prose translations, 70n.

rhetorica: cited, 59–71 *passim*; influence, 93; *Brutus*, 58, 66, 88; *De inventione*, 62, 85; *De oratore*, 57, 59, 62, **82–5**, 89; *Orator*, 66, 85, 88

speeches, **76–82**; *Catilinarians*, 76, 77, 78, 79; *In Pisonem*, 68, 77; *Philippics*, 67, 76, 77, 78; *Post reditum in senatu*, 76; *Pro Archia*, 59, 75; *Pro Caecina*, 67n., 77; *Pro Caelio*, 58, 82; *Pro Cluentio*, 67n., 78; *Pro lege Manilia*, 64, 67n.; *Pro Ligario*, 82; *Pro Marcello*, 58,; *Pro Milone*, 76, 77, 79; *Pro Murena*, 77, 82; *Pro Rabirio*, 67n.; *Pro Sestio*, 76; *Verrines*. 65n., 67n., 68, 76, 77, 78, 79–82

verse, 2–3, 4–5, **71–3**

Cicero, Q. Tullius, 75, 85, 88; works, 73, 84n.

Cinna, C. Helvius, 4; Catullus and, 6, 10–11, 13,

26, 27; his *Zmyrna*, 6, **10–12**, 15, 73; commentaries on, 10 and n.

Claudius Caecus, App., 60

Claudius Pulcher, App. (cos. 54 B.C.), 37

Clodia *see* 'Lesbia'

Coelius Antipater, 95, 96

Colotes (Epicurean), 42

Commentariolum petitionis, 84n.

Cornificius, Q., 6, 13n.

Cotta, C. Aurelius, 59, 83, 91

Crassicius, 10

Crassus, L. Licinius (orator, cos. 95 B.C.), 59, 61, 62, 83–5

Democritus, 38, 51

Demosthenes, 67, 70n., 92

Dicaearchus, 115

Diodotus, 58

Dionysius of Halicarnassus, 66

Duillius, C. (cos. 260 B.C.), 59

Empedocles, 37, 39, 47, 50, 53, 55

Ennius, 9, 54, 72, 73

Epicurus, Epicureanism: Lucretius and, 35–45, 50–5 *passim*; Cicero and, 42, 58, 59, 69; use of letter-form, 73

Epistulae ad Caesarem senem, 95; Appendix as for Sallust

Euphorion, 4, 5, 10, **12–13**

Euripides, 8, 34

Fronto, 93

Furius Antias, A., 10

Galba, Ser. Sulpicius (cos. 144 B.C.), 61, 62

Gallus, C. Cornelius, 4, 11, 12

Gellius, Aulus, 1, 116

Gellius, Cn., 95

Gorgias, 61, 84

Gracchus, C., 62

Gracchus, Tib., 86

Hermesianax, 1

Herodotus, 8

Hesiod, 9 and n., 34

Hippocratic *corpus*, 34

Hirtius, A., 111

Homer, 8, 9, 34, 61

Horace, 23n., 71, 85

Hortensius Hortalus, Q., 62, 66, 67, 71, 76, 77, 83

Hyginus, C. Julius, 117

Invectiva in Ciceronem, 95; Appendix as for Sallust

Invectiva in Sallustium, 95; Appendix as for Sallust

Isidore, 112
Isocrates, 62–3, 73, 84, 98

Jerome, 39–40, 68
Julius Caesar, *see* Caesar
Julius Strabo, *see* Caesar Strabo
Juvenal, 71

Laberius, 119–20, *137*
Lactantius, 93
Laelius, C. (cos. 140 B.C.), 59, 86, 90
Laevius, 1–2, *121–2*
Lentulus Spinther, P. Cornelius, 74, 85
Lepidus Porcina, M. Aemilius (cos. 137 B.C.), 61
'Lesbia', 19, 24–6, 30
Licinus, *see* Porcius
Livy, 92, 95
'Longinus', 25
Lucceius, L., 59, 75, 96, 107
Lucilius, 70
Lucretius, 1, 33–55, *124–5*; knowledge of Greek
    authors, 34, 47, 51; imitates Cicero, 2;
    structure of poem, 21, 43–5; purpose of
    poem, 33–9; compared with Cicero, 34–51;
    attitude to contemporary events, 35–6; relation
    to philosophical sources, 36, 40–1; attitude
    to religion, 36–9; as poet and philosopher,
    39–42; edited by Cicero (?), 39, 58; style and
    metre, 45–50, 72, 105; imagery, 50–5
Lysias, 66, 67

Marcellus, M. Claudius (cos. 51 B.C.), 58
Marius, C., 72, 102
Marius, M. (friend of Cicero), 75
Martial, 69n.
Matius, C., 89
Meleager (and *Garland* of), 1, 9, 20
Melissus of Samos (philosopher), 51
Memmius, C., 6, 33–5, 35, 58
Menippus, 115
Metellus Numidicus, Q. Caecilius (cos. 109 B.C.),
    102
mime, 119–20
Mimnermus, 7, 8
Molo, 65, 109
Moschus, 13, 17

Nepos, Cornelius, 116–18, *136*; relations with
    contemporaries, 19–20, 116; view of Cicero's
    works 75, 116, 118; reputation, 116; style,
    118
    works: *Chronica*, 20, 117; *De viris illustri-
    bus*, 20n., 117–18; poems, 20
New Poets, *see poetae novi*
Nicander, 8
Nigidius Figulus, P., 37
Novius (writer of Atellane farce), 119

Ovid, 48, 77

Pacuvius, 67
Panaetius, 56, 78, 91–2
Parthenius, 10, 11–12, 27n.
Paul, St, 74
Peripatetic doctrines, 56n., 63
Philetas (or Philitas), 1, 7
Philo of Larissa, 56 and n.
Philodemus, 36, 41–2
Philus, L. Furius, 86
Piso Frugi, L. Calpurnius (annalist), 95
Plato, Platonism: Lucretius and, 36, 51; use of
    myth attacked, 42; Cicero and, 58, 59, 63,
    70n., 83, 84, 86, 87, 88; use of letter-form, 73;
    in Sallust's prooemia, 98; Varro and, 116
Pliny the Elder, 113, 116
Pliny the Younger, 78, 93
Plutarch, 118
poetae novi, 1–3, **4–13**
Pollio, C. Asinius, 106, 108, 111
Polybius, 98
Pompeius Magnus, Cn., 77; Cicero and, 78, 87;
    Caesar on, 111; Varro and, 114
Pomponius, L. (writer of Atellane farce), 119
Porcius Licinus, 1, *121*
Posidippus (epigrammatist), 7
Posidonius, 58, 84, 98, 116, 117
Presocratics, 36, 39
Propertius, 1
Publilius Syrus, **119–20**, *137*
Pyrrhus, 60
Pythagoreanism 113, 116

Quintilian, 76; on Sallust, 96, 105; on Cicero,
    65, 71, 79, 93

Rhetorica ad Herennium, 62, 93
Roscius (actor) 65, 84
Rutilius Rufus, P.: memoirs, 95, 107; views on
    rhetoric, 60–1; Cicero and, 85

Sallust, **94–106**, *129–31*; Quintilian on, 96, 105
    style, 66, 69, 71, 104–6; life, 94; relation to
    predecessors, 95–6, 98, 102–3; prooemia, 96–
    9; criticized, 106; influence on Tacitus, 101,
    105
    works: *Catiline*, 94–5, 99–101; *Jugurtha*,
    95, 101–2; *Histories*, 95, 97, 99; spurious,
    95
Santra, 117
Sappho, 1, 24–5, 34
Scaevola, Q. Mucius ('Augur', cos. 117 B.C.),
    59, 83, 85
Scaevola, Q. Mucius ('Pontifex', cos. 95 B.C.),
    90
Scaurus, M. Aemilius (cos. 115 B.C.), 107

Scipio Aemilianus Africanus Numantinus, P. Cornelius, 67; Cicero and, 56, 59, 85–7
Scipio Africanus Major, P. Cornelius, 57, 87–8
Seneca the Elder, 92
Seneca the Younger, 105, 115, 119
Severus, *see* Cassius
Silius Italicus, 21
Siro, 66
Sisenna, L. Cornelius, 95–6, 100, 104
Socrates, 59, 84, 86, 89
Stoic doctrines, Stoics: Lucretius and, 36; Cicero and, 56n., 58, 59, 91 and n.; on language and rhetoric, 60–1, 62, 68; Sallust and, 98; Varro and, 114, 116
Suetonius, 112
Sulla, 58, 107, 119
Sulpicius Rufus, P. (tr. pl. 88 B.C.), 83
Sulpicius Rufus, Ser. (cos. 51 B.C.), 67, 74, 77

Tacitus (historian), 71; influenced by Sallust, 101, 105; *Dialogus*, 68, 93
Terence, 67; influence, 30; Caesar's view of, 67, 110; quoted by Cicero, 58, 75
Terentia (Cicero's wife), 88
Theocritus, 7, 13, 17, 27
Theophrastus, 114
Thucydides: Lucretius and, 34, 46; influence on Sallust, 66, 98, 99, 104, 106

Ticidas, 6, 13n.
Timotheus (statesman), 73
Tiro, M. Tullius, 74, 82
Torquatus, L. Manlius (Epicurean), 35
Tullia (Cicero's daughter), 74, 89

Valerius Aedituus, 1, *121*
Valerius Antias, 95
Valerius Cato, P., 6, 13n.
Varro of Reate, **112–16**, *133–6*; Cicero and, 58, 68, 114, 115; working methods, 112–14; personality and attitudes, 114–16; style, 115
    works: *Annales*, 117; *Antiquitates*, 113, 115–16; *De lingua Latina*, 68, 112, 113; *De re rustica*, 112, 113, 114; *De vita populi Romani*, 113, 115; *Disciplinae*, 112, 113; *Imagines*, 117; *Menippean satires*, 113, 114, 115; other works, 113, 115
Vatinius, P., 5, 66
Velleius, C. (Epicurean), 35
Velleius Paterculus, 104
Virgil, 66; *Georgics*, 9n., 73; *Aeneid*, 14–15, 72, 112
Volusius, 11, 26

Xenophon (historian), 98, 109

14514